Haifa before & after 1948

Narratives of a Mixed City

> # INSTITUTE FOR HISTORICAL JUSTICE AND RECONCILIATION SERIES

Published under editorial responsibility of

The Institute for Historical Justice and Reconciliation

The Hague

VOLUME 6

Haifa before & after 1948

Narratives of a Mixed City

Edited by
Mahmoud Yazbak and Yfaat Weiss

DORDRECHT
2011

Cover design/ Illustration: Studio Thorsten
Photograph: Getty Images/John Philips

This book is printed on acid-free paper.

This project has been sponsored by funding from the Ford Foundation, the Arcadia Trust, the Sigrid Rausing Trust and the Hamburger Institut für Sozialforschung

The views in this book are the responsibility of the author and do not necessarily reflect the views of the Institute for Historical Justice and Reconciliation.

Library of Congress Cataloging-in-Publication Data

ISSN	2211-3061
hardbound	ISBN 9789089790910
paperback	ISBN 9789089790927

© 2011 Institute for Historical Justice and Reconciliation and Republic of Letters Publishing BV, Dordrecht, The Netherlands/ St. Louis, MO. All rights reserved.

All rights reserved. No part of this publication may be reproduced, translated, stored in a retrieval system, or transmitted in any form or by any means, electronic, mechanical, photocopying, recording or otherwise, without prior written permission from the publisher.

Republic of Letters Publishing has made all reasonable efforts to trace all rights holders to any copyrighted material used in this work. In cases where these efforts have not been successful the publisher welcomes communications from copyright holders, so that the appropriate acknowledgements can be made in future editions, and settles other permission matters.

Authorization to photocopy items for personal use is granted by Republic of Letters Publishing BV provided that the appropriate fees are paid directly to The Copyright Clearance Center, Rosewood Drive, Suite 910, Danvers, MO 01923, USA. Fees are subject to change.

TABLE OF CONTENTS

Contributors

Preface
Catherine Cissé-van den Muijsenbergh ix

Towards Mutual Historical Writing: An Introduction to the "Haifa Project"
Mahmoud Yazbak and Yfaat Weiss 1

A Tale of Two Houses
Mahmoud Yazbak and Yfaat Weiss 11

Arab-Jewish Architectural Partnership in Haifa during the Mandate Period:
    Qaraman and Gerstel Meet on the "Seam Line"
Waleed Karkabi and Adi Roitenberg 43

Arabs and Jews, Leisure and Gender, in Haifa's Public Spaces
Manar Hasan and Ami Ayalon 69

Commodities and Power: Edible Oil and Soap in the History of Arab-
    Jewish Haifa
Mustafa Abbasi and David De Vries 99

Historicizing Climate: *Haifawis* and *Haifo'im* Remembering the Winter of
    1950
Dan Rabinowitz and Johnny Mansour 119

"Eraser" and "Anti-Eraser" – Commemoration and Marginalization on the
    Main Street of the German Colony: The Haifa City Museum and Café
    Fattush
Salman Natour and Avner Giladi 149

Haifa *Umm al-Gharib*: Historical Notes and Memory of Inter-Communal
    Relations
Regev Nathansohn and Abbas Shiblak 181

Bibliography 205

Index 217

CONTRIBUTORS

EDITORS

Mahmoud Yazbak is a professor of Palestinian History, head of the department of Middle Eastern History at the University of Haifa. Served as the Chair of Adalah (2008-2011), and headed MEISAI (Middle Eastern and Islamic Studies Association in Israel, 2008-2011). He publishes frequently on social history and issues concerning the modern Palestinian society.

Yfaat Weiss is a professor at the department of History of the Jewish people and is the former head of School of History at the Hebrew University of Jerusalem. The scope of her publication covers German and Central European History, and Jewish and Israeli History.

AUTHORS

Mustafa Abbasi, is a lecturer at Tel Hai Academic College in Upper Galilee. His main fields of research are the Galilee towns Safad, Acre, Nazareth and Tiberias during the Mandate period (1918-1948). He publishes frequently on social history and issues concerning the modern Palestinian society in Galilee.

Ami Ayalon is a professor of Middle Eastern history at the Department of Middle Eastern and African History, Tel Aviv University. His research over the years has dealt primarily with aspects of Arab cultural history in modern times.

David De Vries is professor at the Department of Labor Studies, Faculty of Social Sciences, Tel Aviv University. His research interests are labor and business history and the social history of Palestine and Israel.

Avner Giladi is professor of Islamic Studies in the Department of Middle Eastern History, University of Haifa. His main fields of research and publication are Family History, History of Education and Childhood and Women's and Gender History in medieval Islamic contexts.

Manar Hasan is a lecturer of sociology at Zefat Academic College and the Program for Gender Studies at Bar-Ilan University. Her main research interests are; Urban and Space Sociology, Gender studies, Postcolonial and Colonial studies, collective memory and secular studies.

Waleed Karkabi is head of the building conservation team in the Haifa municipality. He is specialized in building conservation during his

CONTRIBUTORS

second degree (Magister) in Architecture at The Faculty of Architecture of The Building Institute of Leningrad (St. Petersburg Russia).

Johnny Mansour is a lecturer at the History Studies Department at Beit Berl Academic College, Israel. He has written on the philosophy of a two state solution and Palestinian local history. His interests and studies are specifically on the history and development of Haifa.

Salman Natour is an author and playwriter. He is the writer of numerous novels, satires, short stories and articles covering cultural, political and social issues, and Arabic plays that have been performed in theaters across Palestine and the Arab World.

Dan Rabinowitz is an anthropologist writing on ethnicity and nationalism, the Palestinian citizens of Israel, the Arab-Israeli Conflict and the nexus between environment and society. He is a professor of anthropology at Tel-Aviv University and at Central European University in Budapest, Chair of the Israeli Association for Environmental Justice and Vice Chair of Greenpeace UK.

Adi Roitenberg graduated from the Neri Bloomfield Acadamy of Design ("Witzzo") in Haifa as an architectural practical engineer. She is part of the building conservation team of the Haifa municipality.

Abbas Shiblak is a scholar and human rights advocate. He is a research associate at the International Development Centre at the University of Oxford. His main research areas are human rights, migration and minority status.

Regev Nathansohn is a PhD candidate in the Department of Anthropology at the University of Michigan, Ann Arbor. His research focuses on genealogies of coexistence in Haifa, and deals with questions regarding ethnic and racial relations, the politics of history and memory in a multi-cultural society, and the relations between oral and visual representations.

PREFACE

The Institute for Historical Justice and Reconciliation (IHJR) is pleased to present the publication *Haifa, Before & After 1948, Narratives of a Mixed City*. This unique publication is a result of a project that was initiated and implemented under the auspices of the IHJR.

The IHJR was founded in 2004 by Elazar Barkan and Timothy Ryback, with the aim of dispelling myths and misconceptions of history. The IHJR believes that confronting and overcoming distortions of historical reality can provide for a better understanding and can contribute toward laying the groundwork for reconciliation.

The project on the City of Haifa is an endeavor of 14 Israeli and Palestinian scholars and experts – Arabs and Jews –, mostly Israeli citizens, working in the fields of Middle Eastern history, social and economic history, anthropology, sociology and architecture. During meetings from 2008 to 2011 in Salzburg, Hamburg and Tel Aviv, the group collectively conducted research and engaged in the process of writing shared narratives. From the inception of the project, convening scholars and experts from different backgrounds – each with a special connection to Haifa – proved to be challenging. However, throughout its tenure several authors sought rapprochement and in some cases became friends. The development of these friendships became apparent when the group took the initiative to organize a tour along the neighborhoods described in this publication.

The result of this project is a publication incorporating seven shared historical narratives on the economic, social, cultural and political life of Haifa surrounding the period of 1948. The study, *Haifa, Before & After 1948*, examines the liaisons between the Palestinian and Jewish communities in Haifa in an attempt to unravel not only the complicated relations in this mixed city, but also to underscore extensive periods of cohabitation.

The authors explore the events surrounding 1948 on a micro-level, through the lens of architecture and the urban fabric of Haifa. Consequently, they aim at transcending boundaries and to foster a better understanding of the history of the region. This groundbreaking approach serves as an innovative model that could be applied to other mixed cities around the world, such as Sarajevo, Beirut, and Cairo, to name only a few.

I wish to thank the authors for their dedication and continuing work on the project. In addition, I would like to extend my gratitude toward our funders the Ford Foundation, the Sigrid Rausing Trust, the Arcadia Trust and to Ulrich Bielefeld of the Hamburger Institut für Sozialforschung, who

Mahmoud Yazbak and Yfaat Weiss (eds.), Haifa Before & After 1948. Narratives of a Mixed City, ix–x.
© 2011 Institute for Historical Justice and Reconciliation and Republic of Letters Publishing. All rights reserved.

CATHERINE CISSÉ-VAN DEN MUIJSENBERGH

sponsored the two meetings convened in Hamburg, for without their commitment and support this publication would not have been realized.

Catherine Cissé-van den Muijsenbergh
Executive Director

TOWARDS MUTUAL HISTORICAL WRITING:
AN INTRODUCTION TO THE "HAIFA PROJECT"

MAHMOUD YAZBAK AND YFAAT WEISS

This research was initiated early in 2006 when Palestinians and Israelis – Arabs and Jews, mostly Israeli citizens, assembled at the Salzburg Global Seminar under the auspices of the Institute for Historical Justice and Reconciliation (IHJR) with the aim of defining common topics for historical research. The initial meeting was convened by the IHJR's founder, the historian Elazar Barkan, on the strength of his belief in the power of history to create a bridge whereby to facilitate the resolution of ethnic and national disputes, on which he expanded in his book *The Guilt of Nations*. At this complex and moving encounter a number of ideas evolved and several groups were formed, which operated and continue to operate under the IHJR's auspices. Some of the joint projects relating to the Middle East conflict that the participants initiated at the time have proved extremely difficult to bring to fruition. They required participants to reach scholarly reconciliation with regard to a reality that had yet to find a political solution. Perhaps they were ahead of their time. Moreover, many aspects of the political dispute were exacerbated during this period and it appeared as though the prospects for its solution were in fact receding.

The idea of the Haifa Project was born out of the inspiration of this meeting, but we should note that it was from the outset less ambitious, or perhaps more modest. The project did not seek to address the fundamental, overarching big issues, namely the macro. We, the authors, did not, for example, seek to address directly the refugee question, nor that of the holy sites; nor, in fact, any of the burning issues on the immediate political agenda. Rather, we confined ourselves to the restricted micro perspective. We chose to concentrate on a single city, on Haifa. And although it occupies an important place in Palestinian-Jewish-Israeli relations, it is nevertheless only one city.

Irrespective of their national ascription, most local historians would agree that the fall of Arab Haifa along with its approximately 74,000 Arab inhabitants to the Jewish military forces in April 1948 constitutes one of the key events of the Palestinian *Nakba*. From the Palestinian perspective the fall of Arab Haifa symbolizes the end of the vibrant Palestinian urban life that existed during the Mandate period in the three large mixed cities, namely Jaffa, Jerusalem and Haifa. From the contemporary Israeli-Jewish perspective, which ignores the historical event, the city of Haifa continues to constitute a symbol of Jewish-Arab coexistence. Jewish Israelis, we suggest, attach exaggerated importance to the ongoing peaceful urban routine, and in turning the Palestinian existence in the city into folklore they in fact remain oblivious to the true condition and identity of the Palestinians of Haifa, both in the past and in the present. A different, more reconciliatory approach, would argue that despite past residues and the traumatic experience of 1948, and despite the long shadow that this casts in the form of the as yet unresolved conflict, in the conditions pertaining in Israel today, Haifa, with its relatively secular and liberal atmosphere, constitutes practically the only alternative for a shared Palestinian-Jewish-Israeli existence based on mutual respect extending to all social classes. The "Haifa Project" departed from the point of tension between the events of the past and present awareness, and thus established from the outset a clear link between the city and its people's civil affiliation, bearing in mind the issues of civil society and civility.

The first joint session of the "Haifa Project" was held in Salzburg in February 2009, attended by sixteen colleagues. We arrived at the first meeting without any structured template, with no list of topics, and with no guiding principles other than this one – that each article within the project would be written by two colleagues who did not share a national affiliation, namely, by a Palestinian and an Israeli Jew. This is a somewhat arbitrary principle, since the political affiliation and identity of the authors is not exclusively or directly derived from their national affiliation. Yet nevertheless, in our quest for a joint narrative we chose to adhere to this principle, however mechanical or rigid it may be. The absence of a pre-agreed structure immediately resulted in an open discussion and enabled the various topics to develop according to the dynamic generated among the participants and their areas of expertise. It goes without saying that this meeting was a particularly intricate one. Some of the participants felt that the project was adopting a particular slant. One of the participants dropped out after this session since he/she "was not prepared to compromise on his/her narrative." Not all the linkages worked out, and some prosaic difficulties, such as the inability to adhere to a time-table, also cropped up.

The project assumed its current shape, reflected in this collection of articles, between the first and the second meeting, which took place in the summer of 2009 in Hamburg under the auspices and with the support of the Hamburger Institute for Social Research (HIS). Four participants left the project while three others joined it, and the group began to crystallize. The list of topics was likewise finalized following the six-month interval between the meetings, which we used to visit various libraries and archives and to engage in a comprehensive survey of the existing documentation and to take note of its limitations. At this second and subsequent meeting we discussed the documentation and the nature of the available sources, and it was these archive materials, press reports, interviews and ethnographic studies that in many cases determined the research questions. Most of the project participants are professional historians, three are sociologists and anthropologists, two are architects and one is a writer. The majority of our group, both Jews and Palestinians, live in Israel. One Palestinian refugee lives in London. The political escalation in the area as the group was working has regrettably made it difficult to co-opt participants living in the areas of the Palestinian Authority or in the *Diaspora*. Many of the group's members are currently researching the history of Haifa or have done so in the past, while others are personally connected to the city. The professional and the biographical aspects defined differing and complementary links between participants and the topic, and some of us consciously chose to express this in our writing.

In February 2010 the group returned to Salzburg to discuss the final outline of each article. At this stage it appeared as though none of the articles would address the events of 1948 directly and exclusively. Yet at the same time, there is not a single article that is not in some way connected to these events. The state of affairs at that juncture reflected the group dynamics that developed among its members, and in particular the intuitive understanding that an excessively direct and hasty attempt to clarify the traumatic event and to directly address the violent moment was liable to generate opposing camps and to establish rigid positions emanating from the discourse of legitimacy on both sides of the dispute. If the very publication of the book at this time is to be considered a success, this stems from the slow pace and the caution with which the group members proceeded to conduct their mutual contacts and, paradoxically, from the knowledge that this project has nothing whatsoever to do with resolving the conflict.

In August 2010 we gathered at the Hamburger Institute for Social Research for the final writing session and took this opportunity to present the project to a small audience of scholars under the auspices of the HIS. This meeting enabled us to assess the considerable progress we had made as a group. This was in fact the fourth week that we had spent together over the past two years and these contacts had led to a deepening of relationships. It was perhaps because of this closeness or due to the moment of truth of writing that the year 1948 reappeared in all its force. He/she who had dropped out at the beginning saying that he/she was not prepared to forego his/her narrative was right. Collaborative writing does indeed demand compromise. Unlike the oral presentation of the articles at the Salzburg and Hamburg meetings, writing does not allow for speaking in two voices. By its very nature writing is an act of synthesis, and the semantics expose the authors' identities as well as their decisions as to the interpretation of the event. The text is thus an act of compromise, in the case of each individual article and in their joint presentation.

The articles in this book address the time before and after. The significance of these periods derives, as mentioned, from the year 1948, which hovers over all the book's pages. The relations between the national groupings, the contacts and the tensions between them, lie at the foundation of the articles dealing with the Mandate period, which examine the limits of the existence of civil society amidst a national conflict. These articles may, either consciously or not, impose a dimension of contra-factual history on readers; as they address the contacts among the various national communities they indirectly point to the historical option that did not come to pass, and which may possibly have evolved in circumstances of non-sovereignty. Some of the articles that address the post-1948 period in Israeli Haifa examine the life of the Palestinian community that remained in the city, or alternatively, the impact of the Mandatory Palestinian community on the memory of the contemporary city. This, then, is a project that addresses history and memory and the links between these issues and individual and collective identity in the pre and post eras. Just as engagement with memory does not follow the chronological axis of time, we chose to arrange the articles thematically rather than chronologically, along a path that moves from the individual to the community and then returns to the individual.

The book begins with the article by Mahmoud Yazbak and Yfaat Weiss, which traces on a small scale the narrative of Haifa's urban Palestinian society prior to and following the *Nakba* through the stories of two houses built in the city in the 1930s. The symbolic power of the house in the narrative of the destruction of Palestinian society in 1948 in general and in the cities in particular requires no elaboration. While the home of the Muslim Shiblak family represents the story of Palestinian refugees who were prevented from returning to their home and their city, thereby symbolizing the fate of the Palestinians in general, the story of the home of the Christian Swidan family, which returned to settle in the city against all odds is a very different and exceptional one. It is this exceptionality that undermines the common label of "coexistence" that conceals more than it reveals.

Houses, their fate and the fate of their builders likewise constitute the central topic of the article by Waleed Karkabi and Adi Roitenberg. They reconstruct the cooperation and unusual friendship that developed between the Jewish architect Moshe Gerstel and the Muslim entrepreneur, businessman and public figure, Hajj Tahir Qaraman. The article traces the fate of the buildings that the Muslim entrepreneur Qaraman and the International Style architect Gerstel built, separately and jointly, on the Jewish-Arab seam line during the 1930s and 1940s, which were destined to find themselves in the no-man's land of the civil war only a few years after they were built.

The article by Manar Hasan and Ami Ayalon likewise addresses the relations and social ties between Arabs and Jews in Haifa in the 1930s and 1940s, a period during which a new public space took shape in the city as a result of the processes of modernization. The article examines Haifa's public spaces as areas of social change and Arab-Jewish cohabitation in times of national conflict. It observes the presence of men and women in the city's public places, especially those associated with cultural activities. Such places were located in different parts of the city and accessing them often entailed crossing geographic and other inter-communal boundaries. To what extent, the chapter asks, did Arabs and Jews feel comfortable sharing their leisure spaces with each other? And in what measure was such sharing affected by the political vicissitudes of the period?

Alongside the sphere of culture and leisure, the labor market constituted a major area of contact between Jews and Palestinians in Mandatory Haifa. In their joint article on the oil and soap industry and trade in Mandatory Haifa, Mustafa Abbasi and David De Vries demonstrate the material foundations of some of the political changes that beset the mixed town of Haifa in the 20th century. Examining this symbolically and politically charged economic branch, the authors expose the forces and factors that operated prior to 1948 to separate Haifa's Palestinian and Jewish communities. At the same time the article exposes a lesser known dimension in the historical literature of Haifa: the relative capacities of the oil and soap producers and merchants in the Arab and the Jewish communities to survive and compete within the wider regional economic context of this branch. These relative capacities testify to the reciprocal relations between the local and the political spheres on the one hand and the spatial-Mediterranean dimension on the other.

The article by Daniel Rabinowitz and Johnny Mansour observes the residents of the city of Haifa and the Palestinian refugee *Diaspora* in the year 1950 through a shared but divisive moment. Beginning with the unusually cold weather that hit the Middle East in February 1950, the authors focus on the manner in which this resonates in the memories and narratives of *Haifo'im* (Israeli residents of Haifa) and *Hayfawis* (Palestinians from Haifa, both residents and exiled refugees). Locating the event and its memory in the historical, political and cultural context of Haifa in the immediate aftermath of the war of 1948, the article highlights the impact that outstanding climatic events can have on periodization, temporal suspension and place making.

Whereas the previous article accompanies the *Hayfawis* to their places of exile, the joint article by Salman Natour and Avner Giladi, which addresses memory and identity, is situated in two locations on one of the main avenues of Haifa's German Colony. These are the Haifa City Museum, a municipal educational institution that aspires to foster a local identity in the spirit of the dominant Zionist ideology, and Café *Fattush*, which, with the modest means at its disposal, expresses the historical account and cultural aspirations of the city's Palestinian minority. Employing historiography as well as ethnography, the authors trace the steps taken and the efforts made by these two different institutions to define the city's history and cultural identity.

The book's final article brings the discussion back to the individual, his/her memories and home. The article written jointly by Regev Nathansohn, on the basis of interviews that he has conducted in recent years with Haifa residents born in the 1930s (Jews and Arabs alike), and Abbas Shiblak, on the basis of secondary literature and his own family's experiences seeks to show Haifa's twofold experience of solid inter-communal relations and strategies of segregation. The article challenges the experience of national segregation in Haifa, seeking to examine to what extent it indeed existed in an unequivocal form during the 1930s and 1940s and the manner in which it is reflected, reproduced or challenged in later memories and historical narratives as configurations of memory.

We take pleasure in thanking the *Institute for Historical Justice and Reconciliation* under whose auspices this group was formed, and its Executive Director, Catherine Cissé-van den Muijsenbergh, who initiated the process, was deeply involved in the work of the group, and facilitated the publication of this research.

We are grateful to the *Hamburger Institute for Social Research* and to Ulrich Bielefeld, Director of the Research Unit *Nation and Society* for most generously hosting two of the scholars' meetings, for intellectual inspiring and placing at our disposal the HIS's excellent information and library services and for enabling us to present the project for the first time to a scholarly audience last year.

Our final thanks go to the participants in the group for their endurance, devotion and the great interest that they showed in this complex project during each of its stages.

Historical Mile Stones

The following short historical introduction offers a brief chronology of the city's development since the mid-19th century and might be read by those who miss a clear historical background.

When, in 1840, the Ottomans resumed their hold over Palestine, Haifa's administrative position was upgraded and became a center of a *qada`* (district). In parallel, Haifa's importance as one of Palestine's main harbors and centers for foreign trade grew rapidly from that time on.[1]

When the German Templars began migrating to Palestine in 1868 they set up in Haifa their first settlement to be known as the "German Colony", in expectation of the city's future development. Migration of European Jews to northern Palestine began in the 1880s and the Jewish neighborhood gradually grew within the Islamic quarter (*al-Hara al-Sharqiyya*). Soon afterwards, the Baha`is established their first homes in Haifa following their expulsion from Iran. European merchants and officials who worked in European consulates and in missionary organizations began to spread around the city. With Haifa's increased administrative importance, and as the economic infrastructure expanded, so the number of immigrants increased from inside and outside Palestine, both urban and rural people, and from various religious communities. This human diversity became a characteristic of the city. Palestinians gave Haifa the name of *Umm al-Gharib* (Mother of the Stranger).

Construction of the Hijaz railway started in 1892 and, on 1 October 1905, celebrations marked the line's opening. It connected Haifa with Damascus in the north and with the Hijaz in the south. The Ottoman administration chose Haifa as the major rail terminus and brought with it railway maintenance works and the railway administration offices. Endless projects and programs to expand the port followed. Investors, both locally-based and from abroad, set up heavy industry in Haifa because of its excellent infrastructure.

By the beginning of the 20th century, Haifa had become the leading city in northern Palestine. As a result, Jewish immigrants settled there in

---

[1] For a detailed study of Haifa during the Ottoman Period, see Mahmoud Yazbak, *Haifa in the Late Ottoman Period: A Muslim City in Transition 1864-1914* (1998).

the new Herzliya neighborhood, at the foot of Mount Carmel, the first specifically Zionist planned area. An indication of the city's importance to the future Zionist project was the opening of the first academic Jewish institute in 1912, the Technion. In addition, the arrival of Jewish-owned heavy industry changed the city's economic base.

Merchants with businesses in Beirut or Damascus relocated to Haifa or set up branches and warehouses there. The expansion of industry and commerce in Haifa and the presence of the railway network encouraged many wealthy Palestinian families by the early 20th century to invest in Haifa and to live there. In addition, people from the countryside moved to the city in search of work. New neighborhoods appeared, a process speeded up with the end of World War I and the beginning of the British Mandate.

The rapid change in the social and economic infrastructure of Haifa from the late Ottoman Era onwards was reflected in cultural developments. When the Ottoman authority permitted in 1908 publication of newspapers, Haifa emerged as a center of journalism. By 1914 nine newspapers and magazines were published in Haifa, the most important of which was the *al-Karmil* newspaper owned and edited by Najib Nassar. It became well known for its anti-Zionist views.

Under the British Mandate (1918-1948) Haifa became the administrative capital of northern Palestine. The region's largest factories were built in Haifa during the first decade of British rule, *Le Grand Moulin*, Shemen for soup production, *Nesher* for cement, al-Hajj Tahir Qaraman's factory for cigarettes and tobacco, as well as many others.

Initiatives by the British Mandate included building a new and modern harbor to give Palestine a main maritime port, constructing a large airport, establishing a new railway workshop, building pipelines for transporting oil from Iraq and establishing a refinery in the bay of Haifa.

The expansion of the economic structure of the city during the British Mandate years made Haifa a very attractive city for immigrants, both Arabs and Jews. The population increase completely changed the city's character.

Haifa's social evolution during this period, demonstrates a fascinating process of urbanization, due to the heterogeneous nature of its component people: villagers from various areas, Christians of all churches, Muslims, Jews, Syrians, Lebanese, Jordanians, Egyptians, Sudanese and Europeans intermingled together in Haifa's daily life.

Haifa's population growth, from approximately 22,000 in 1918 to more than 50,000 in 1931 and to more than 140,000 by 1947, dramatically changed its demographic character. The most phenomenal change during the Mandate period was in the Jewish community. While Jews made up approximately one-eighth of the population in 1918, their number grew to one-quarter in 1922, to one-third in 1931, and to over one-half of the total inhabitants of Haifa in 1947. This dramatic increase can only be explained by the number of Jewish immigrants that flooded Palestine in successive waves in the 1930s after the emergence of National Socialism in Germany and the persecution of Jews in Europe.

The Arab population had also grown tremendously during the 1930s as a result of natural increase and immigration. It is estimated that the Arab population of Haifa increased from 34,148 in 1931 to more than 50,000 in 1938. Both the British Mandatory administration and the Arab private sector initiated a number of projects that attracted Arab workers, skilled and unskilled. Hence, what had been a relatively small town at the beginning of the Mandate period had become one of the largest cities in Palestine over the course of 39 years. The population growth changed the balance of the town's communities, stripping the Arab community of the social and psychological power it had previously enjoyed in its majority status.

A serious slump in the building industry in the spring of 1936 deeply affected both Arab and Jewish unemployment. The Arab strike which started in Haifa in April 1936, resulted in a take-over by Jewish labor in segments of work that had previously been purely Arab. Following the strike and the coming three years of the rebellion, Arab building and its allied industries came to a total standstill, which further deepened unemployment among the Arabs. These were mostly day laborers who were unorganized and quickly lost their jobs to the *Histadrut* (the Jewish Labor Organization), which was fighting to capture such areas of work, leaving many unskilled seasonal Arab workers to return to the familiar cycle of poverty. Approximately 50 percent of the Arab population in Haifa was reported to be living in slums, characterized by overcrowded living conditions, poor sanitation, and low income residents.

Sheikh 'Izz al-Din al-Qassam, a religious and charismatic leader, who agitated among the urban poor, won the trust and adulation of the rural immigrants in Haifa. His armed activity, first evidenced in November 1935, set a precedent based on understanding the readiness and ability of the embittered poor immigrants to carry out a rebellion. For them it would be a release of the social pressure and perpetual economic hardship. The mass support of al-Qassam's activity was seen as the start of a process of shaking free from the prolonged distress. The long-simmering social and political agitation reached boiling point with al-Qassam's death (November 1935). His disciples and friends, who understood this well, let the spark that caused a three-year rebellion (1936-1939). As the situation of the rebels in early 1939 grew more difficult, owing to government attacks and lack of funds and arms, their violence was increasingly directed against the most vulnerable elements – the Arab civilian population and those considered to be the cause of their plight. Their attacks reflected the bitterness of the peasants and poor immigrants in a state of lawlessness.

The end of the revolt in Haifa, as elsewhere, irrespective of its negative aspects, was a triumph for the Mandatory administration and the Jewish National Home policy. It was also a minor victory for the mercantile Arab class, which could now resume its business and its residence without concern for what the future might hold. However, it was a moral and political defeat of Arab society as a whole. In Haifa the balance had tipped in favor of the Jewish character of the city, and it was set on a course which was dramatically achieved with the tragic expulsion of the Arab population in 1948. If by the end of World War I the Arab population stood at roughly 17,000 and the Jews numbered approximately 3,000, in 1947 there would be approximately 74,000 Arabs and a similar number of Jews living in the town.

Hostilities broke down in Palestine when on 29 November 1947 the United Nations accepted Resolution 181, which envisaged the partition of Palestine into an Arab and a Jewish state. When less than six months later, on 15 May 1948, the Jewish leaders proclaimed the State of Israel in those parts of Palestine that were allocated to it in the Partition Plan as well as in the parts of which the Israeli armed forces had taken control by then, there were barely 2,000-3,000 Palestinians left in Haifa.

A TALE OF TWO HOUSES

MAHMOUD YAZBAK AND YFAAT WEISS[1]

PREFACE

Haifa's Palestinian residents endured great suffering during the course of the war of 1948. Their distress became particularly intense in April, when the city fell to the Jewish forces, and was manifested in the forced mass departure from their city and their homes. Of the approximately 74,000 Palestinian residents who had lived in Haifa prior to its conquest only some three thousand remained, dispersed among the city's neighborhoods. Upon proclamation of the establishment of the State of Israel in May 1948, the provisional government of Israel refused to allow these people to remain where they were and forced them to leave their homes and neighborhoods, assembling them in one area, *Wadi al-Nisnas*, in order to facilitate control over them. Jewish residents who had arrived in Israel, initially from Europe and subsequently from Arab countries, were housed in place of the original householders who had abandoned their homes owing to the war or were forced to vacate them in its wake. What happened to the Palestinians' houses and their property? How did the State of Israel deal with this property and what part does it play in Palestinian consciousness? In the aftershock of the *Nakba* (catastrophe), the property that had belonged to those Palestinians who had become refugees did not constitute a major concern within Palestinian political, juridical, intellectual and academic activity, and remained in the shadows for many years. With the stirring of a more active Palestinian leadership in the first half of the 1960s, the Palestinians began to address these issues in earnest in an endeavor to establish evidence of their prior existence among the public at large and amid a dismissive public opinion, as part of a general move toward the establishment of an independent Palestinian political entity. Israeli institutions, on the contrary, systematically endeavored to erase Palestinian history and its remnants within the newly created Israeli space: the state destroyed Arab villages whose inhabitants had recently become refugees,

---

[1] The authors wish to thank Gal Oron and Ziyad Dahir for their assistance.

covered many of them through forestation and located Jewish settlements in these areas. The Palestinian and mixed cities endured a systematic process of destruction of the Arab neighborhoods and the establishment of Jewish neighborhoods in their stead. Transformation of the space was accompanied by the changing of the names of streets and neighborhoods as part of a general process of "Hebraization of the map." Haifa's Arab quarters fell victim to this policy of "Hebraization," and the erasure of Palestinian collective memory and its replacement by an alternative memory that ignored the Arab one. This was an Israeli memory that established the perspective of the victor while annulling the memory of the vanquished.

This article seeks to restore that which has been repressed by exposing two Palestinian houses built prior to the 1948 war and which represent on a small scale many of the components of Palestinian memory prior to it. The stories of these two houses represent the narrative of urban Palestinian society prior to and after the *Nakba*: the Shiblak family house represents the story of Palestinian refugees who were forbidden to return to their home and city, while Swidan House represents the story of the Palestinian minority that remained in Haifa, continually engaged in a Sisyphean struggle for the *de facto* realization of *de jure* rights derived from a formal civil equality that does not in fact exist.

THE HOUSE OF FADIL AHMAD SHIBLAK: 1 LOD ROAD

Entrepreneurship

In 1926 Fadil Shiblak purchased from his brother-in-law Husayn al-Qazaq a small plot of land of 372 square meters located between Hadar ha-Carmel and the upper extremity of Wadi al-Salib, in an area that would soon become a seam line, in order to erect on it a house for himself and his new wife Zahiyyah. Toward the end of the twenties he built a small house on part of the land, to which he moved from his family home in the *Wadi al-Nisnas* neighborhood in the western section of the city. Once his finances had improved, in autumn 1935 Fadil Shiblak requested the engineering office of Ahmad Faris and Taufiq Mannasi to prepare for him a plan for the construction of a large house on his entire plot of land.

In those days, during the time of the British Mandate, Haifa was at the height of a building boom and a period of economic entrepreneurship. The building of a new harbor – the largest in the Middle East – the connection of the oil pipeline from Iraq to Haifa, and the construction of the oil refinery, alongside the massive imperial investments in which both the Jewish and Arab business and private sectors participated, had turned it into a city that was attracting more manpower than any other. In parallel, and in the wake of the Nazis' rise to power in Germany and its negative impact on the condition of European Jews in general, the pace of Jewish immigration to the city picked up in the 1930s. As a result of the growing tide of

Fig. 1: The Shiblak House in Lod Road 1 (September 2010)

migration – both Arab and Jewish – the city was experiencing an acute shortage of housing, and the price of houses was spiraling accordingly. Due to these circumstances, many of the city's wealthier residents began to invest in constructing apartment buildings for rental purposes. Among them was Fadil Shiblak, who, like many others, decided to erect his building in the upper regions of *Wadi al-Salib*. The construction of housing earmarked primarily for rental gave birth to new patterns of construction and architecture: instead of the traditional Palestinian building constructed according to the al-'Aqid method – the arched ceiling – and rather than the extended family home surrounded by a wall and inner courtyard, the thirties witnessed the construction of houses comprising a number of stories, each containing several apartments designed for families unconnected by family ties. Fadil Shiblak's house accorded with this building pattern, initially adopted in the Jewish neighborhoods and which rapidly became prevalent also in the new Arab neighborhoods.

From where did the Shiblaks come? As far as we know they moved in the early 20th century from the crowded city neighborhoods within the wall that enclosed the old city to *Wadi al-Nisnas* in the west of the city, where the family's homes stand to this day. The Shiblaks were related by marriage to the al-Qazaq family, which owned extensive agricultural tracts of land in the west of the city, watered by the "al-Qazaq spring" named after them, located on the upper reaches of the area later known as the "German Colony."[2] The Shiblaks prospered along with the city's development. Ahmad, Fadil Shiblak's father, erected a new quarry on the summit of Mount Carmel in the area known as Jabal Iskandar, close to *Wadi al-Siyyah* in the vicinity of the village of Kababir. The quarry was designed to meet the demand for building blocks in the early 20th century, which could no longer be satisfied by the ancient quarries situated on the land of al-Fakhura on the western slopes of the Carmel in the direction of Stella Maris.[3] Convoys of camels transported the stones to Haifa for construction of the houses of the expanding city. The Shiblaks were well known in the early 20th century as investors and owners of quarries in the Kababir and *Wadi al-Siyyah* area. In addition to Fadil Shiblak, who, following the birth of his first son Khalil acquired the name Abu Khalil, Hasan Shiblak (Abu Nayif), whose house still stands in *Wadi al-Nisnas* and who was among the largest road construction contractors and the owner of a contracting company named "Shiblak and Abd al-Fattah," likewise gained a reputation.[4] Hasan Shiblak, incidentally, was among the upper echelon of the city's Palestinian political leadership. He joined the leadership of the Shaykh 'Izz al-Din al-Qassam movement, which led the revolt in Haifa in the mid-1930s, and his name resurfaced as a member of the city's Arab national leadership with the intensification of the Arab-Jewish struggle toward the end of the British Mandate.[5] The Shiblaks benefited from the building boom and its expansion. When the British authorities began to build the harbor in the early 1930s, there was a sharp rise in the demand for

---

[2] Mahmoud Yazbak, *Haifa in the Late Ottoman Period, 1864-1914: A Muslim Town in Transition* (1988), pp. 212-228.
[3] Testimony of Mrs. Zahiyyah Shiblak, March 1991, Tunisia.
[4] See www.zochrot.org/index.php?id=526.
[5] *Al-Difa' 'An Hayfa Wa-Qadiyyat Filastin, Mudhakarrat Rashid al-Hajj Ibrahim* (Defending Haifa and the Palestinian Question, Memoirs of Rashid al-Hajj Ibrahim), Introduced by Walid al-Khalidi (2005), pp. 50, 62, 75-76 and 128; Bayan N. al-Hut, *Al-Qiyadat wal-Mu'sassat fi Filastin 1917-1948* (1984), pp. 327 and 386.
The Shiblak family owned a number of buildings dotted around Haifa's Arab neighborhoods. Hasan Shiblak (Abu Nayif), who made his home in *Wadi al-Nisnas*, was the best known member of the family in Haifa.

building stones and quarry laborers, most of whom came from the Nablus area, a city that would acquire great importance in the life of the family.

From Roof to Beams

Over a short period, between the construction of Fadil Shiblak's small home in the late 1920s and his decision in 1935 to add two stories, the *Wadi al-Salib* neighborhood underwent profound changes: the brushwood bushes (*Billan*) that had covered the slopes of the ravine had recently vanished, and together with them the original name of the slope, *Ard al-Billan* (Land of Brushwood) was forgotten by the residents. New stone houses gradually climbed the stony slopes of the ravine from its outlet and the railway station toward its highest points, and with them the name Wadi al-Salib slowly became established. As the density of population increased, long lines of vertical steps were built. Building activity increased at the same time also in the *Hadar ha-Carmel* neighborhood, extending along the lateral axis connecting the German Colony in the west of the city to *Wadi al-Salib* in its east. The location of Fadil Shiblak's house in fact constituted a "meeting point", which would soon turn into a "seam line" and a boundary separating the Jewish *Hadar ha-Carmel* neighborhood from the Arab *Wadi al-Salib* Quarter.[6]

In early September 1935 the engineers Ahmad Faris and Taufiq Mannasi submitted a construction plan and an application for building permission for the Fadil Shiblak house to the Building Licensing Department in the City Engineer's Bureau. The department's clerks opened a building file, which to this day bears the number 35/1510, even though the entire Shiblak family is no longer present in the city.[7] Upon the opening of the file the applicant paid a sum of 2.5 Liras as a deposit for the required license. In testimony that they would submit many years later Mrs. Zahiyyah Shiblak, Fadil's wife,[8] in exile in Tunisia, and her first-born son Khalil,[9] in exile in Beirut, noted that the management of Barclays Bank in Haifa had agreed to provide Fadil with a loan of 5,000 liras for the building of the house on the strength of a recommendation and guarantee given by Zahiyyah's father Hasan al-Qazaq, a well-known Haifa grain merchant. Fadil Shiblak furthermore mortgaged his house until completion of the repayment of the substantial loan, which was returned in monthly

---
[6] Yfaat Weiss, *A Confiscated Memory: Wadi Salib and Haifa's Lost Memory* (2011).
[7] Haifa Municipality, Archives of The Conservation Department, file no. 35/1510, p. 32.
[8] Testimony of Mrs. Zahiyyah Shiblak.
[9] Testimony of Khalil Shiblak, Beirut, 1 November 2009.

installments of 30 Liras that Fadil Shiblak continued to pay regularly up to the events of 1948 and the loss of his home.

The building file of Shiblak House shows that toward the end of October 1935 the City Engineer's Bureau considered the plans for the expansion of Shiblak's house and returned them to the engineers for correction. The Bureau made the granting of building permission conditional on the clear demarcation of the sewage lines. It appears that Fadil Shiblak did not await the conclusion of the prolonged discussions of the City Engineer's Bureau and began construction work in earnest before receiving permission. At the end of January 1936, with building nearing completion, the head of the City Engineer's Bureau issued an official building permit that bore the number 1538/1510/35. The permit stipulated that a stone wall be built to enclose the plot of land on which the house was built. Before issuing "permission to occupy the building" according to the municipal Law, the City Engineer's Department demanded that changes be made to the wall surrounding the plot of land. On 23 March 1936, after meeting the demands of the Engineering Bureau, Fadil Shiblak submitted a second request for permission "to occupy the building," following which two municipal inspectors, the sanitary inspector and the building inspector, went out to inspect the house at close quarters. The former reported that all the sanitary conditions had been complied with, while the latter lodged an objection owing to the additions made by the owner on the basement floor, namely the small apartment that Fadil had built without permission toward the end of the 1920s. These additions had been made in order to enlarge the area of the basement and thereby the area designated for rental, and they resulted both in the building inspector's refusal to grant permission to occupy the building,[10] and in the submission of a lawsuit by the City Engineer's Bureau against the owner.[11] The documentation in the building file shows that Fadil Shiblak succeeded in persuading the court that the basement had been built prior to the passing of the municipal laws and their implementation, and the municipality subsequently granted Mr. Shiblak permission to occupy the house in July 1936.[12]

Fadil Ahmad Shiblak's house is two stories high, each of which covers an area of 140 square meters. They are constructed on top of a basement covering an area of 111 square meters.[13] The building's facades

---

[10] Haifa Municipality, Archives of The Conservation Department, file no. 35/1510, p. 83.
[11] Ibid., p. 77.
[12] Ibid., pp. 84 and 88.
[13] Ibid., the building plans.

are made of white stone and each story has two verandahs, one facing east and the other north, with a view of Haifa Bay and the port. At the time of their construction each of the two upper stories contained four rooms, two kitchens, two shower rooms and two toilets. The basement floor likewise contained four somewhat smaller rooms, as well as a kitchen, a shower room and a toilet. The inner division of Fadil Shiblak's house into apartments and its external appearance were characteristic of the pattern shared by many other houses designed by the same engineers, namely, the conventional pattern for houses of Haifa's middle class in the 1930s and up to the *Nakba*.

The Tenants

The population density experienced by Haifa during the 1930s and 1940s, produced by the many waves of Arab and Jewish migration to the city, was clearly felt also in Fadil Shiblak's house. In 1942, so file 35/1510 reveals, in addition to the landlord, nine families comprising a total of 47 individuals lived in the house that had initially been built as a profit-generating investment.[14] In order to contain so large a number of tenants the house had undergone a process of re-division. Instead of the five apartments included in the house when it was built, there were now, in 1942, nine apartments. The reduced area of the apartments expressed primarily the growing demand for rental accommodation in Haifa. Fadil Shiblak's investment was thus a particularly successful one, exceeding his expectations and enabling him to make the regular repayments on the loan that he had taken out from the bank for construction of the house.

As previously mentioned, owing to its location at the eastern extremity of the Jewish *Hadar ha-Carmel* neighborhood, the Shiblak House, like many other Arab houses built as an investment in this area, attracted both Arabs and Jews, who rented rooms in the same apartments and lived therein side by side, sharing the toilets, kitchens and showers. Recalling the names of the house's tenants 43 years after becoming a refugee, the landlady Mrs. Zahiyyah Shiblak, formerly Qazaq, remarked: "Among the tenants was Umm Musa, an Arab Jewess who lived on the ground floor. There was also a [Jewish] Romanian family with a son named Re'uven. There was also Subhi al-Khadra from Gaza. There were others whose names I do not presently recall."[15] The documents in the archive of

---

[14] Ibid., pp. 38 and 91.
[15] Testimony of Mrs. Zahiyyah Shiblak, March 1991.

Haifa Municipality mention the names of further tenants, Sarah Katiri, Giza Goldstein, Rahamim Lugashi and Tsurel Yona.[16] Zahiyyah Shiblak remembered the social ties between the Arab and Jewish occupants as having been very good. In this respect Mrs. Shiblak noted that Re'uven, the son of the Romanian Jewish family, was a personal friend of her brother, Subhi al-Qazaq.[17] Re'uven's name was likewise mentioned in the testimony submitted recently by Khalil, Fadil Shiblak's eldest son, in Beirut, in which he noted that "Our neighbor on the floor on which we lived was a Romanian [Jewess] and she had two young sons, one named Re'uven and the other, the younger, was named Otto. We maintained very good relations with this family. I later learned that Re'uven joined the *Haganah* and was killed in the fighting in Haifa."[18]

The tenants' peaceful existence was first disturbed with the outbreak of World War II. With British strategic and military installations located in its vicinity, Haifa became a preferred target for bombing by Axis war planes, and particularly by Italian planes. The apartment buildings and civilian installations in the city were totally lacking in shelters that could protect residents from these bombings, and the Mandatory Government quickly issued a number of regulations that obliged residents to construct shelters in their homes so as to protect themselves.[19] As was to be expected, many did not or could not comply with the regulations, while those who could afford to do so generally chose to distance themselves from the danger and to leave the city until peace returned. During the war years many of the city's wealthier residents moved inland and to villages in the vicinity of Haifa, which did not endure attacks by the Axis powers' planes.[20]

Over the years Fadil Shiblak had established good connections with the city of Nablus and also maintained good relations with the residents of its nearby village Lubban-al-Sharqiyya, several of whose residents had migrated to Haifa and worked in the family's quarry at Jabal Iskandar in the city. Because of the life threatening circumstances and continued bombing of the city, and since he had been directly injured by one of the raids when caught in a barber shop in the city center,[21] he decided in 1941 to leave town temporarily and move to Nablus, with the intention of returning to

---

[16] Haifa Municipality, Archives of The Conservation Department, file no. 35/1510, p. 89.
[17] Testimony of Mrs. Zahiyyah Shiblak, March 1991.
[18] Testimony of Khalil Shiblak, Fadil's first-born son, Beirut, 1 November 2009.
[19] Haifa Municipality, Archives of The Conservation Department, file no. 35/1510, p. 38.
[20] 'Abd al-Latif Kanafani, *15 Shari' al-burj – Haifa, dhikrayat wa-'ibar* (1996), p. 85.
[21] Testimony of Mr. 'Abbas Shiblak, Oxford, January 2010.

Haifa with his family at the end of the war. The family remained in Nablus for over three years, where the daughter Ra'isa and the son 'Abbas were born. The paterfamilias Fadil would briefly travel to Haifa every so often to collect the rent for the apartments that served as a source of income for the upkeep of the family members in Nablus, where there were few opportunities to make a living.

His absence did not absolve Fadil Shiblak from having to look after the property. During the time that Fadil Shiblak and his family were staying in Nablus, the Jewish tenants submitted a complaint to the mayor of Haifa on 25 February 1942 owing to the lack of a shelter in the building for the protection of its occupants, and demanded that the landlord be ordered to build a shelter.[22] A few days subsequent to the neighbors' application an urgent demand on the part of Haifa Municipality to build a shelter in his Haifa house with an area of no less than 20 square meters in order to protect the tenants from aerial bombing was dispatched to Fadil Shiblak's address in Nablus. On the strength of the recommendations of the Municipal Emergency Committee it was decided to convert one of the rooms in the house for this purpose, and the Municipality peremptorily issued a permit to begin work. From his place of sojourn in Nablus Fadil Shiblak authorized a relative of his wife's, Mr. 'Abd al-'Al al-Qazaq, to undertake the project. Owing to the matter's importance, the Municipal Emergency Committee agreed to provide the property owner with the required construction materials, which were subject to rationing because of the emergency and the war. Work on reinforcement of the shelter's external walls was soon completed, prior to the commencement of work on the inside. In light of the delay in continuing the job and the pressure exerted on the Mayor by the tenants, and after Giza Goldstein had submitted a signed complaint to the High Commissioner in person,[23] Haifa Municipality issued a lawsuit against Fadil Shiblak in order to compel him to complete the construction of the shelter. During the course of the hearing held in the Haifa court Fadil Shiblak succeeded in proving his sincere desire to continue the construction work and to reinforce the walls of the designated room from within. However, he noted, he had encountered opposition on the part of the Jewish tenant living in this room, who had flatly refused to vacate the room for the sake of the designated shelter. Since the tenant could not, according to the existing laws, be compelled to vacate the

---

[22] Haifa Municipality, Archives of The Conservation Department, file no. 35/1510, document no. 18, 25 February 1942.
[23] Ibid., document no. 27, 20 July 1942.

apartment, the City Engineer emphasized in his report that "there are many situations similar to this, and this issue should be resolved by means of the passing of new laws."[24] When the Shiblaks returned to their home in Haifa toward the end of World War II in late 1944 the shelter that may have protected the tenants from the bombardments of the next war, which would take both the house and its occupants by surprise in 1948, had not yet been built.

Exceptions

Apart from the shelter, Fadil Shiblak was called upon to address a further particular request made by one of the tenants. In light of the increasing severity of the shortage of accommodation in the Jewish neighborhoods of Haifa, he was approached while in Nablus by Mrs. Sarah Katiri, a Jewish tenant who, with her husband, had rented the northern room of the building's ground floor, and who now requested permission to house her two elderly parents in her room. Fadil Shiblak voiced no opposition and did not demand any money in return. Since Mrs. Katiri's room was extremely small, her parents turned the open verandah into their living space during the summer months. With the advent of the winter of 1944 this arrangement was no longer sufficient, and with the authorization of the owner Mrs. Katiri erected a wooden fence, 4.5 meters long and 1.5 meters wide, around the verandah so as to protect her parents from the cold.[25] The City Engineer's Bureau opposed the change made by Katiri and the owner of the property without obtaining the appropriate permit, and in January 1945 issued a lawsuit against them demanding that they demolish the "illegal [addition] that has become a living room."[26] In response Sarah Katiri submitted a supplicatory letter to the City Engineer in which she noted the harsh conditions endured by her parents as a result of the severe shortage of accommodation in Haifa, which had left her no choice but to house them in her room. In her pleading she expressed her willingness "to remove the wooden wall upon the ending of the war and the ending of the time of anger and shortage of apartments," adding that "the demolition of the wooden walls will leave my parents without a roof over their heads."[27] In fact, and

---

[24] Ibid., file no. 35/1510, document no. 30, 1 October 1942.
[25] Ibid., document no. 35, 17 October 1944.
[26] Ibid., document no. 38, undated, marked B\26\45.
[27] Ibid., document no. 36, 2 November 1944.

despite the court's decision calling for the demolition of this addition[28], the wooden wall remained in place until the end of World War II.

The shortage of housing in Haifa became ever more acute in the mid-1940s in the wake of the increasing waves of immigration from within the county of those seeking employment in Haifa, but also because of the waves of residents returning to their city and the swelling ranks of Jewish immigrants from central Europe after the ending of World War II. With the increased demand for housing and the rise in rents the phenomenon of neighborhoods of tin shacks spread through Haifa as did the erection of tin rooms on the roofs of buildings for the sake of rental and generation of profit without having to obtain municipal permission. The attempts of the City Engineer and the activity of the City Council failed to put an end to these phenomena even when the courts were utilized for this purpose and issued wholesale demolition orders.[29] The records of Haifa Municipality show that when Fadil Shiblak returned to his Haifa home from Nablus he had acted in a similar manner. In early 1946 he erected on the roof of his building "a small room, its walls made of blocks and its ceiling of tin plates, for the purpose of rental, without obtaining the appropriate permit from the municipality." Since he did not respond to the City Engineer's warnings to demolish the small room, the municipal bureau responsible for inspection of building lodged a formal complaint against Fadil Shiblak to the court and obtained a demolition order. Shortly thereafter the Municipality again applied to the court regarding the same issue and obtained a further demolition order, but Fadil Shiblak ignored this as well. Haifa Municipality could not, in fact, offer alternative solutions to the shortage of housing and therefore failed to display resolve in implementing the demolition orders.[30]

The shortage of housing in Haifa encouraged the owners of buildings intended for rental to make major changes in the inner division of the apartments they owned in order to reduce their size and increase the number of lessees. This trend is clearly apparent in the documents pertaining to Fadil Shiblak's house; the basement floor of his building, which originally comprised four living rooms, two shower rooms and two kitchens designed for the domicile of two families, underwent a change in 1946, in the wake of which it contained eight living rooms, two shower

---

[28] Ibid., document no. 27, 20 July 1942.
[29] Mahmoud Yazbak, *Al-Hijra al-'Arabiyya Ila Hayfa fi zaman al-Intidab* (1988), pp. 132-143.
[30] Haifa Municipality, Archives of The Conservation Department, file no. 35/1510, document no. 42, undated, marked B\1001\47.

rooms and one kitchen shared by all the occupants of the floor.[31] On the eve of the 1948 war Fadil Shiblak's house was thus crowded with tenants of various ethnic origins: Arabs, Arab Jews and Ashkenazi Jews, as Zahiyyah Shiblak testified. The number of families living in the basement varied between nine and twelve, where they resided under extremely harsh conditions and in a very confined space, sharing a kitchen, a shower and toilets. Having no alternative, the tenants in the building regularly encountered one another, and during the attacks of the planes of the Axis nations they sat in fear together, perhaps quarreling and laughing together in turn. Fadil Shiblak's house, in fact, represented one case among many of a pattern that repeated itself in most of Haifa's Arab neighborhoods, and in particular in those located along the "seam lines" that separated the Arab and Jewish neighborhoods. This phenomenon occurred in one direction only; neither historical documentation nor oral history document a similar case regarding a Jewish owned building. One may assume that, even when built by private initiative, Jewish construction was designed to build the national home. With the onset of the winter of 1947 the human mosaic of Fadil Shiblak's tenants and that of other similar buildings began to change rapidly; violent incidents were on the rise in Haifa, as in the other parts of the country, and at the beginning of 1948 the majority of Jewish families abandoned the buildings and moved behind the "seam lines," crowding together with the Jewish population, with the exception of one stubborn tenant, Mrs. Sarah Katiri (see Nathansohn and Shiblak's paper).

Exile

As we have mentioned, Shiblak House was located at a strategic point, not merely because this was the 'seam line,' but also because it overlooked all of the *Wadi al-Salib* area lying beneath it and stretching all the way to the eastern railway station. This station of the Ottoman Hijaz railway, which connected Haifa with Damascus in the North and with Hijaz in the South, is an icon in the annals of the city of Haifa. When it was ceremoniously opened in 1905 in the presence of a large number of invited guests, it symbolized the beginning of a series of profound changes that had commenced in the city several decades beforehand. With its establishment, the eastern area of Haifa began to attract investors and merchants, who erected their stores, warehouses and factories, and its construction provided a strong impetus to the city's economy and trade. The building of Fadil

---

[31] Ibid., the building plans of 1946.

Shiblak's house had been a part of these developments; yet now, on the verge of the confrontation between Jews and Arabs in the city, its location was to its detriment. The landlady, Mrs. Zahiyyah Shiblak, was keenly aware of the strategic location of the house, when, in her testimony recorded in 1991, she noted that her home "was surrounded by four roads, overlooked the Jewish area and the Carmel in one direction and *Wadi al-Salib* in the other, and the Jews had thus 'marked' it from the outset."[32] With the outbreak of hostilities in Haifa toward the end of 1947, the area of the house and the nearby buildings became a focus of intense military activity on the part of the Jewish and Arab forces.[33] In mid-February 1948 the *Haganah* forces invested considerable effort in improving their positions on the high ground overlooking the Arab neighborhoods, during the course of which they gained control over Fadil Shiblak's house and other houses in its vicinity at the head of *Wadi al-Salib*. As the danger to his family grew, the head of the family decided, as did thousands of other Arabs, to leave the city temporarily and to seek a safer place to live until such time that the hostilities subsided and the danger to his family passed, when he would be able to return to his home. One may well conjecture that, when he made the decision to leave his home in mid-February 1948, Fadil Shiblak clearly remembered the departure from the house at the time of the Axis powers' plane attacks on Haifa during World War II. Like thousands of other Arab Haifa residents, he most probably believed that he would return home shortly, as he had returned only a few years previously.

Among the impressions of the shooting, the mortars and the bombardment, the following images are etched in the memory of 'Abbas, at the time the youngest of Fadil Shiblak's children, who was aged five when his family left Haifa:

> On that day I was squashed together with my parents and three brothers into a small black car. We took a few belongings with us that filled the car. Among the objects we took was a Singer sewing machine that my mother had used for many years, and we took along also an *'ud*, a musical instrument that my parents really loved ... among the objects there was also a wooden box, which originally served as a container for sweets. I later understood the significance of this box, which contained precious things such as the keys to

---

[32] Testimony of Mrs. Zahiyyah Shiblak, March 1991.
[33] Tamir Goren, *Arab Haifa in 1948: The Intensity of the Struggle and Dimensions of the Debacle* (2006) (in Hebrew), see the daily reports of the *Haganah* in Haifa, pp. 105, 106, 346 and 349.

the house, land registry documents, the documents of ownership of the house and other documents, including the birth certificates of the family members.[34]

The black car left Fadil Shiblak's house on 1 Lod Road, Haifa in the direction of Nablus, to the house of Sabih al-Nabulsi opposite the famous *al-Hammuz* café, in which the Shiblak family had stayed when it left Haifa during World War II. The family had continued to rent this house after their return to Haifa at the end of the war since the eldest son Khalil, who had been sent to Nablus to study at al-Najah College, was living in the city, and members of the family frequently visited him, with the house in Nablus serving as lodgings during their visits.

Fadil Shiblak never returned to his house in Haifa. His legal status changed once the State of Israel was declared. According to international law he and the members of his family became refugees, while the State of Israel regarded them as enemies and prohibited them from returning to Haifa. During a short period of refuge in Nablus, which became part of the Kingdom of Jordan owing to the results of the war, the Shiblaks lost their sources of income. Given the new circumstances, the family's breadwinner could naturally no longer collect the rental from the tenants in the apartment building that he owned in Haifa. At the same time, and due to these changed circumstances, he was no longer able to pay the rent for the house in Nablus, nor to meet his family's basic needs of existence. For this reason he was compelled to accept the food aid distributed by United Nations Relief and Works Agency for Palestine Refugees in the Near East (UNRWA).[35] In order to reduce expenses, and since he refused to live in one of the refugee camps surrounding Nablus, Fadil Shiblak and his family moved to the village of Lubban al-Sharqiyya nearby Nablus, a place in which he knew many of the residents who had worked in the quarries on Jabal Iskandar in Haifa prior to the *Nakba*. Fadil Shiblak likewise lacked a source of livelihood or employment during his sojourn in the village of Lubban al-Sharqiyya, and spent his time in the village café. The members of his family had to make do with the little basic foodstuffs and the financial aid provided by UNRWA.[36] During the family's sojourn in Nablus another son, Hamza, was born to Fadil and Zahiyyah, a brother to Khalil, Ra'isa, 'Abbas and Ra'ifa. When the head of the family realized that they would not be able to return to Haifa, he left the village in 1952 for Amman and then moved on to Irbid in search of employment and suitable schools

---

[34] Testimony of 'Abbas Shiblak, 15 February 2009.
[35] Ibid.
[36] Ibid.

for his sons and daughters. Khalil, the oldest child, had meanwhile quit his studies in order to seek work and assist in the upkeep of the family. He found employment in Saudi Arabia, and used his salary to support his family in Irbid.

Like many of the Palestinians of their generation, following the '1967 *Naksa* (debacle)'[37] the Shiblaks participated in political activity in support of the resistance movement led by the Palestine Liberation Movement. During the family's stay in Jordan the daughter Ra'isa Shiblak completed her studies and began work as a teacher, while the son 'Abbas began to study at the law faculty of Cairo University up to the outbreak of the Black September hostilities in 1970 between Palestinians and the Jordanian forces. In the wake of these hostilities the Shiblak family moved briefly to Syria and then on to Lebanon, where they were reunited with the other members of the extended family, who had left Haifa in 1948 directly to the refugee camps in Lebanon. After the death of the paterfamilias Fadil Shiblak in Beirut, and with the outbreak of the civil war in Lebanon in 1975, a bloody battle that seriously harmed the Palestinians, the wooden box that Fadil Shiblak had taken with him upon leaving Haifa was burned. The documents of ownership of the house in Haifa were thus destroyed, as were the family members' birth certificates and the marriage certificate of Fadil Shiblak and his wife Zahiyyah. In 1982, when Israeli forces invaded Beirut and forced the evacuation of the Palestinian leadership from the city to Tunisia, the Shiblak family embarked upon a fresh wandering. Part of the family – Ra'isa, 'Abbas and their mother Zahiyyah – moved to Tunisia and later continued from there to Oxford in England. Ra'ifa came to Cairo and lives there. Khalil emigrated to Canada, while Hamza moved to Saudi Arabia. In July 2007 Zahiyyah's odyssey came to an end in far away Oxford, where she was buried, 3,200 kilometers from her home in Haifa.

The Former Occupant

What became of the house of Fadil Shiblak, we enquired in an official letter to the bureau of "The Custodian of Abandoned Property," a body subservient to the Israeli Ministry of Justice. "[…] an examination conducted by our office has failed to locate properties under the name of

---

[37] The terms *Nakba*, denoting the Palestinian catastrophe of 1948, and *Naksa* (debacle), denoting the defeat of the armies of Egypt, Syria and Jordan in the 1967 war against Israel have been preserved in Arab and Palestinian consciousness.

Shiblak Fadil that are administered by us."[38] The reply surprised us, since we had noted in our application the full address of the house: Haifa, 1 Lod Road. Even though this property may not be registered under the name of the "absentee," according to Israeli terminology, namely the Palestinian refugee, as far as we know it is registered according to the address, which has remained unchanged from 1935 to this day. Continuing our search for the registration of the house, we found that ownership of the building had passed to the "Development Authority," which had empowered the Israeli governmental company Amidar, the National Housing Company in Israel, to administer this property.[39] The registration of the house contains the address of the property, its number and details concerning the plot of land on which the building stands according to the records kept by the Land Registry Bureau: lot number 10852/29/1. Incidentally, according to record number 2747 of the Haifa Land Registry Bureau, on 24 August 1957 the Custodian's Bureau transferred ownership of Fadil Shiblak's property in its entirety to the "Development Authority." Following completion of the registration of the property, the following remark appeared in the registry log: "The property is frozen for resolution ...", namely, resolution of the Palestinian-Israeli conflict.[40] The "Development Authority" transferred the title to this property to Amidar, which engaged in housing Jewish tenants who had recently immigrated to Israel in the houses of the Palestinian refugees. The records of Amidar for 1995 show that eight Jewish families and one Arab family[41] were housed in Fadil Shiblak's house, which it had begun to administer in 1957. The western apartment on the third floor, which had served as lodgings for the Fadil Shiblak family until they became refugees, was sealed and remains so to this day, sealed with breeze blocks. The Haifa Land Registry documents show that Amidar was not content to let the apartments in the building and to collect the rent, but on 3 August 1999 sold and transferred ownership of one of the apartments on the ground floor to one of the occupants,[42] in contravention of the terms of the "Custodian of Absentees Property" law. The blocking off of the

---

[38] Israel Ministry of Justice, the General Custodian, National Location Department, 17 March 2009.
[39] Declaration of sale/purchase of land right, file no. 99127137, dated 20 July 1999.
[40] For further reading consult Ronald W. Zweig, "Restitution of Property and Refugee Rehabilitation: Two Case Studies", *Journal of Refugee Studies* 6:1 (1993), pp. 56-64.
[41] Amidar, Haifa and Northern Branch, Property Information Department, bloc 10852, lot 29, house number 12, 17 July 1995, 14 May 2001.
[42] Israel Ministry of Finance, Purchase Tax Department, Haifa, file no. 99127137, 20 July 1999.

apartment, the freezing of the property, the transfer of the title, the letting of the apartments and the sale of one of them finalized the Shiblak's loss of their property Shiblak House thus met a fate similar to that of the vast majority of Palestinian houses within the territory of the State of Israel. The fate of the Swidan House, which is traced in the following section, was different.

HANNA SWIDAN HOUSE: 33 CRUSADER STREET

A Monument

Standing on Ben-Gurion Avenue, the main street of the Templar colony, with one's back to the sea and facing the mountain, one beholds a splendid sight. The Baha'i Gardens spread out from the base of the mountain almost to its summit. The shining golden dome of the Shrine of the Bab glitters at the center of the gardens. Should one's eye insist on wandering eastward of the gardens, beyond the marble walls and ornamental iron gates, it would come across an assortment of structures, a true hodgepodge comprising an international style of building dating from the 1920s and 1930s as well as projects that emerged from the various public housing workshops of subsequent decades. Here and there a developer's ambitious initiative defiantly protrudes, lacerating the general texture ostentatiously, disproportionately and with an inappropriate style. This jumbled agglomeration, incidentally, is rather characteristic of large tracts of Haifa's construction, which consistently ignores the city's singular topography. A similar picture reveals itself also to the west of the gardens, albeit less crowded and forlorn than that on the eastern margins. Yet above all, one's eye is caught by a large building adjacent to the Baha'i Gardens, prominent in size and style; this is Swidan House.

The singular nature of the structure, so it appears, is a function not of some subjective esthetic preference or inclination on our (the authors') part. It was recognized already in 1992 by an independent outside body. Swidan House was included on Haifa Municipality's list of conserved buildings as a "monument," "*any work on it*, including renovation of its facades, must be undertaken *according to the conservation guidelines*," (emphasis in original) it was stipulated on 31 March 1992 on the Mini Sheet, the documentation of ongoing activity in the building file.[43] Haifa, incidentally, was among the first cities in Israel to compile a tentative list of buildings and sites worthy of conservation within its jurisdiction as early as

---

[43] The Municipality of Haifa, The Conservation Department, Building File 3822/33.

1984. This was a local initiative that predated country-wide initiatives, yet this does not necessarily indicate concern for the city's Arab architectural past. The inclusion of Swidan House in this original list, however, may certainly be regarded as an exceptional recognition of its singularity. Moreover, the unidentified inspector's decision to recognize the structure as a "monument" furnishes further evidence of its special status. One may learn more about this status and the building's conservation over many decades in a city devoid of awareness of historical conservation from a further incidental reference; namely, an application on the part of two students to Haifa's City Engineer late in 1966. This, too, is recorded in the building file kept in the main archive of the Engineering Administration; a sequential file, number 3822/33, which contains the annals of the structure from its construction in the mid-1930s up to the present day, its continuity articulating a blunt reproach to the fragments collected within it.

"Dear Sir," the two boys write to the City Engineer,

> we, two pupils in the sixth class of high-school at the Reali School in Ahuza, have decided to undertake an independent project on a house in Haifa that is of particular interest to us. The house is situated on Crusader Street, and can be seen from United Nations Avenue. We understand that the house is called 'Swidan House' but are not sure about this. It resembles a castle with two turrets facing the sea, and is painted yellow-brown. We should be most grateful if you would send us material pertaining to the said house or suggest an alternative source from which we may obtain the necessary details.[44]

There is thus no doubt that, with its impressive facades facing Haifa Bay, its twin turrets and unusual ochre coloring, Swidan House caught the eye, and in this instance the eyes of two inquisitive youngsters. "A mansion, on the slopes of the Carmel, known as Swidan House," is how the building was described at a court hearing held that same year in the Rental Court affiliated to Haifa Magistrate's Court.[45] Beyond the sweeping agreement as to the grandeur of the house, the reference in the Mini Sheets in 1992 and the incidental application on the part of two youngsters in 1966 as well as many further references in earlier years testify that Haifa's residents referred to the building as "Swidan House," even though the Swidans, who

---

[44] Ibid., File 3822/33, from Carmel Storlezi and Raphael Yoeli to Haifa City Engineer, 7.11.1966.
[45] Ibid., Building File 3822/33, Rental Court affiliated to Haifa Magistrate's Court. Rental File 133/65 Yishai First of 33 Crusader Road Haifa, applicant, against the heirs of Hanna Swidan, Malik Swidan, 33 Crusader Road, 20.3.1966.

built and owned the house, were for several decades prevented from living in it.

Mismatch

When, in 1992, once the Knesset had passed "Amendment 31 to the Planning and Construction Law" (the Conservation Law), Swidan House was declared a listed building, the Swidan family's descendants were already living in many of its apartments, having succeeded in regaining their rights through a Sisyphean process. The facades of the house, as they appeared to the two youngsters in 1966, concealed more than they revealed, since, according to the conventional meaning of ascription, Swidan House was not at that time the house in which the Swidans lived. For several decades the Swidans had employed market forces in order to regain the property. While their ownership was indeed not contested *de jure*, it was wrested from them *de facto* when, in 1948, they were deprived of the possibility of living in the property, of populating it in other words. During the decades before they regained the right to live in their home the Swidans were frequently compelled to deal with tenants who sought to adapt the property in which they resided to their needs by virtue of a rental contract or key money. This kind of tension between the owners and the tenants would endure over the entire period, as the bulging building file attests. Let us who browse over these shabby small claims in lower courts not be deceived by them, even though they appear to be ordinary disputes between property owners and tenants in the property market. These proceedings reveal the upheaval that Haifa underwent from being a "mixed city" with a strong Arab bourgeois stratum rich in property to a Jewish city of laborers that, amid the immediate pressing needs, housed a jumble of impoverished and destitute Jewish migrants.

Indeed, the disparity between the Arab bourgeois past and the Israeli-Jewish present became apparent, for instance, in the claim submitted by the tenant of the turret Yishai First against Hanna Swidan's heir, his son Malik Swidan, to the Rental Court affiliated to Haifa Magistrate's Court in the month of March of this same year, 1966.[46] The turret's picturesque appearance, which imparted to the building a special aura within the urban milieu, alongside its numerous other decorative elements (which in turn generated horrific fables of a sinking house, an engineering error and a suicidal architect), provided a stark contrast to the quality of life of the

---

[46] Ibid.

tenant who had resided therein since 1952. The trials of tenant First are related over the course of a prolonged correspondence, beginning in the late 1950s and continuing into the latter half of the 1960s. First sought to adapt the two spaces in which he resided on the roof of Swidan House, namely the turret and a room further along the roof, to the needs of his family. He set out his troubles at length in his application to the City Construction Department of Haifa Municipality in 1958:

"My wife and I together with our three children live in two rooms of 11 and 12.5 square meters. Apart from their small size, the rooms are also not side by side, but are separated by a distance of 4 meters, which the two older children cross in winter: in driving rain and tempestuous winds whenever they leave their room."[47] The tenant Y.First mobilized the assistance of well-wishers, such as the Welfare and Culture Officer in the Trade and Industry Ministry, who visited the family's home and lost no time in reporting to Haifa's Deputy Mayor that:

[…] I visited his apartment and was astounded at the conditions in which the said family is living on the roof. The area of the two-room apartment is 24 square meters, the distance between the rooms is 4 meters without a roof covering and wall, and 5 souls live in this small area, including 3 children aged 13 to 5. The congestion is such that the older children sleep on armchairs. In the absence of a passage way the family suffers from the sun in summer and in winter from winds and rain and sometimes from flooding.[48]

A glance at the original plans of the building prepared in 1933 shows that the structure on the roof was not originally designated for human domicile. It most probably served as a laundry room and contained toilet facilities. This structure, together with the turret, was turned into a living unit of sorts owing to the chronic shortage of accommodation in the city. The city engineer was prepared to agree in part to the tenant's wishes providing that the connection of the living spaces would not detract from the appearance of the house. The negotiations addressed the disparity between the tenant's accommodation needs and the esthetic qualities of the singular structure. In this context the original uses of the turret, or "tower" as it is called in some of the documents, came under discussion. Malik Swidan, son and heir to the original owner of the property Hanna Swidan, sought in his testimony to establish cultural and historical rights in order to protect the appearance of the structure, contending before the Rental Court

---

[47] Ibid., File 3822/33, Yishai First to the City Construction Department, July 1958.
[48] Ibid., Building File 3822/33, letter from Y. Shumert, Welfare and Culture Officer with the Trade and Industry Ministry to Haifa Deputy Mayor Mr. Fleeman, on 22.10.1958.

affiliated to the Haifa Magistrate's Court that "the room in the tower served his late father as a prayer house."

The son added that

> I am sure that were my father alive today he would not agree to any change in the tower, when we have 36-37 tenants in the house. If everyone should want to do whatever they desire they will turn the house into a market. If the requested change is made, this will transform the entire appearance of the tower. I oppose any change being made to the tower, even if the change is made up to the height of the door.[49]

The historical rights in the name of which Malik Swidan demanded that no changes be made to the tower fell on deaf ears. The claimants were unimpressed by the mention of the prayer room and asserted that the said tower had ceased to serve as a prayer room even in the lifetime of the deceased himself and that the deceased had let the tower to the applicant for the purpose of accommodation. The outcome of this juridical contest cannot be established from the documentation.

Yishai First was one of many tenants living in Swidan House who initiated various changes to the inner partitioning of the building so as to adapt it to their needs. The Swidan family was frequently required to contest the tenants' initiatives to introduce these changes, which were undertaken by circumventing the owners of the property and were facilitated in part by the fact that they did not at the time live in or nearby the building. Mrs. 'Afifa Swidan applied to the City Construction Committee to issue a demolition order against a tenant of hers on the ground floor who, without her agreement, without applying for a license and making use of her building stones had constructed an additional room.[50] Thus too, by means of repeated applications written in English on the official notepaper of his import-export company, did Jean M. Swidan seek to prevent the tenant Yosef Levy from constructing a kitchen and additional room in the basement apartment.[51] The class discrepancy between the erstwhile urban Arab bourgeoisie and the impecunious Jewish immigrants manifested in the use of English and the notepaper as symbols of class is

---

[49] Ibid., Building File 3822/33, Rental Court affiliated to Haifa Magistrate's Court. Rental File 133/65 Yishai First of 33 Crusader Road Haifa, applicant, against the heirs of Hanna Swidan, Malik Swidan, 33 Crusader Road, 20.3.1966.

[50] Ibid., Building File 3822/33, Afifa Swidan, owner of the house at 151 Mountain Road to the City Construction Committee, 29.12.1960.

[51] Ibid., Building File 3822/33, Jean M. Swidan to the Haifa Municipality, Engineering Department, 2.6.1950.

further emphasized by the details of the case, since Nissim Ben-Yosef Levy, a recent immigrant and "a clear welfare case," was in desperate need of exceptions to the building regulations. As the documents note, he was living with his asthmatic father who also suffered from angina pectoris, with a brother suffering from tuberculosis, and with a further eight individuals, and sought to isolate the ill brother in order to protect the remaining family members from infection by fashioning an apartment by means of enclosing part of the column floor of Mr. Hanna Swidan's house. Since this was not a designated building zone, his request was rejected.

The severity of the conflicts of interest and the conflicting needs of the property's owners and the new tenants are demonstrated by the case of another tenant, Peter Bondi. An Auschwitz survivor, Bondi had passed through five different German concentration camps between 1941 and 1945. On the basement floor of Swidan House, which he shared at the time with the immigrant Nissim Ben-Yosef Levy, Bondi built an apartment for himself and his ailing wife with the money he had mobilized through the sale and pawning of the meager belongings that he had managed to bring with him, and with the help of loans made by friends. Bondi invested all his means in this construction project. The Czechoslovak Immigrants Association supported his application to permit him to complete this illegal construction, testifying that "the immigrants from Czechoslovakia who came in 1949 had no way of bringing with them money or other property apart from the few objects that could be brought in one crate. The aforementioned Mr. Peter Bondi also brought just one crate containing his personal belongings, and apart from these he has no means whatsoever here in the country."[52] The City Engineer rejected the application since the area had been designated solely as a sports pavilion, and the construction of an apartment on this location would constitute an infringement of the building regulations.[53]

Swidan House and its many tenants – down and outs and destitute Jewish immigrants – serves as one of many examples from the period beginning in late 1948 of the transformations undergone by stately Palestinian homes in the city in the wake of their owners' departure and the forced concentration of those who remained in the city in the *Wadi al-Nisnas* neighborhood as their homes were placed at the disposal of new

---

[52] Ibid., Building File 3822/33, to the Mayor of Haifa from the Czechoslovak Immigrants Association, 13.1.1950, signed by the Secretary, Engineer Y. Fraenkel.
[53] Ibid., Building File 3822/33, Y. Proshenski, City Engineer to the Czechoslovak Immigrants Association, 6.6.1950.

tenants. With the end of the war of 1948 many families were housed in the apartments of Swidan House and in many other apartments and houses that had in the past been designed as a single family unit. As time passed the tenants were compelled to improvise additions, and to add toilets, bathrooms and kitchens in the passage ways and areas that had originally been designed as public spaces. In any event, they lacked the means for ongoing upkeep of the expensive structures. "Mismatch" is how the literature terms the disparity between these high quality buildings and the low economic status of the new tenants.[54]

The Basement and the Courtyard

Many of the changes undergone by the property occurred on the basement floor of Swidan House, which emerges as the weak point of the grand building. In the original design, to which we shall return later, this floor was left empty, without a specified function. It would appear that Hanna Swidan chose to utilize the building area allotted to him in the well ventilated spaces facing the sea. The basement was naturally not part of these. Yet this way of thinking was the product of a time of plenty, and was irreconcilable with the acute hardship generated in the city in the wake of the 1948 war, and in fact, as witnessed in the case of Fadil Shiblak's house, already prior to it. Given the lack of available housing, these open spaces constituted an ever-present provocation, if not a veritable breach. In the mid-1950s Mr. Swidan had hoped to legalize a number of structures constructed without a license toward the end of the 1940s and which now served as kitchens, toilets and storerooms to the tenants residing on the ground floor and in the basement, as well as to an exterior building erected in the courtyard and which served as living quarters at the time.[55] His request was rejected, despite the position taken by the City Engineer's inspector, who had noted a year earlier that "this building has undergone many transformations on its way to becoming a slum," and that since "we are in any case unable to prevent the building from becoming a slum," it would be preferable to impose a number of steps to improve sanitary conditions by means of legalization.[56]

---

[54] Amiram Gonen, *Between City and Suburb: Urban Residential Patterns and Processes in Israel* (1995), p. 51.
[55] The Municipality of Haifa, The Conservation Department, Building File 3822/33, Office of the City Engineer to Mr. Hanna M. Swidan on 8.11.1956.
[56] Ibid., Building File 3822/33, 21.9.1955.

Conditions in the mid-1950s were most probably far better than those pertaining in the basement and courtyard in 1950. In that year a number of employees of Steel Brothers & Co., whose offices occupied part of the building, complained of the unbearable stench caused by the housing of 18 individuals on the ground floor verandah without any sanitary infrastructure whatsoever, as well as the breeding of chickens, dogs, rabbits and pigeons in the courtyard.[57] These apparently fantastical assertions are borne out in the Building Department's order to the tenants and landlord to clean the courtyard, install a platform for garbage containers and to remove the chicken coops.[58]

It would be a mistake to attribute all these changes to the war and its aftermath, although it had, no doubt, played a decisive part in the conversion undergone by the mansion in later decades. Over-population, it appears, was prevalent already in the mid-1940s, owing to the general shortage of housing in the city among both Jews and Palestinians. This over-population was likewise evident in the Shiblak House. Already in 1945 Mr. Hanna Swidan submitted an application through the architects Rais and Canaan to convert the column floor into an area of domicile. The City Engineer was reluctant to approve the application. He too referred to the danger that the building may turn into a slum owing to over-population.[59] Around a decade after its construction, so it would seem, a cloud began to hover above Swidan House, which may be distilled into the keyword "slum."

The origin of the dwelling in the courtyard, incidentally – the same structure that Mr. Swidan sought in vain to legalize in the mid-1950s – pre-dated the dramatic events of April 1948 by several months. In June 1947 Mr. Swidan requested permission to build a tennis court and a pavilion,

---

[57] Ibid., Building File 3822/33, Steel Brothers & Co. to the Chairman, Haifa Municipal Council, 31.8.1950.
"Part of the ground floor verandah is now undergoing structural alterations to convert the open verandahs into extra rooms. There are now about eighteen people living on this verandah or in the storeroom adjacent thereto without any adequate sanitary facilities. The stench on a hot day is overpowering. [...] Chickens, dogs, rabbits and pigeons are also being bred there. Their droppings add to the general filth and squalor."
[58] Ibid., Building File 3822/33, 19.9.1950.
[59] Ibid., Building File 3822/33, Government of Palestine, District Commissioner's Offices, Haifa District, Haifa, A.D. Lebhar to the City Engineer, Haifa 23.5.1945.
"My own view is that as the Sweidan (*sic!*) House is already several floors in excess of regulations no concession should be granted to increase the density of the population of a building that already bids fair to become a slum."

which would include two shower rooms, a verandah and two toilets.[60] The timing appears somewhat strange when one reads the narrative from its conclusion. From its beginning it reads merely as a real estate initiative on the part of a versatile man. Mr. Swidan's application was approved in July 1947, with the stipulation that the court be built first.[61] In early September 1947 Mr. Swidan received final approval together with a demand that he implement the plan during the following six months, before this authorization would become invalid.[62] It appears that the work was not completed, since in August 1949 a sports club, a Jewish one of course, called "The 105 Sportsclub", did indeed operate on the site. It is unclear what infrastructure was available to the club in the courtyard of Swidan House, but tennis courts were not built.[63] The application submitted by the new users, "for a crafts and industries license for the club – Hanna Swidan" as officially noted in the documents, for the sale of alcoholic beverages, was rejected. Hanna Swidan and his family were no longer living in the building at that time. Like all the Arab residents of the city, some 3,000-3,500 in number, they were compelled through an act of forced settlement to reside on the Western side of the city, in the area of Wadi al-Nisnas and the adjacent streets.[64]

Rupture

Swidan House's building file in the archive of Haifa Municipality's Conservation Department may be likened to a facade that conceals the history of its occupants. The upheaval in the lives of Hanna Swidan and his family shortly after they received authorization for the tennis court project

---

[60] Ibid., Building File 3822/33, extract from minutes of the 114th meeting of the Haifa Local Building and Town Commission held on 10.6.1947:

"Mr. Hanna Swidan, requesting permission to erect a tennis-court with a pavilion comprising two rest rooms and a verandah, two showers and two latrines, in the courtyard behind his building at Crusader Street (Parcel 202, Block 10813). Resolution: The application was recommended for approval."

[61] Ibid., Building File 3822/33, Government of Palestine, District Commissioner's Offices, Haifa District, Haifa to Mr. Hanna Swidan, 21.7.1947.

[62] Ibid., Building File 3822/33, Municipal Corporation of Haifa, City Engineer's Department to Mr. Hanna M. Swidan, 1.9.1947.

[63] Ibid., Building File 3822/33, the City Secretary to the City Engineer, 15.8.1949.

[64] The local Palestinian population, incidentally, experienced the forced settlement completed in July 1948 as an insensitive and unjust step, with some even referring to it as ghettoization. Born of immediate military-security logic, this action in retrospect ironically contributed to the evolution of a Palestinian milieu as the area expanded and developed over the years and became the preferred Palestinian neighborhood in Haifa.

is not recorded therein, and to the extent that this left any remnants they are to be found in a different archive, in the Israel State Archive. The painful correspondence between Hanna Swidan and his new rulers begins with a letter penned by the paterfamilias "to the head of the State of Israel, the esteemed Mr. Ben-Gurion," on 3 July 1948, in which he seeks to protect his life and property:

> I am Hanna Mubadda Swidan, born in Haifa to an ancient family, and a trader in food and beverages, who despite the Arab boycott persisted in buying from Jews. I have always maintained correct relations with the Jews of Haifa. As a citizen of the State of Israel I request my rights. I have been told that the defense forces are preparing to invade my house on the slopes of the Carmel. May your honor please issue the appropriate orders in order to protect us from all aggression on the part of the military, and cultivate me as one of his people and assist his servant.[65]

No wonder that Hanna Swidan expected the Jewish state to protect his rights. His position opposing the Arab boycott was consistent, and he had adhered to it over some two decades despite persistent internal pressure and direct threats to his life. Perusal of the Jewish press reveals that Swidan's position was well known in both Jewish and Arab society. The journal *Filastin* published in Jaffa reported in late 1929 that Hanna Swidan had been threatened by the Black Hand – a secretive and extreme organization founded in Jaffa in 1919, which established a branch in Haifa a year later – warning that were he to continue to enjoy the services of the Electric Company his life would be placed in danger.[66] *Filastin*, incidentally, was among the leaders of the campaign against Ruthenberg and the Palestine Electric Company already in the early 1920s in Jaffa. It failed there just as it failed in Haifa in the mid-1920s, because the bourgeois elite desired electricity and hooked up to the grid despite the pressures. Swidan chose to ignore the threat and to inform the governor and the police, in the clear knowledge that the British regime supported Ruthenberg's Zionist initiative and was taking action against its opponents. In 1930 Swidan persisted in his refusal, when he declined to participate in a trade stoppage initiated by the Muslim Association, and in a riposte in the form of a pamphlet that he issued of his own accord he announced that he would make do with a stoppage of only two hours.[67] It would appear that, as

---

[65] Israel State Archives, Hanna Swidan to David Ben-Gurion on 3.7.1948 – 310/11.
[66] "The Black Hand", *Davar*, 17 December 1929.
[67] "The Arab Stoppage", *Davar*, 24 August 1930.

in the cases of many other Christians,[68] he persisted in his refusal to join the boycott also during the "Great Arab Rebellion," since in 1938 a customer of his, Dr. [N]ajib Khury, son of Haifa's former Municipal Physician, was mistakenly shot in his store. The local press surmised that the shots had been targeted at the owner of the store and were fired in the wake of a threatening letter he had received a few days previously.[69] Hanna Swidan himself, incidentally, drew a pistol and pursued the attacker in vain, as he succeeded in escaping by forcing an Arab taxi driver at gun point to drive him in the direction of Balad-al-Sheikh.

That which was known to the readers of *Davar* two decades prior to the *Nakba* no longer worked in his favor in 1948. His direct application to Ben-Gurion was transferred from the Haifa branch of the Ministry of Minorities to the main office in Tel Aviv. A few days later a response was received instructing "to receive him and to handle his affairs as you see fit and to the extent that this matter does not compromise the interests of the military."[70] Hanna Swidan did not give up his attempt to endear himself to the new rulers, and in early January 1949 he approached the State President, Chaim Weizmann. In the conventional style of correspondence between a subject and the ruler, particularly in cases that seek the direct protection of the rulers in the face of harassment by local officialdom,[71] in a letter studded with panegyric and in the spirit of religious kinship on which he dwelled expansively, he declared that "I am proud of you and love you and hope that you will receive us amongst you and we shall be faithful and obedient." "I shall be delighted," he wrote, "together with my family and servants, to live under the protection of your state."[72] Asked by the Minorities Ministry to express an opinion on this application, the Foreign Ministry remained cool. "This man is not considered to be a particularly respected or important person," they assessed there, "in our opinion a polite

---

[68] Benny Morris, *1948: The Annals of the First Arab-Israeli War* (2010), p. 28.
[69] "A Daring Assassination in Haifa. Christian Arab Seriously Injured", *Davar*, 17 June 1938.
[70] Israel State Archives, The Ministry of Minorities at the Kirya to Mr. Moshe Yitah, Ministry of Minorities Haifa Branch, 13.7.1948, C – 310/11.
[71] Yuval Ben-Bassat, "On Telegraph and Justice: The Petitions of Residents of Jaffa and Gaza to the Great Wazir of Istanbul in the Late Nineteenth Century", *The New East* 49 (2010), pp. 30-52.
[72] Israel State Archives, Hanna Mubadda Swidan to President of the State of Israel, Dr. Chaim Weizmann, 12.1.1949, C – 310/11.

response is sufficient, with a formal acknowledgement of his letter (in Arabic, of course)."[73]

A polite response, however, could not meet Hanna Swidan's true requests, nor could it alleviate his pressing tribulations. The Swidan family was dispersed in all directions in 1948. The father and brother remained in Haifa, the mother and five children – three sons and two daughters – fled to Egypt, while the events surrounding an additional son – Malik – Malik defender of the turret, took a dramatic turn. On the same day that he approached the State President, Hanna Swidan wrote a further letter to the Minorities Ministry in Haifa in which he submitted two requests: to enable his son Malik to move from Fassuta to permanent residency in Haifa, and to allow his family to return to the country from abroad, namely Egypt.[74] The 21 year old Malik had traveled to Fassuta on 13 April 1948 to recuperate from two operations and following a bout of typhoid.[75] Mr. Hanna Swidan agreed to deposit any warranty required of him for the transfer of Malik and also to guarantee his livelihood. Regarding the matter of the return of his family, Hanna Swidan was ordered to submit a return request to the Immigration Committee, which would in turn require the authorization of the Ministries of Foreign Affairs, Security, Police and Minorities. The matter of the son initially appeared to be simpler: on the basis of a warranty of 250 Israeli Liras and the medical certificate he was permitted to dwell in Haifa.[76] His father meanwhile submitted an application to the Transfer Committee for permanent residency. But at this point things spun out of control. At midnight on 17 March 1949 military police and other security personnel appeared and asked Malik to accompany them on suspicion of being an infiltrator.[77] In his distress, Hanna Swidan approached the director of the Minorities Ministry in Haifa. The security personnel, he related, had slapped his son and had threatened another son, Farid, with a pistol when he tried to unravel the reason for the arrest. He now felt helpless after having turned in vain to the *Wadi al-*

---

[73] Ibid., Y. Shimoni, Foreign Ministry, Middle East Desk to the Secretary of the President of the State Council, 23.1.1949, C – 310/11.
[74] Ibid., Minorities Ministry Haifa Branch to Minorities Ministry, Ha-Kirya, 12.1.1949, C – 1318/73.
[75] Ibid., Minorities Ministry, Ha-Kirya to Minorities Ministry Haifa Branch, 27.1.1949, C – 1318/73.
[76] Ibid., Intelligence Service Haifa Base to Minorities Ministry Haifa Branch, 28.12.1948, C – 1318/73.
[77] Ibid., Minorities Ministry Haifa Branch to Intelligence Service 3, Haifa Base 18.3.1949, C – 1318/73.

Nisnas police in search of his son.[78] Some three days later Hanna Swidan returned pleading to the Minorities Ministry in the city – in all probability one of the very few addresses to which he could turn with any degree of confidence in these dramatic circumstances. His son Malik, it transpires from the letter, had been led to the village of Mansura after being divested of his belongings, 36 Liras, a gold watch, a Parker fountain pen, spectacles and identity card.[79] "He was then ordered to run and since he suffered from a fracture and was ill he was unable to run so they shot at him and hit him in one spot only a centimeter from the heart and in a second spot on the knee." His injured son, so the father wrote to the authorities, was carried on a donkey to the village of Rumaysh, where he was treated by a doctor who subsequently accompanied him in a taxi to the hospital in Tyre for further treatment. "Mr. Yitah," wrote Hanna Swidan, "I turn to you in the name of humanity and ask you what is the reason for all this attack. You are our representatives here and what should I do."

House of Dreams

Mr. Hanna Swidan chose to position his house 181 meters above sea level. The carefully designed plan prepared by the local architect and contractor Eng. I. Haggar was submitted to the City Engineer on 30 August 1933. The structure was to be erected in the Bab al-Manatir quarter, or Guards Gate, which was not actually a quarter in the conventional sense. The schema presents a first house, standing alone, on an unpopulated and as yet unprepared tract of land. The house was erected prior to the paving of the road, which would later be known as Crusader Road. It would appear that the man was a true entrepreneur. Hanna Swidan was a man of vision. In the original plan the road is called Tanzim Road, a Turkish name of uncertain origin. The road, in any event, never bore this name. Hanna Swidan, incidentally, was not pleased with the name "Crusader" given to the road. Apparently well aware of his singular contribution to the development of the road, on 5 June 1945 he applied to the Mayor of Haifa, requesting him to consider the issue of the name chosen by the municipality for the road. "I request," he wrote, "that you name the road Hanna Swidan and ask you to correct it."[80]

---

[78] Ibid., Hanna Swidan to the Minorities Ministry Haifa Branch, 18.3.1949, C – 1318/73.
[79] Ibid., Hanna Swidan to the Minorities Ministry Haifa Branch, 23.3.1949, C – 1318/73.
[80] Haifa City Archives, Hanna Swidan to the Mayor of Haifa, 5.6.1945, document 1541 – 9/2. I thank Johnny Mansour for drawing my attention to this document.

The sketches and sections of Swidan House indicate a measure of technological innovation. Apart from a pit for the collection of water that appears in the original plan, which may not eventually have been implemented, the house contains no traditional elements whatsoever. This is not a stone house, the conventional style at the time among both Jews and Arabs, but is made of concrete, which requires modern construction technology that was then only evolving. The appearance is exceptionally beautiful and has obviously been carefully thought out. The many decorative elements as well as fine details, such as the sliding doors and their tracks, indicate great attention to detail, a clear awareness of quality, an expensive and assured esthetic taste, imagination and daring. The carefully crafted building diagram enables the observer to share the dreams of the entrepreneur and owner, Hanna Swidan, at a remove of over seventy years.

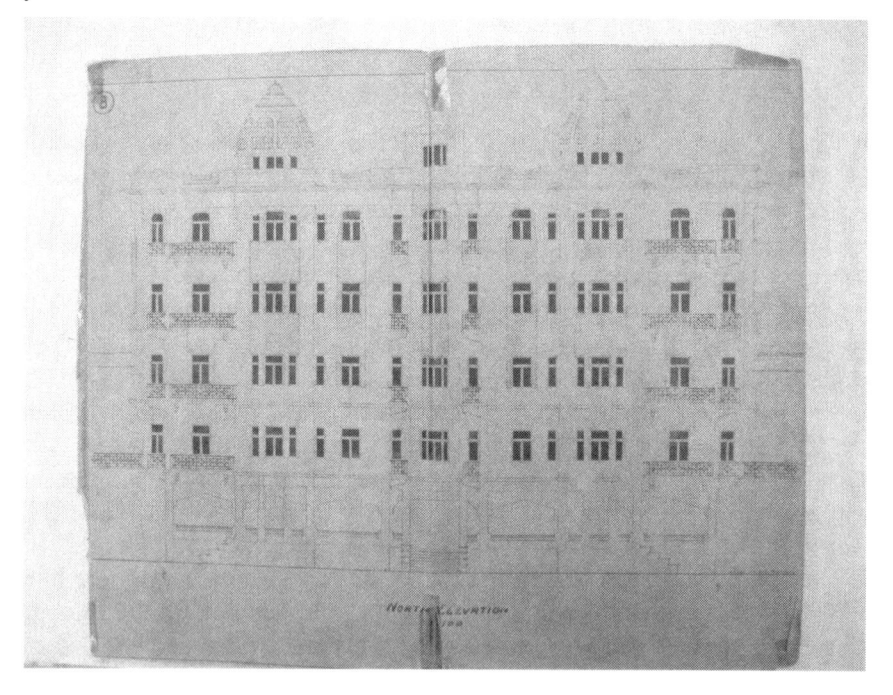

Fig. 2: The Swidan House

Source: Municipality of Haifa, the Conservation Department, Building File 3822/33

It appears that the owner and architect spared no effort, neither in planning nor in financing, in seeking to take in the splendid landscape to be seen from all possible angles of the building. Constructed on exceptionally steep and dramatic topography, on a slope of approximately 45 degrees, the building called for complex solutions. That chosen was to erect retaining walls, which facilitated maximum congruence between the contour of the mountain and that of the structure. To this solution was added the construction of a floor of columns beneath the building, adorned with pointed arches as a decorative element. Devoid of all use, according to the original plan of course, the column floor was designed for one objective alone: raising the building, making it taller, that is, and enhancing the built area's exposure to the scenery. In later years, with the passing of the golden age, numerous eyes were set on this floor, born in plenty and culminating in paucity, its existence provoking those seeking a roof over their heads, a motley collection of needy and impatient immigrants and refugees.

Once the building had been raised, all of it faced the landscape. Unlike many of the buildings constructed at that time in the Jewish section of the city, Swidan House utilizes the majority of the building area allocated to it to face the sea, in a grand and open façade facing Haifa Bay. All its floors and sides sport numerous porches suspended on concrete ledges: the open verandahs face the sea, while the enclosed balconies face east and west, toward the Baha'i Gardens, the western Carmel, and on the side of the entrance bridge on Crusader Road, toward the upper slopes of Mount Carmel. The verandahs and balconies were decorated with attractive and precise iron work in art deco style, complemented by a multitude of windows, both single and triptychonic, likewise adorned with applied art nouveau elements, such as the glass panels installed with a wooden frame in the upper third of the window, alongside elements that were not eventually applied, such as the decoration by means of a rough plaster finish that sets the windows off against the smooth plaster ubiquitous on the finish of all the outer walls. The many different styles allow us to characterize the house as an eclectic building, a trait typical of many of the buildings constructed at that time in Palestine.

The house was handsome, and most handsome too were the rooms that spread out in a central structure and two perfectly symmetrical wings. From a surprisingly simple stairwell that was almost incompatible with the general magnificence one could enter spacious living quarters. The inner entrance hall and the corridor at one end led to five mostly square and in some cases rectangular living rooms, whose proportions were attractive to the beholder. They were spacious, had many windows and most led directly on to a verandah or balcony. The 3.91 meters high ceilings, in line with the conventional ancient Arab style of building, far exceeded the usual height of contemporary structures, which tended to be some 3.2 meters in height.

The construction of the wings naturally enhanced the exposure to the landscape and likewise to the breezes blowing from different directions. Swidan House was a spacious and well ventilated house, looking out on to splendid scenery, which at the same time delighted those who looked upon it.

Engineer Haggar submitted the initial plans on 30 August 1933. On 21 November 1933 the plan was approved, and on 20 February 1935 an application was submitted for a license to occupy the building, which was received in April of that year. The pace of progress was thus very rapid. Surrounded by a fence that would be badly damaged by the rains of February 1946 and subsequently rebuilt, Swidan House came into being.

ARAB–JEWISH ARCHITECTURAL PARTNERSHIP IN HAIFA DURING THE MANDATE PERIOD

QARAMAN AND GERSTEL MEET ON THE "SEAM LINE"

WALEED KARKABI AND ADI ROITENBERG

The state [Israel] did not go out of its way to conserve most of the Arab monuments ... but there is another reason [for their neglect] in my opinion. Several of the most important buildings that my father built are located in the border area between the Arab and Jewish [parts] ... the area became a slum.

Interview with architect Prof. Leopold Gerstel, 2009[1]

INTRODUCTION

As one enters the city of Haifa from the east and approaches the *Hadar ha-Carmel* neighborhood one passes old structures and neglected courtyards. Among the concrete projects constructed in the 1950s and 1960s stand stone buildings that display a rich variety of architectural detail characteristic of urban Arab architecture, such as arched windows and protruding balconies, wide stairwells lit by glass windows and the use of various types of stone finish. The arched openings of most of the buildings are nowadays bereft of their windows, the balconies adorning the facades have lost a support or two, and the stylized iron railings have rusted or disappeared. Time has not been kind to the buildings that survived the Palestinian *Nakba* (catastrophe) of 1948; their facades are laden with piping, cables and billboards. Over many years, a variety of materials has been used to make improvised additions to most of the structures and to enclose their balconies. The few remaining architectural details bear witness to the architectural quality of the original structures and to the considerable care taken by their Palestinian owners at the time of their construction in the 1900s and 1940s.

---

[1] This article is based partly on our conversations with the late Prof. Leopold Gerstel, the son of architect Moshe Gerstel, conducted in Haifa in 2009.

M. Yazbak and Y. Weiss (eds.), Haifa Before & After 1948. Narratives of a Mixed City, 43–68.
© *2011 Institute for Historical Justice and Reconciliation and Republic of Letters Publishing. All rights reserved.*

Approaching the city from the east, one passes through the *Halissa* and *Tel-'Amal* neighborhoods and crosses *Wadi Rushmiya* on the way to *Hadar ha-Carmel* in the West. In order to ease the congestion caused by the heavy traffic ascending toward Hadar ha-Carmel a bridge was constructed over the course of *Wadi Rushmiya* in the late 1980s, which nowadays carries the traffic flowing toward *Hadar ha-Carmel*, while the historic *Rushmiya* bridge built in the 1920s serves the traffic leaving the neighborhood. Trucks carrying earth for the construction of new roads constantly ply their way through the course of *Wadi Rushmiya*, which is undergoing rapid and extensive transformation. New roads are appearing that traverse and transform the *Wadi*'s natural layout while the retaining walls erected alongside them obscure the topography's natural contours altogether. Upon crossing the bridge that spans the *Wadi* one moves along the main artery entering *Hadar ha-Carmel*, which was the heart of Jewish Haifa during the British Mandate and one of its most elegant neighborhoods, meticulously laid out according to the principles of the garden suburb. This transport axis constitutes a rough upper boundary between the old established Jewish neighborhood of *Hadar ha-Carmel* and the Arab neighborhoods *Wadi Salib* and *al-burj* below it.

Standing close to the entrance to the *Hadar ha-Carmel* neighborhood, an expansive structure that curves along the topographical contour of Mount Carmel overlooks *Wadi Rushmiya*. This is *Beit ha-Ta'asiya* (Industry House), designed in 1945 by the architect Moshe Gerstel.[2] The building comprises two five-story wings on either side of a central octagonal main wing.

One of the structure's distinctive characteristics is its elongated narrow windows that face *Wadi Rushmiya*. Industry House is located on the seam line between the Arab and Jewish neighborhoods. A mere two years after its construction this was to become a front line, and from its elevated position the building commands a view of the main artery entering the city from the East and of the historic *Wadi Rushmiya* bridge. As the conflict between Arabs and Jews escalated in December 1947 the British placed an observation post on its roof. The structure's location likewise afforded a strategic advantage to the *Haganah* fighters who took up position on it as they prepared to take control of the Eastern theater in April 1948.[3] Part of

---

[2] Industry House was built as a center for light industry, craft workshops and storage on the margins of the *Hadar ha-Carmel* neighborhood.
[3] Tamir Goren, *Haifa ha-Aravit be-Tashah: Otzmat ha-Ma'avak u-Meimadei ha-Hitmotetut* [*Arab Haifa in 1948: The Intensity of the Struggle and the Dimensions of the Collapse*] (2006).

the Industry House building nowadays serves as a storage space and houses small craft workshops, while the rest lies in neglect. Some of its facades still bear pockmarks that recall its location on the firing line in 1948.

Fig. 1: The Industry House (2011)

Another of architect Gerstel's buildings lies about one kilometer from Industry House as the crow flies. This is the abandoned *Talpiot* Market building located at the heart of the erstwhile seam line area, which likewise attracts one's attention. Over the past decade the structure has ceased to constitute a focus for commerce but it is still an impressive presence in the urban landscape. The market's construction in 1940 constituted one of the prominent achievements of its initiators, the *Hadar ha-Carmel* Committee, signifying progress and modernity in Haifa in particular and in the country in general. Gerstel's design for *Talpiot* Market won first prize in a design competition that drew entries from some one hundred leading architects. The building is a fine example of the International Style of architecture in the area. It was one of the first urban commercial centers to be established in the country, combining a rich food market, stores selling a variety of goods, an exhibition hall, warehouses and garages. A restaurant was located on its roof.

Fig. 2: The Industry House (A perspective by Leopold Gestel)

Moshe Gerstel was among the prominent and influential modern architects who shaped Palestine's urban complexion during the 1930s and 1940s. Other members of this group included Erich Mendelssohn, Richard Kaufmann, Yosef Neufeld and Arieh Sharon, adherents of the International Style of architecture that developed in Europe in the early 1920s. Upon arriving to Mandatory Palestine they developed and adapted this style to the local needs, landscape and climate. Like them, Moshe Gerstel has left his singular architectural imprint on the urban space. He worked mainly in Haifa, designing and constructing buildings on Mount Carmel, on the seam line, in the downtown area and in the '*Abbas* neighborhood. On the seam line the Jewish architect Moshe Gerstel encountered a man who would become his colleague and friend, the Muslim entrepreneur, businessman and representative of the public, Hajj Tahir Qaraman. This article recounts the story of their meeting against the backdrop of Haifa's urban space.

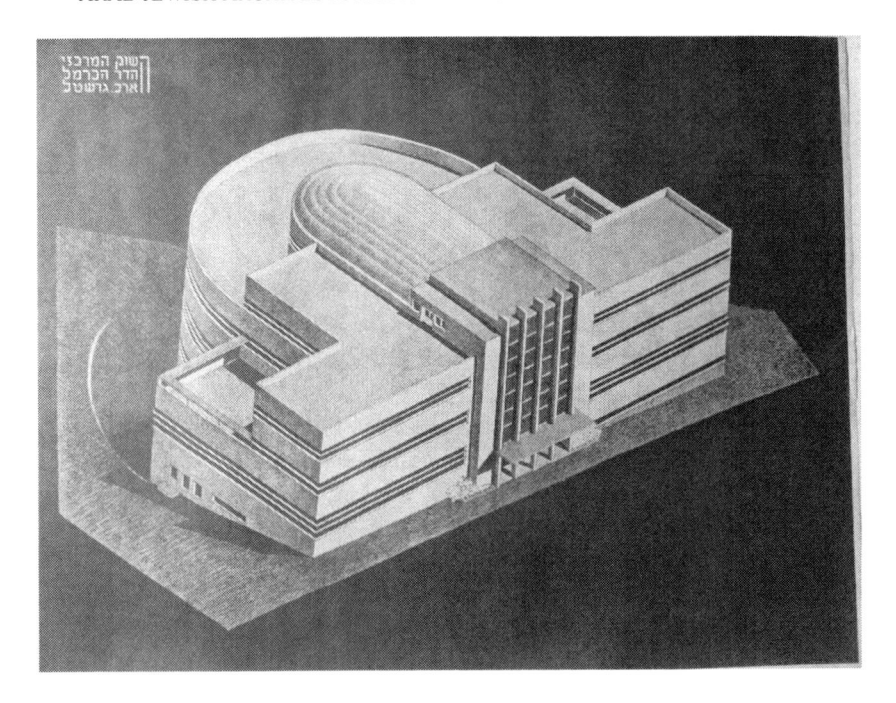

Fig. 3: Talpiot Market

FROM LOCAL ROMANTICISM TO INTERNATIONAL PERSPECTIVE

Following the accession of the Nazis to power in Germany in the 1930s a considerable number of Jews arrived from Europe to Mandatory Palestine in general and to Haifa in particular. Among them were leading Jewish architects in their countries of origin. They found in Haifa a pre-existing planning infrastructure to which they applied the new International Style of architecture that had begun to develop in Europe after World War I. Haifa's economic and urban development reached its peak at this time. Construction began on new neighborhoods on the basis of modern planning principles, as presented in the report of the English town planner Prof. Patrick Geddes to the British Governor of Haifa District Alexander Stanton in 1918-1920. The fledgling urban planning began to encompass the spheres of water provision, transportation, and the location of the port and industrial area. Detailed plans were likewise drawn up for the various areas of the Carmel: Central Carmel, Western Carmel and Southern Carmel, as well as *Hadar ha-Carmel*.

The new neighborhoods now under construction constituted the most appropriate and natural locations for the erection of buildings in the new International Style. Underlying this style was a coherent idea grounded in a comprehensive world view encompassing sociology, civil engineering, political thought, design and economics that accorded with the spirit of the times. Moshe Gerstel operated in Haifa during the 1930s alongside a number of architects familiar with the International Style, the most prominent of whom were Erich Mendelsohn, Leopold Kracauer, Benjamin Chaikin, Theodor Menkes and Binyamin Orell. In parallel to these Jewish architects – some of whom were teachers and students at the Bauhaus School who migrated to Palestine when it was closed down in 1933 by the Nazis – a number of Arab architects who had been educated abroad began to work in Haifa. They too were imbued with the new spirit of world architecture, the Art Deco style born at the beginning of the 20th century, which gained momentum between 1920 and 1930. And they were likewise influenced by modern architecture, which introduced the ideas of the International Style. Among the Arab architects who worked in Haifa were Ahmad Faris, who had studied in Canada, and Emile Bustani, who had studied in Boston in the USA. In 1936 architect Emile Bustani built a modern house on Haifa's shoreline for his uncle, the lawyer and intellectual Wadi' Bustani, and in the same year designed a home for Dr. Musallam Sa'd in the prestigious *'Abbas* neighborhood.[4]

Brought to the city by architects from Europe, the International Style of architecture took Haifa by storm and made its mark on both Jewish and Arab construction activity. Arab architects and entrepreneurs adapted this style to the spirit of the local tradition. This is apparent in the integration of new elements such as vertical windows generally placed on the structure's common stairwell; spacious hanging balconies protruding from the facades, which coincided with the disappearance of the traditional stone supports; pergolas on the roofs, which manifested the use of traditional Arab architectural elements; and various forms of stone finish on the facades. Many examples of this mixed architectural style are to be found in the *'Abbas* neighborhood on the Lower Carmel, in the *ha-Nevi'im* Steps area, including a collection of the Tuma family[5] houses, the

---

[4] The Musallam family home, the Municipal Engineering Administration Archive, Building File no. 3828/36.

[5] On the Tuma family's buildings on *Ma'alot ha-Nevi'im* Street, see Nili Bar On and Idit Shelomi (Architects and Town Building), *Beit Tuma Simtat ha-Nevi'im 3 Haifa* [*Tuma House, 3 ha-Nevi'im Lane Haifa*], Documentation File, Sites Conservation Unit, Haifa Municipality (2010).

Majdalani houses[6] in today's *Yavneh* Street and the Hasan Dik houses on today's Hasan Shukri and Ibin-Sina Streets, as well as in the *Wadi al-Jimal* (*Ein ha-Yam*) neighborhood near the seashore.

As the International Style took hold in Haifa from the mid-1930s onward, Jewish architects of European origin began to cooperate with Arab entrepreneurs. The architect Binyamin Orell[7] and the engineer Yehezkel Zohar, for example, built a spacious and innovatively designed mansion in which Haifa's first elevator was installed for the Salam family. Toward the end of the 1930s a distinctive public housing project for employees of the refinery was built on the edge of the German Colony by the entrepreneur Raja Rayyis, designed by the renowned architect Antone Thabet. The project was planned in conjunction with the British-Jewish architect Benjamin Chaikin.[8] The architect Moshe Gerstel likewise designed residential structures and apartment buildings for the Palestine elite, including the 'Asfur, Habibi, Shabib, Abinadir and Qaraman families.

Moshe (Morris) Gerstel was born into an orthodox Jewish family in April 1886 in the town of Novy-Yarchev located not far from the city of Lemberg in Western Galicia. He acquired his education in architecture at the University of Lemberg in Poland (nowadays part of the Ukraine) between 1908 and 1914. He completed his studies toward the end of World War I, during which he served as an officer in the Austrian army, obtaining his degree in architecture from Vienna University in 1917. While working on a public housing project in Amstetten in Lower Austria, Gerstel formulated novel ideas regarding design. This innovative complex of residential buildings was designed as a public project that created an "atrium," or common inner courtyards, for the use of all residents of the complex. Following his success in constructing projects in conjunction with a local entrepreneur, Gerstel left Vienna in 1922 in order to work in Romania. He opened his own architectural office in Bucharest, working mainly on the design of residential buildings, and there he met his wife to be, the daughter of an architect. In 1933, Gerstel, his wife and two young sons arrived in Palestine and settled in Haifa. They lived in a room in the

---

[6] On the Majdalani home on *Yavneh* Street, see Dalia Levy, *Seker Shimur Beit Majdalani, Rehov Yavneh 3, Haifa* [*Conservation Survey of Majdalani House, 3 Yavneh Street, Haifa*], Sites Conservation Unit, Haifa Municipality (2001).

[7] On the architect Binyamin Orell, see Aluf Orell and Dror Orell, *Binyamin Orell: Adrikhal Lelo Diploma* [*Binyamin Orell: Architect without a Diploma*] (2008).

[8] On the architect Benjamin Chaikin, see Danny Raz, and Semadar Raz (Conductors of the Survey), *Heikhal Iriat Haifa – Seker Miqdami* [*The Haifa Municipality Building – Preliminary Survey*], Shiqmona Company for Haifa Municipality (2008).

Teltsch Hotel on Mount Carmel. A year later Gerstel's wife and sons left the country and returned to Romania in the wake of a crisis in his personal life.

It is difficult to establish with any certainty what motivated Gerstel to leave Europe. "His migration to Palestine was not a result of purely Zionist motivation," his son Leopold noted in an interview. "He did not belong to the Zionist movement and was not identified with any particular political party".[9] Yet he apparently nevertheless sensed the winds of change blowing in Europe. The migration from Europe to Palestine affected him deeply and greatly influenced Gerstel's works as an architect and a painter. It is evident that the unfamiliar scenery of the land and its local figures made a powerful impression on him upon his arrival. He expressed his impressions of the new surroundings in charcoal and pencil drawings and watercolors of the local Carmel landscape and the figures of the local peasants, the stonemason with whom he worked and local Arab dignitaries.[10]

Gerstel's architectural style likewise underwent a transformation, acquiring a new and local expression. The landscape is the birthplace of the building, and Gerstel began to study the place and the local landscape. The planning process was bound up with his familiarization with the existing environment and the local material. He was, however, also receptive to the innovative concepts offered by the International Style, and like many of the architects working in Palestine he invested considerable resources in maintaining connections with Europe through visits and by reading professional literature and journals.[11] And like most of the pioneers of the International Style in Palestine, Gerstel by no means abstained from using local elements. He made use of traditional materials such as stone, introducing varied adaptations and details while integrating subdued geometrical shapes derived from the International Style and seeking to minimize the use of non-functional, decorative elements. His architectural works were guided by the principles of simplicity. At every opportunity, his son Leopold related, he would reiterate: "One must design as inexpensively

---

[9] Interview with Leopold Gerstel, 2009. This section is based on interviews conducted with Moshe Gerstel's son, Prof. Leopold Gerstel, architect and artist, lecturer at the Faculty of Architecture in Innsbruck, Austria and at the Technion in Haifa (2009).

[10] Plans, perspectives, sketches and drawings from the architect's estate in the possession of the Gerstel family in Haifa.

[11] Michael Levine, *Ir Levana, Adrikhalut ha-Signon ha-Beinle'umi be-Yisra'el, Diuqanashel Tequfa* [*White City: The Architecture of the International Style in Israel, Portrait of a Period*] (1984), p. 33.

as possible in order to provide housing for as many people as possible." In designing his buildings he combined heavy rectangular structures with flat roofs. He adapted the apertures to the local light and heat, providing shade by moving the windows back from the facade of the structure and using pergolas and canopies that resembled eye shades.

Upon his arrival to Haifa Gerstel found most of his clients among the city's wealthy Arabs. In 1936 he designed a residential mansion for Hanna 'Asfur.[12] The house is located on the main road of the French Carmel neighborhood, on the way to Stella Maris, and its presence exudes grandeur and singularity to this day. In designing this mansion Gerstel succeeded in creating a synthesis between eastern and western styles. The use of high arches on the building's corners and the stone finish on the facades imbued it with an "eastern" character; yet these were combined with modern western forms, such as the division of the aperture by installing a vertical window in the stairwell, and the use of rounded verandahs protruding beyond the building's facade, and criss-crossing iron banisters on the girders of the roof.

Fig. 4: Villa 'Asfur

On the plot adjacent to the 'Asfur home Gerstel designed a villa for the family of Jamil Habibi, a Palestinian judge. In 1938 he built a villa for Mrs. Agnes Huri. During its construction Gerstel fell out with the client owing to inaccuracies in the implementation of the project and their joint

---

[12] Hanna 'Asfur was a Protestant Haifa lawyer whose career prospered by virtue of his special relationship with the British.

venture was thus interrupted owing to his pedantic and uncompromising character. Gerstel consequently did not regard this building as one of his and its construction was completed by the Italian architect Giovanni Borra, who resided in Palestine at the time while engaged in planning a project for the Carmelite order nearby *Sahat al-Khamra (Khamra Square)* in Haifa's downtown.

In these mansions on the Carmel, Gerstel made elegant and original use of the elements characteristic of the International Architecture Style. The structures are simple cubes devoid of ornamentation; the apertures of the buildings are rectangular and functional, integrating the modern material of glass and creating divisions by employing Belgian frames in the stairwell openings. His distinctive architectural signature was manifested in a curved element on the balconies, which he adorned with a simple iron railing. Gerstel learned to appreciate the qualities of traditional stonemasonry and used it on the finish of the facades of his buildings. By combining the rough *tobzi*[13] stone with the more delicate elaborations of *musamsam*[14] and *matabbi*,[15] Gerstel succeeded in elegantly and naturally integrating the innovative international forms with the traditional, local material. Further examples of projects that Gerstel constructed for Arab clients are to be found in the *'Abbas* neighborhood, located on the slopes of the Carmel between *Shari' al-Jabal* (Mountain Road) and the lower reaches of *al-Karma* Street (nowadays *ha-Gefen* Street). This area underwent rapid development from the end of the thirties and the early forties onward and soon became the elite neighborhood of Haifa's Christian Arab population.[16] At the upper end of *'Abbas* Street Gerstel constructed an apartment building for the Sahyun family,[17] and at its lower end built one for Subhi

---

[13] *Tobzi* processing leaves the stone with a rough surface and is widely used in Arab construction.

[14] *Musamsam* is a delicate form of processing.

[15] *Matabbi* is a very delicate form of stone processing which produces a speckled surface.

[16] On the urban development of the *'Abbas* neighborhood, see Tova David and Tzilla Reiser (Practicing architects and conductors of the survey), *Seker eikhuyot le-Shimur be-Shekhunat Abbas be-Haifa* [*Qualities Survey for Conservation in the Abbas Neighborhood of Haifa*], Haifa Municipality, Engineering Administration, Long-term Planning Department, Building Conservation Unit (2009).

[17] The Sahyuns were a well-known Haifa family that owned many properties in and beyond the city. Several of its members took part in the urban and political activity of Palestine (Johnny Mansour, "Ha-Aravim be-Haifa be-Tequfat ha-Mandat ha-Briti, Hitpathuyot u-Temurot Hevratiot, Kalkaliot ve-Tarbutiot" ["The Arabs of Haifa during the Period of the British Mandate: Social, Economic and Cultural Developments"], in Dafna Sharfman and Eli Nahmias (eds.), *Tei al Mirpeset ha-Qazino, Du-Qium be-Haifa be-Tequfat ha-Mandat*

Lamam. In these residential buildings Gerstel made use of elements derived from International Architecture Style while finishing the facades with various applications of traditional stone material. This combination would, in later years, become one of Moshe Gerstel's trademarks.

Gerstel and Qaraman Meet on the "Seam Line"

The encounter between architect Moshe Gerstel, the European Jewish immigrant, and his colleague the Palestinian-Arab entrepreneur Hajj Tahir Qaraman, occurred in the mid-1930s. Tahir Qaraman was born into a Muslim family in Nablus in 1890. The paterfamilias, Darwish Qaraman, traded in goods purchased in Nablus, which he sold in the nearby villages. The family's financial circumstances deteriorated upon the death of the father and in 1899 they were invited by Tahir's step-brother Hajj 'Arif to move to Haifa. Only a boy at the time, Tahir came to Haifa with his younger brother 'Abd al-Ra'uf Qaraman, his three older sisters and his mother. Following the move northward Tahir began to work in Hajj 'Arif's store. With his diligence and cleverness he endeared himself to the clients who visited the store, soon took leave of 'Arif's business and opened a small kiosk not far from *Sahat al-Khamra* in the old city. He quickly established a reputation as an honest and hard-working merchant and his business began to flourish, yet:

> Tahir had never learned to read and write. He asked one of his clients, a sheikh who was a teacher of Arabic, to teach him to read and write in exchange for merchandise that he supplied to him. At the end of the working day the sheikh would come to the kiosk and once the doors were closed they would sit and study together. He soon learned to read and write and this enabled him to conduct his affairs more efficiently.[18]

The camel convoys that passed through Haifa would on occasion break their journey and replenish their stocks at Qaraman's kiosk. If they lacked the means to pay for the goods they would pawn their robes. Tahir marked the robes with colored threads of wool, green, red and yellow, so as to identify their owners. When they returned to the city and paid their debt he

---

ha-Briti 1920-1948 [*Tea on the Casino Verandah: Coexistence in Haifa during the British Mandate Period 1920-1948*] (2006), p. 273).

[18] Interview with Su'ad Qaraman and her son Tahir Qaraman, Ibtin, 2009. This section is based on interviews conducted with Mrs. Su'ad Qaraman, an educationist and intellectual, the niece and daughter-in-law of Tahir Qaraman (the widow of his first-born son Darwish Qaraman) in January 2010 and October 2009. She lives with her family and son Tahir on a farm at Ibtin.

would return their garments. Once he had established his business Tahir began to trade with Syria and Egypt and built up partnerships with well-known merchants in Syria such as Hunayni and Saraqibi, inducing them to come to Haifa. Through his reliability and efficiency he established his reputation throughout the region. In close proximity to Tahir Qaraman's store was a halva factory owned by Sha'ban el-Bard. Tahir's younger brother learned from him the secrets of halva production. Qaraman later purchased the halva factory from Sha'ban el-Bard and imported the raw materials from Nablus, considered to be the "mother of halva." Qaraman furthermore developed a good working relationship with the Mandate government and began to supply the British army. His finances were in good order and he was able to meet all his commitments and schedules.

In 1922, before he became acquainted with Gerstel who was living in Romania at the time, Tahir Qaraman purchased a large plot of land in the upper area of *Wadi al-Salib* bordering on the lower part of the *Hadar ha-Carmel* neighborhood, on which he erected an abode for his extended family. The Qaraman family home still stands at Syrkin Street 29, in the heart of the "seam line" neighborhood, its two facades facing the bustling market beneath it. The structure is excellently designed, displaying great attention to detail and meeting the highest standards of quality. It is made of stone, with a flat roof and three high-ceilinged residential floors above the ground floor.

Each floor was built for one of Tahir's brothers. Hajj Tahir lived on the top floor with his two wives and four sons and daughters. Over the years he married four wives, as befitting his social stature. The first, the mother of Darwish (Su'ad Qaraman's husband) was a good woman; the second was a beauty; the third spoke English and the fourth was a socialite. Su'ad Qaraman's father, 'Abd al-Ra'uf (Hajj Tahir's younger brother) lived on the ground floor with his wife and eight sons and daughters. Hajj Tahir's mother lived with them, while the intermediate floor was always let to tenants.[19] A flourishing garden was cultivated next to the house:

> A vine pergola shaded a fountain amidst a pool, surrounded by stone seats. The family would congregate here of an evening to enjoy the summer breeze and to warm themselves on sunny winter mornings. On occasion musicians such as Rawi Kammash and Usama al-Shawwa were invited to play and sing. Reciters of the Qur'an and religious dignitaries were invited during the month of Ramadan. Fruit trees and bougainvillea shrubs were planted in the garden

---

[19] Diala Khasawneh, *Memories Engraved in Stone: Palestinian Urban Mansions* (2001), pp. 52-60.

in addition to the vegetables. A bird cage containing a collection of rare species was placed in it. The garden played an important role in the family's day to day life. It is now covered in ugly asphalt and has become a parking lot for people who come to the market.[20]

Fig. 5: The Qaraman House

Qaraman's splendid home served as a meeting place for his numerous friends and acquaintances among the Palestine elite. Social and cultural gatherings as well as political and business meetings were held there.

Qaraman was one of the first Palestinian industrial entrepreneurs in Haifa. With his two partners Dik and Salti he founded the largest cigarette factory in the country in 1925, under the name.

---

[20] Ibid., pp. 57-58.

Fig. 6: Qaraman, Dik and Salti's Cigarette Factory

The facility employed fifty workers and occupied an impressive building at Haifa's eastern entrance on the road to Nazareth. Qaraman furthermore established a factory for the production of kitchen salt and an additional business dealing in the marketing of rice (the Eastern Rice Marketing Company). In 1933 he purchased a Jewish-owned factory that produced nails and began to manufacture iron grilles as well. In light of his commercial success Qaraman began to devote time to social and political activities within public, financial and social organizations. He was a founding member of the Palestine Arab party and became a member of the Haifa Chamber of Commerce founded in 1920. He was also a leading member of the Islamic Association, Head of the Association of former Nablus residents and Head of the Haifa Association for Assistance and Education.[21]

The Qaraman family was involved in additional businesses and enterprises in Haifa and its environs. One of these was the lime furnace and quarry in the Carmel Mountain, founded in 1926 in partnership with the

---

[21] Mahmoud Yazbak, *Arab Immigration during the Mandate Period* (1996) (in Arabic); Goren (2006), p. 502; Mansour (2006).

Even va-Sid company.[22] Qaraman purchased land adjacent to the city and established an agricultural farm in Ibtin that included a grain mill and dairy, which evolved into a thriving business.[23] In 1931 Tahir Qaraman was elected to Haifa's Municipal Council. In 1940 he was appointed one of the deputies to the first Jewish mayor, Shabtai Levi, and filled the role of Deputy Mayor until late 1949.[24] His friend and fellow city councilor David ha-Cohen relates in his memoirs: "He was a man of considerable talent, quick on the uptake, had an ability to disentangle commercial intricacies and was a master of compromise and of finding a common language with partners who were so different from him in culture, education and outlook".[25] Nonetheless, part of the Qaraman family became refugees in Jordan after 1948.

Tahir Qaraman was Moshe Gerstel's major client. The architect designed two buildings for investment purposes in the "seam line neighborhood." This was also the location of two buildings that Gerstel built for Zionist institutions, namely *Beit ha-Ta'asiya* and *Talpiot* Market. The seam line neighborhood was located on the eastern fringes of *Hadar ha-Carmel*. The urban seam line demarcated the boundary between Haifa's Jewish and Arab neighborhoods, crossing the city from east to west. The line ran roughly along the natural topographical contour at which the Carmel's moderate incline begins, marking the lower boundary of the Jewish *Hadar ha-Carmel* neighborhood and the upper boundary of the Arab *Wadi al-Salib* neighborhood. This was a quiet residential area on the margins of *Hadar ha-Carmel*. It contained two- and three-story apartment buildings; the plots were enclosed by fences containing a tapestry of courtyards and gardens containing trees and vegetation. Prosperous Arab families began to purchase plots of land here in the 1920s, on which they erected grand mansions as well as buildings for investment purposes, combining commercial facilities on the ground floor with residential apartments on the upper floors. This process whereby Arab families left the

---

[22] David Hacohen, *Et Lesaper* [*Time to Relate*] (1974), pp. 44-46.

[23] Su'ad Qaraman, *Hoveret Ma'amarim: Haifa Maqom le-Ta'asiya, Atidam shel Mivnim Histori'im* [*Collection of Articles: Haifa as a Site for Industry, the Future of Historic Buildings*] (2009), pp. 12-13.

[24] Eli Nahmias, "Aravim ve-Yehudim be-shuq Avoda Dinami ve-Energeti be-Haifa ha-Mandatorit" ["Arabs and Jews in a Dynamic and Energetic Labor Market in Mandatory Haifa"], in Dafna Sharfman and Eli Nahmias (eds.), *Tei al Mirpeset ha-Qazino, Du-Qium be-Haifa be-Tequfat ha-Mandat ha-Briti 1920-1948* [*Tea on the Casino Verandah: Coexistence in Haifa during the British Mandate Period 1920-1948*] (2006), pp. 59, 90-91; Goren (2006).

[25] Hacohen (1974), p. 45.

confines of the traditional Arab neighborhoods gained momentum with the evolution of a bourgeois-urban class as a result of the tremendous economic development in Haifa during the period of the British Mandate. In the streets containing the neighborhood – *Eqron*, *Lod* and *Yehi'el* – urban stone houses were built that combined varied architectural elements. Along these streets could be found properties owned by Arab and Jewish families alike: the families of Shafiq Saraqibi, 'Usman 'Abd al-Ghani, 'Awad Ahmad Mansur, Khalil Malas and Fadil Shiblak alongside the families of Avraham Greenberg, Haya Brock and Haya Shalom, David Simhon, Natan Zucker, Avraham Klibanov and the Sharbiv family.[26]

In 1938 Moshe Gerstel designed a building for Qaraman and his business partner Shafiq Saraqibi in the heart of the "seam line neighborhood". The structure comprises two wings made out of two separate cubes, one of which is finished in delicate *taltish* stone, while the other is finished in rough *tobzi* stone.

Fig 7: Qaraman & Saraqibi building

---

[26] Danny Raz and Semadar Raz (Architects and Conductors of the Survey), *Seker Shimur Mivneh be-Rehov Eqron 15* [*Conservation Survey of the Building on 15 Eqron Street*], in association with the Sites Conservation Unit, Haifa Municipality (2010).

Fig. 8: Qaraman & Saraqibi building

This was a building of impressive quality, and alongside it Moshe Gerstel completed the construction of *Talpiot* Market in 1940.

In the early 1930s Tahir Qaraman divided the plot on which he had built the family home into two sub-sections, and in 1937 Gerstel erected an apartment building intended for investment in the western corner. Its design followed the curved corner of the plot, resulting in a continuous "n" shaped structure with an inner courtyard. The structure has three main entrances and is serviced by three separate stairwells. The building comprised three residential floors located above a commercial floor.

The stairwells are spacious and obtain natural light through vertical glazed windows. Some of the apartments have their own entrances through corridors that display arched elements. This building originally contained some thirty apartments, an unusually high number at the time. The three stairwells emerged onto an extensive flat paved roof, contained within a balustrade and a concrete pergola providing shade. The building's facades were simply designed, devoid of special decorative elements but with horizontal cordons of stonework of various styles (done mainly in *taltish* and in *matabbi*). Small rounded balconies were located on the corners of the structure.

Construction activity entered a serious recession during World War II, during which building activity was greatly curtailed and there was a severe shortage of building materials such as cement and iron. Moshe Gerstel did not evade this crisis. The number of his commissions declined and many projects were put on hold, including a building for Sulayman Qutran in the German Colony. "He had no work during those years," his son Leopold related, "he entered a design competition for a cinema and failed to win the prize." Hajj Qaraman came to Gerstel's assistance at this time. "We lived on the roof of Qaraman's house for perhaps three or four years," his son Leopold reminisces, "with father alone after we arrived in the country." As an act of human kindness Hajj Tahir proposed to Gerstel that he construct two additional rooms on the roof of the structure in which to reside with his two small sons who arrived from Europe in 1942. The official notepaper of Gerstel's office carried the address "Qaraman House." A portrait of Hajj Tahir Qaraman drawn by Gerstel with colored pencils was found in Gerstel's estate.

Fig. 9: Portrait of Qaraman by Gerstel

As the friendship between the two men blossomed Gerstel often frequented the Qaraman home and became Qaraman's "house architect," designing for him a complex of seven apartment buildings on the family's land in *Neveh Sha'anan*, although this project did not materialize. In the German Colony Gerstel constructed an apartment building for investment purposes that contained stores and a center for the distribution of milk. Gerstel then designed the "Qaraman farm" adjacent to the village of Ibtin. Here the family lived in single story villas surrounded by gardens containing ornamental as well as fruit trees. The farm provided agricultural produce to the area and included a small tobacco factory, a press for the production of olive oil and soap, a grain mill and living quarters for the employees. A "social center" was planned for the farm, comprising accommodation for employees and communal services such as a laundry and dining hall (which did not materialize).

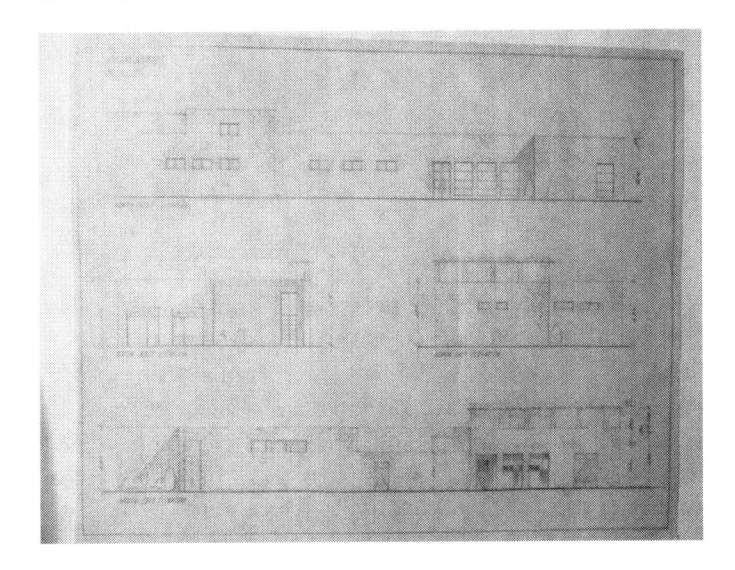

Fig. 10: Social Center

Gerstel's professional activity declined after 1948. His Arab friends and acquaintances were forced to abandon their homes and properties and were expelled or fled from Haifa. "Prior to the war the majority of his clientele was made up of Arabs and he did not have much of a clientele thereafter … to the Zionists he didn't really belong to the family … unlike the architects Sharon and Rechter who had clients at the time when Zionism was evolving," his son Leopold testified.

Fig. 11: Moshe Gerstel

When the confrontation between the nationalities culminated in the founding of the State of Israel, the Arab-Jewish architectural cooperation that had endured under the British Mandate came to an abrupt end. The narrative of the encounter between Qaraman and Gerstel was founded on friendship and mutual respect and it therefore continued beyond the cataclysm experienced by Haifa in 1948. Gerstel maintained close contact with the family even after the death of Tahir Qaraman in 1952, and in 1956 he designed the final project for the Qaraman family, a residential villa for one of the Qaraman sons on the Ibtin farm. Yet Gerstel reduced his architectural activity following the establishment of the state of Israel until his death in 1961. Since then Gerstel's name has been forgotten and is no longer part of Haifa's local public awareness or of the national scene. Only a few references are to be found in contemporary Israeli architectural literature to his singular works and his architectural activity. Yet his distinctive architectural touch is still clearly apparent in the buildings that he designed and constructed in Haifa. Gerstel was among the most prominent architects who worked in Haifa during the British Mandate. Among the well-known public buildings he constructed in the city are the Old Carmel Hospital, the *Talpiot* Market structure and *Beit ha-Ta'asiya*.

Fig. 12: Carmel Hospital – Staircase

Archival material testifying to the scope and quality of his architectural endeavor remains in the private possession of his family and has yet to be revealed to the general public. While writing this article we gained a glimpse into this private archive, which comprises a collection of original plans, sketches, drawings and perspectives as well as many photographs, all of which demonstrate the extent of his activity.

After the *Nakba*, fortune did not smile on Tahir Qaraman either. He was forced to leave Haifa upon the outbreak of the 1948 war. Several members of his extensive family, including the wives and children, were sent to a temporary safe haven in Lebanon, while others made their way to Egypt and some found refuge on the Ibtin farm. Like all the other abandoned Palestinian properties, the family's buildings were placed under the responsibility of the "Custodian of Absentees' Property," which transferred them to "new" Jewish tenants. The grand structure at 29 Sirkin Street in the heart of the Market neighborhood stands in disrepair, neglected and desolate, in the wake of physical changes brought about by improvised additions that disregarded its original character and the sealing of some of its sections. The structure's original function as the Qaraman family's home underwent transition over the years. During the 1960s the Jewish community of immigrants from Aleppo living in the neighborhood requested that the second-story apartment in the building be transformed into the "Aram Tsova Synagogue." The plan submitted to the municipality's licensing department by Engineer A. Rosenthal proposes changes to the apartment's original internal divisions that called for the demolition of the walls of the living rooms. It furthermore proposes to block off the original windows on the eastern facade, thereby closing the exit to the balcony in order to facilitate the positioning of the Holy Ark toward the east, as is customary. The proposal also calls for the demolition of rooms to make way for a central hall in which a raised prayer dais would be placed, in the style characteristic of Sephardic synagogues. In order to enlarge the area of the women's section, the members of the synagogue committee requested that an exterior verandah supported by columns and protruding three meters beyond the structure's outline be added on to the building's western front. This request was refused, most probably because the municipality officials understood the destructive effect that this addition would have on the building's distinctive character. Internal changes to the building were made, however, some with the authorities' approval but most without any authorization whatsoever. To this day the synagogue serves the small Jewish community that attends services mainly on the Sabbath and on religious holidays. In 1972 a Mr. Ya'akov Reznik applied to the municipality requesting to renovate his butcher's store located on the building's ground floor. He wished to make major alterations to the building's facade – to demolish a stone wall, install a metal shutter along the entire length of the opening, lower the level of the floor and demolish some steps. The licensing official recommended that the request for alterations to the facade be rejected, "since the place is within the sphere of renewal and the internal alterations detract from the building's facade."[27] Yet two years later, in 1974, a fresh comment was registered that authorized the requested alterations, which transformed the complexion of the ground floor beyond recognition.

EPILOGUE – "THE LIGHT OF MEMORIES"

The *Nakba* experienced by the Palestinian Arab residents of Haifa put a sudden end to the continuous Arab urban activity in the city extending from the beginning of the 19th century to the end of the Mandate period. Haifa's Arab community underwent a radical transformation in size and ethnic composition between the end of 1947 and April 1948. The physical features

---

[27] Engineering Division Archive, Haifa Municipality, Building File no. 36/3828.

of the Arab part of the city were likewise significantly altered, clearly manifesting the destruction of the fabric of the traditional urban population.[28] The demolition of the old city that began in July 1948[29] conclusively severed the urban continuity of the Arab city, disrupting the constellation of Arab neighborhoods. The physical connection between the *al-Hara al-Sharqiyya* (Eastern [Arab] neighborhood) beginning with *Wadi al-Salib*, through the alleys of the old city extending to the outskirts of the western neighborhoods was finally terminated.

Unlike the Arab neighborhoods that were deliberately demolished during the war and upon its conclusion, the buildings along the "seam line" were not demolished, since this was primarily a Jewish neighborhood. The buildings abandoned by the Arab population were soon occupied by new tenants. These were local Jewish neighbors who took them over or recent immigrants to the country who sought to improve their living conditions by moving out of disadvantaged impoverished neighborhoods, primarily from the downtown area. During the 1950s the properties were placed under the responsibility of the "Custodian of Absentees' Property," and subsequently transferred to the Development Authority. After dividing the apartments originally designed for a single family into sub-units for a number of families, this body let the properties to new Jewish tenants, charging a low monthly rental. Various elements and installations including piping of different sorts were attached to the buildings' facades, balconies were enclosed, and improvised toilets, storerooms and canopies were added on the roofs and balconies. The disadvantaged population rapidly housed in these overcrowded apartments was unable to maintain the structures. "An incompatibility or 'mishmash' evolved, expressing the disparity between the low economic status of the new tenants and the superior quality of the buildings".[30]

The buildings soon fell into neglect and deteriorated owing to the rapid turnover of tenants and the temporary structural improvisations. In recent years the "seam line" neighborhood has experienced a process of physical deterioration and an exodus of population. Residents whose financial circumstances have improved have left to live in more attractive neighborhoods in the city. Many buildings have been evacuated, their upper stories abandoned. Commercial activity is conducted on the ground

---

[28] Goren (2006), p. 195.

[29] The Absentees' Properties Law passed in 1950 stipulated that the properties should not be sold, but could be transferred to the Development Authority. See Yfaat Weiss, *Wadi Salib: ha-Nokheiah veha-Nifqad* [*Wadi Salib: A Confiscated Memory*] (2007), pp. 87 and 89.

[30] Weiss (2007), p. 76.

floors of these structures during the day, mainly along *Sirkin* and *Yehi'el* Streets, while the sidewalks have been taken over by stands and the streets are crowded with vehicles and pedestrians. As evening falls the stores close and the area becomes deserted. The "seam line" neighborhood is now populated primarily by people of low socio-economic status; immigrants from the former Soviet Union, most of whom are elderly or singles, Arab families from the outlying villages and a new community of labor migrants, known as "foreign workers."

> This was once a good neighborhood ... we lived here all together, the Moroccans with Romanians and Poles ... we came here from Stanton Street in 1953, after the Arabs left ... I live here in the building, our neighbor was Rabbi Ohanna [Rabbi Nissim Ohanna, the Chief Rabbi of Haifa] ... here on the corner (she points to the Qaraman family home) there was a Polish family ... their daughter used to play for us on the violin. She fell in love with my son ... we were good neighbors, we celebrated holidays together ... on Shavu'ot we would throw water on one another ... Arabs? There were none here ... there was *Talpiot* Market, it was a good neighborhood ... a number of grocery stores and small stores ... later they spoiled the street ... all the stands sprung up here ... nowadays all kinds of ... riffraff has come to the apartments ... Russians and also Arabs ... wherever someone moves out, undesirables come in ... and they destroyed the beautiful house here on the corner ... the municipality destroyed it.[31]

The architect Sharon Rotbard has written about the linkage between the city's history and geography. He maintains that

> the decision to demolish an old building, to construct a new one or to conserve an existing building determines what is destined to be forgotten, what is retained as a remnant and what is worthy of remembrance. There is thus a clear and essential link between the history of the city and its geography. The city's geography preserves that which history tells it to remember and erases that which it tells it to forget. It occasionally also chooses to emphasize certain chapters of its narrative that are deemed worthy of special note....[32]

The seam line neighborhood was destined by its topography to be forgotten. In Haifa, the link between the geographical layout (the topography) and the physical condition of the structures worked in favor of the structures built on the Carmel, while those located in the downtown

---

[31] Interview with Mas'uda Ben-Simhon, resident of *Yehi'el* Street adjacent to the Qaraman family home, 2010.
[32] Sharon Rotbard, *Ir Levana, Ir Shehora* [*White City, Black City*] (2005).

neighborhoods and along the seam line were condemned to neglect and oblivion. This fate was shared by the houses that Gerstel designed. Those located on the Carmel survived and retain their splendor, while the buildings that he erected along the seam line for the institutions of the *yishuv* and for his friend Qaraman have lost their aura and continue to deteriorate in the twilight zone to this day.

ARABS AND JEWS, LEISURE AND GENDER IN HAIFA'S PUBLIC SPACES

MANAR HASAN AND AMI AYALON

A colorful aspect of the grand shifts Haifa experienced during the Mandate was the emergence of new public spheres that attracted increasing segments of the population. As the city was growing and modernizing, its social and cultural life was becoming richer and more varied. Novel forms of pastime were introduced, and new facilities appeared in the city's landscape, from theater halls to football fields. Leisure institutions of more traditional type, primarily cafés and restaurants, were likewise rapidly proliferating. Both old and new entertainment places were now frequented by crowds far bigger than before, among them – another remarkable novelty – many women and youth. On the whole, the city's leisure modes were being transformed. They were becoming more public.

Our chapter examines Haifa's public spaces as areas of social change and Arab-Jewish cohabitation in times of a national conflict. It looks into the presence of men and women in the city's public places, especially those associated with cultural activities. Such places were located in different parts of the city and accessing them often entailed crossing inter-communal boundaries, geographic or otherwise. To what extent, we shall ask, did Arabs and Jews feel comfortable sharing their free-time spaces with each other? And in what measure was such sharing affected by the political vicissitudes of the time?

Haifa's circumstances during the Mandate were in many ways different from those of other cities in Palestine. Arab newcomers, mostly from the rural periphery, and Jewish immigrants, mostly from Europe, entered the city in ever-increasing numbers, and a spirit of perpetual change marked its public life. Haifa's residents at any given point were predominantly new: most of its 1940 residents had not yet arrived in 1930; most of the 1930 residents had not been there in 1920. The shared sense of a promising future, spawned by the city's dynamic growth, typified the general atmosphere and sometimes overcast inter-communal differences. These circumstances were reflected, among other things, in Haifa's spatial expansion: beside separation on the macro level (everyone knew which parts were basically "Arab" or "Jewish"), there were areas of mixed

---

M. Yazbak and Y. Weiss (eds.), Haifa Before & After 1948. Narratives of a Mixed City, 69–98.
© *2011 Institute for Historical Justice and Reconciliation and Republic of Letters Publishing. All rights reserved.*

residence, where Arabs and Jews cohabited in one street, even one building, and used the same bus lines. It was also seen in the joint management of the city's municipal affairs and in Arab-Jewish collaboration in labor struggles.[1] Sharing the city's public leisure spaces was yet another aspect of this. As we shall see, it was shaped by multiple factors, of which the political-national conflict was only one.

The social, economic and cultural changes in Mandatory Haifa reflected a process of urbanization that affected Palestine as a whole. Generated by world capitalism during the 19th century and accelerated under British colonialism,[2] the process was notable on several plains: demographic growth;[3] shifts in the city's morphology and public spaces; and changes in social relations. Especially visible were changes in gender relations and the growing visibility of women, married and unmarried, in public places, including spaces designed for cultural and leisure activities.[4] The notion "public space" (or "sphere") has a broad range of meanings, of course, and its intention – as Charles Goodsell has noted – depends on the user's field of scholarship.[5] A definition relevant to our concern here emphasizes the physical aspects of urban public spaces, which "function as sites of public use and citizen interaction." Their importance is in that they are "allowing residents to escape the stress and hubbub of city life; promoting connectedness among citizens and groups; helping to create a sense of community identity; and furnishing a site for political dialogue and protest."[6]

Palestine's entry into the world capitalist market in its industrial age – under colonial circumstances and in inferior conditions – had a direct impact on the development of modern leisure, its designed public spaces and the culture associated with it. The historian Peter Burke, who has

---

[1] For a discussion of Arab-Jewish coexistence in Haifa, see Yosef Vashitz, *Tmurot hevratiyot ba-yishuv ha-'aravi shel haifa bi-tqufat ha-mandat ha-briti*, unpublished PhD Dissertation (1993), pp. 68-90, 194-204.

[2] Manar Hasan, *Ha-Nishkahot: ha-'Ir ve-hanashim ha-falestiniyot, ve-hamilhama 'al ha-zikaron*, unpublished PhD Dissertation (2009).

[3] Mahmoud Yazbak, "Ha-hagira ha-'Aravit le-haifa, 1933-1948: nituah kamuti 'al pi mekorot 'arviyim", *Katedra* 45 (1987), pp. 131-146; Gad Gilbar, "Megamot ba-hitpathut ha-demografit shel 'arviyei eretz Israel", *Katedra* 45 (1987), pp. 43-56.

[4] See the interesting discussion of this issue in Hans Chr. Korsholm Nielsen and Jakob Skovgaard-Petersen, "Introduction: Public Places and Public Spheres in Transformation – The City Conceived, Perceived and Experienced", in Hans Chr. Korsholm Nielsen and Jakob Skovgaard-Petersen (eds.), *Middle Eastern Cities 1900-1950* (2001), pp. 12-13.

[5] Charles T. Goodsell, "The Concept of Public Space and Its Democratic Manifestations", *American Review of Public Administration* 33/4 (December 2003), p. 361.

[6] Ibid., pp. 363-364.

studied the "invention" of leisure in early modern Europe, has noted that the modern distinction, or "regular alternation of work and leisure, was a product of industrial capitalism."[7] An elite (especially men) privilege at first, time off work gradually became available to other social groups, who adopted a routine of "regular doses of daily or weekly recreation".[8]

In a volume that focuses on inter-communal relations in a "mixed" city, exploring leisure practices entails a promising advantage. Spending one's free time is a voluntary human activity whose nature, location and frequency are readily changeable, more so than the choice of a residence or a place of employment. Since people alter their recreational patterns at will according to changing circumstances, this part of their life routine should be an especially sensitive indicator of their feelings and thoughts. But there is also a serious shortcoming to this choice of activity as a field of inquiry: sources for the study of past leisure practices are notoriously problematic. Like most aspects of people's daily life, recreation is seldom documented; when it is, the accounts are perforce sketchy and often overly personal. For certain kinds of pastime – cinema, theater, sports events – newspapers and casual documents sometimes provide credible information on location and schedule, but they rarely consider the human experience involved. Other kinds of leisurely activities, e.g. spending free time in restaurants, cafés, on the beach, or in public parks are hardly ever recorded. Furthermore, the scanty evidence available to us is inevitably tainted by the accumulating dust of time, which in the present case is especially tricky: both Arabs and Jews tend to view pre-1948 daily realities through the loaded prism of subsequent events. Such problems limit our ability to recover an accurate picture. A conscientious reading of available testimonies may allow us to reconstruct the scene's general contours and main characteristics, but perhaps little beyond that. Their limitations remain considerable and should be borne in mind.

HAIFA LEISURE

In late-19th century Ottoman Haifa, a small town then, public entertainment was limited in sites and practices. Haifa's surroundings, engulfing mountain and sea, pleasant forests and exquisite vistas, offered its residents diverse natural areas for enjoyable outing. There were also man-made facilities designed for recreation. A popular form of pastime, mostly among

---

[7] Peter Burke, "The Invention of Leisure in Early Modern Europe", *Past and Present* 149 (February 1995), pp. 136-150.
[8] Ibid., p. 148.

Arabs, was sitting in a café for sipping tea or coffee, smoking, and company, and sometimes listening to storytellers (*Hakawati*). By 1900, quite a few cafés were lined up along the old city's Jaffa-Umayya main artery parallel to the seashore. There were operators of street puppet-shows (*qarqoz/karagöz*) and "magic boxes" (*sanduq al-'aja'ib* – peeping into a box with hand-rolled pictures). After the turn of the century, a modest theater activity appeared in some, mostly private, schools.[9] For the city's Jewish community, a similarly limited free-time activity was reported. "Each person is a world unto itself, completing the day's work and returning home to spend the rest of the day with the family," a 1909 account noted, somewhat gloomily, and mentioned a library as the only local cultural institution.[10] These, and the beaches in the city's southwestern area, made up the range of leisure options in pre-Mandatory Haifa.

The scene began to change after World War I. By 1921, the Jewish-owned *Coliseum* Cinema was already operating on Allenby Street (downtown), with a pianist accompanying the silent motion pictures. Soundless movies were likewise introduced in several cafés nearby, employing some crude technology,[11] and by 1926 two other silent movie theaters were in operation, *Eden* and *Empire*.[12] Local Arab drama bands began performing in improvised arenas and the large gardens of some cafés.[13] Organized sport was another new kind of recreation, introduced in Haifa before World War I and gaining momentum thereafter. Football, played in Palestine sporadically since the onset of the 20th century, soon became a popular pursuit with British encouragement and participation. Teams were assembled as sections of social-cultural clubs or otherwise – e.g., the railway workers and Haifa Christian scouts on the Arab side, *Maccabi* and *Hapo'el* on the Jewish side.[14] Already in the early 1920s, an

---

[9] Salim Tamari, "The Vagabond Café and Jerusalem's Prince of Idleness", in Salim Tamari, *Mountain against the Sea: Essays on Palestinian Society and Culture* (2009), pp. 176-180; Johnny Mansour, "Ha-'aravim be-haifa bi-tqufat ha-mandat ha-briti", in Daphna Sharfman and Eli Nahmias (eds.), *Tei al Mirpeset ha-Qazino, Du-Qium be-Haifa be-Tequfat ha-Mandat ha-Briti 1920-1948 [Tea on the Casino Verandah: Coexistence in Haifa during the British Mandate Period 1920-1948]* (2006), pp. 284-285.

[10] A report from Haifa in *Ha-Tzvi* (Jerusalem), 21 September 1909, p. 2.

[11] Yaakov Davidon, *Hayyo hayta haifa* (1952), pp. 23-27, 137-139; Arthur Koestler, *Arrow in the Blue* (1952), p. 180; Bulus Farah, *Meha-shilton ha-'othmani la-medina ha-'ivrit*, translated by Udi Adiv and Yusuf Mansour (2009), p. 21.

[12] E.g., *Hatzafon* (Haifa), 26 March, 28 May 1926.

[13] Mansour (2006), pp. 285-287.

[14] Tamir Sorek, *Zehuyot be-mishaq* (1996), p. 24. The Jewish sports organization *Maccabi* was founded in 1906 and its Haifa branch in 1913. *Hapo'el* was a post-World War I organization (1923), its Haifa club opened in 1924.

annual football tournament was held in the city, with Arab, Jewish and German teams competing for a championship cup,[15] and game fields were improvised on school and communal club grounds. Alongside such novelties, leisure sites of more traditional nature also expanded. Cafés, rapidly proliferating, came to comprise a rainbow of institutions – from humbly furnished places that offered coffee, water-pipes and table games to fancy ones, with a capacity for scores or hundreds of people and spacious enough for dancing and artistic performances. A notable example of the latter kind was *Bustan al-Inshirah* Café and gardens, which also included a theater arena, opened in the mid-1920s between Jaffa and Allenby Streets. A facility of a different kind was Gan Binyamin, opened in 1925 in a Jewish section of *Hadar ha-Carmel*, a large public park accessible to all.[16] Haifa's fast growing populace – doubling in size during the 1920s (from c. 25,000 to c. 50,000), mostly through the influx of newcomers – displayed increasing appetite for recreation. The city came to feature a scene of public leisure sites markedly richer than it had been in Ottoman times.

Varied as this activity was in the 1920s, it was not nearly as colorful as it would become during the following decade (when the city's population would again double), and in the 1940s. The arrival of speaking films, a novel thrill, prompted the expansion of cinema halls, starting with *'Ein Dor* in the lower city, in 1930. By the mid-1930s, over half-a-dozen movie theaters were operating in Haifa, among them *Eden*, *Aviv* and *Gan ha-'Ir*, known in Arabic as *Bustan al-Balad* on or close to Jaffa Street in downtown, Hertzliyya, Armon, Ora, and the roofless Amphi in *Hadar ha-Carmel*. They kept mushrooming in the 1940s, now also in the upper Carmel (*Moriya*, *Amin*), in response to a palpable public demand. "Eighty-thousand Haifa Arabs go to the cinema every month," an advert for a theater-building company noted in 1946, apparently somewhat wishfully but indicating the activity's growing popularity.[17] Cinemas offered a mixed choice of films: European and American, typically shown in the Hadar and Carmel theaters (which featured "the latest in cinema hall architecture, film

---

[15] *Haaretz*, 24 November, 8 December 1924. The November report announces the assembly in Haifa of a five-team league "as in every year." A "Palestine Football Association", comprising Arab, Jewish and British teams throughout the country was founded in 1928; Sorek (1996), pp. 24-27. See also Davidon (1952), pp. 147-156.

[16] *Hatzafon*, 26 February, 18 June 1926 (reporting events in *Bustan al-Inshirah*); Tamir Goren, "Ganim tziburiyyim ve-tipuah ha-'ir bi-tquftat ha-mandat", *Haifa* (Haifa History Association Bulletin), No. 5 (December 2007), pp. 5-12; 'Abd al-Latif Kanafani, *15 Shari' al-burj – Haifa, dhikrayat wa-'ibar* (1996), pp. 34-35; Farah (2009), pp. 21-22.

[17] *Al-Difa'*, 5 March 1946.

programmes and entertainment," as one observer noted);[18] and Arab, primarily Egyptian, mostly in downtown places. Those in foreign tongues often had locally produced handwritten translations, usually in Hebrew, accompanying the movie on a side screen. The bigger halls also hosted theater plays, concerts, and various other public activities. So did several other facilities opened in the city, most prominently the posh Casino event hall, inaugurated in the Jewish neighborhood of *Bat Galim* in 1934.

Public sports, an exciting activity evoking group-solidarity and local patriotism, also grew popular. More football teams were formed, among them those of the Catholic and Greek-Orthodox clubs and the football clubs of *al-Ittihad, Shabab al-'Arab, al-Tirsana,* and *al-Nadi al-Riyadi al-Islami.* Game fields were now better organized and by the early 1940s some of them had come to host intra- and inter-city matches regularly. Three of these were concentrated in the southwestern Haifa area known as *al-Mawaris* (today's Qiryat Eliezer).[19] Drawing players and fans in increasing numbers, football became a lively kind of public-sphere action. Other sports activities, notably boxing, basketball, and swimming,[20] were also becoming common though not as much as football. Concurrently, Haifa's cafés and restaurants burgeoned everywhere: a *Haganah* report of the mid-1940s listed no fewer than 68 Arab cafés and 59 Arab restaurants in the city, most of them downtown along the Jurayna-German Colony axis and on Kings Street, but also in other parts.[21] Jewish immigrants opened such facilities in the Hadar and Carmel areas, on the premises of hotels or independent of them. In their foods and drinks, decoration, and music, these were more reminiscent of places in the owners' old home-countries than of their Arab counterparts in the lower city. They added a European flavor to Haifa's expanding public spaces.

ARABS AND JEWS IN THE LEISURE SPHERE

No formal or physical barriers separated Arab entertainment areas from Jewish ones. Geographic distances within the city were fairly small and moving from one section to another on foot or by bus posed little difficulty.

---

[18] P.J. Vatikiotis, *Among Arabs and Jews* (1991), pp. 24-25.
[19] Kanafani (1996), pp. 105-113.
[20] Ibid., pp. 113-116.
[21] *Haganah* Archive, 105/279 – an undated document, apparently written in the 1940s. See also Mustafa Kabha, "Hayei ha-tarbut be-haifa ha-'aravit be-shilhey ha-mandat", in *Haifa be-1948* (2008), p. 22. Kabha relies on another *Haganah* document and more sources in discussing some important cafés.

Members of the two groups could come to the same football fields and movie halls, cafés and restaurants, gardens and beaches, and spend their fun time in each other's company whenever they felt comfortable doing so. Alternatively, they could choose to spend their free time in mutual exclusivity.

Arab-Jewish sharing of leisure spaces in Haifa was reported throughout the Mandate, in collective and individual activities. It occurred all over the city but especially in *Hadar ha-Carmel*, the area adjoining the city's downtown, with a mixed population on its outskirts, where Arabs and Jews met regularly during their free time and at other times. Such space-sharing occurred in eating and drinking places, where the range of tastes on offer in one community's restaurants was alluring to members of the other. Attracted to oriental foods, sweets, and beverages, Jews frequented Arab restaurants and cafés in the city's Arab quarters,[22] and Arabs, typically of the upper social class, came to Jewish eating places on the Carmel – for, as one observer noted, "what could appeal more to the 'emerging' Arab townsman than a European nightclub-restaurant with a variety of food, drink and entertainment run by charming Hungarians?"[23] We hear of an Iraq-born Jew opening a café on Kings Street, in the heart of an Arab area;[24] of Arabs attending a Jewish Purim evening party at *'Ein Dor* hall, where they "danced till sunrise";[25] and of "very many Jews" among the audience of the opera *Samson and Delilah*, performed in Arabic by an Egyptian team in *Bustan al-Inshirah*.[26] Arabs and Jews met in public gardens and on the beach (the *Khayyat* Beach was usually used by both groups),[27] in cinema halls and football fields.

How common were such encounters? It depends who you ask. As already noted, past patterns of social behavior are a thorny matter, mostly because much of the extant evidence on it is typically personal and subjective: what for some people was an era of cordial coexistence, replete with amiable exchanges, could be one of stressful estrangement in other

---

[22] E.g., Davidon (1952), pp. 57-63; Mordechai Ron, *Haifa shel yemei yalduti* (1993), p. 29.
[23] Vatikiotis (1991), pp. 24-25. See also Ron (1993), pp. 92-93; Daphna Sharfman, "Ha-anashim, ha-eru'im veha-meqomot she-'assu historya", in Daphna Sharfman and Eli Nahmias (eds.), *Tei al Mirpeset ha-Qazino, Du-Qium be-Haifa be-Tequfat ha-Mandat ha-Briti 1920-1948 [Tea on the Casino Verandah: Coexistence in Haifa during the British Mandate Period 1920-1948]* (2006), pp. 196-197.
[24] *Davar*, 24 November 1936.
[25] *Davar*, 24 March 1932.
[26] *Hatzafon*, 18 June 1926. Similarly, *Davar*, 24 March 1932.
[27] *Haaretz*, 2 September 1924; *Davar*, 18 October 1929 (a vivid description of an Arab-Jewish friendship evolving on the Haifa beach); Kanafani (1996), pp. 36-37.

peoples' memory. That Haifa's Arabs and Jews shared spaces of free-time activity is amply confirmed by available testimonies. But to what extent this was habitual and widespread is more difficult to ascertain. We will try to examine this issue by focusing more closely on two kinds of leisure activities: movie-going, an individual practice; and football, an organized one.

CINEMA: SHARING A DARKENED SPACE

Going to the movies was a personal pursuit, practiced upon one's choice and not necessarily related to one's social links or political sentiment. Logistic considerations, such as location and cost, informed that choice along with cultural ones, such as language and taste. It was an activity conducted mostly in the dark, which masked those present from each other throughout much of the event. Films fixed the spectator's gaze on the screen; other viewers, even those in adjacent seats, were only marginally relevant to one's entertainment. Yet there was also a part that facilitated mutual awareness: the time before and after the show and during intermissions, when everyone met openly in one public site.

Accounts of Arabs and Jews sitting side by side in the same hall before, during, and after movies come from different points in time throughout the Mandate. Haifa's first silent movie theater, the *Coliseum*, is reported to have been attended by members of the two communities together, from its outset in the early-1920s, apparently on a regular basis. A street crier would announce the day's show in Arabic, while the translation attached to the film would normally be in Hebrew.[28] Such joint experiences are reported for later years as well. One lively account is by P.J. Vatikiotis, the renowned scholar of Middle Eastern history and politics who grew up in Haifa during the 1930s and 1940s. Vatikiotis relates in his memoirs how Arabs from his *Wadi al-Nisnas* neighborhood and elsewhere used to come regularly to Jewish movie halls in *Hadar ha-Carmel*, where quality entertainment was offered. These places, he noted, "served everyone who paid: Jew, Arab, Englishman and foreigner. And they welcomed money from any nationality. The biggest spenders were the Arabs."[29] More city residents in the 1940s, interviewed orally, likewise attested to Arabs and Jews spending their leisure time under the same cinema roof.[30]

---

[28] For vivid descriptions, see Davidon (1952), pp. 23-27.
[29] Vatikiotis (1991), pp. 24-25.
[30] Ron (1993), p. 42; interviews with Haifa residents: Meir Elbaz, Hanna Abu Hanna (both interviewed by Amir Kulick, Haifa, 16 April 2008 and 18 May 2009, respectively); 'Abd

Arabic and Hebrew newspaper announcements of movies might be an additional, if indirect, source for such space-sharing in the cinema. They would tell us what cinema owners considered to be the films' potential audiences. If a movie was listed in both Hebrew and Arabic papers, we may assume that those who advertised it regarded members of the two groups as likely customers – and, plausibly, that some (or many) of them on both sides actually were. Such a source would be useful even if not systematic enough to permit quantification. During the 1920s and 1930s, notices on cinema events in Haifa appeared almost exclusively in the Hebrew press, which rarely listed Arab films and shows. Arab papers seldom carried ads for any movies in Haifa then, and began doing so only in the early 1940s. A comparative examination of such ads in Hebrew and Arabic newspapers during that last decade of the Mandate reveals that the same movies were sometimes concurrently announced to readers of both languages. For example, both the Arab and Jewish press advertised the foreign film *Tunis Victory* (Arabic *intisar tunis*, Hebrew *ha-nitzahon be-tunis*), along with a matinee (*batalat bariz/giborat paris*), shown in Armon at *Hadar ha-Carmel* in July 1944.[31] For another, the Egyptian film *al-bayh al-muzayyaf* (*The Phony Bey*), shown in *'Ein Dor* theater in March 1946, was announced by *Filastin* and by several Hebrew papers (as *ha-bey ha-mezuyyaf*).[32] Again, it goes without saying that ads of this kind are no indication of what actually took place in the movie halls. But added to the testimonies cited above, they seem to enhance the impression regarding Arab-Jewish leisure-space sharing.

But how common was this sharing? Our exploration of press adverts also reveals another salient facet: Arabic and Hebrew papers were far more systematic in posting events specifically designed for their respective, separate constituencies than in promoting those suitable for all. Arabic journals listed primarily Arabic-speaking films, concerts, plays and shows by Arab artists, both local and foreign;[33] Hebrew papers advertised movies, theater plays, music concerts, and lectures in Hebrew and

---

Akram Tuqan (interviewed by Aviv Deri, Haifa, 8 September 2009); Emile M.[..] and Ibrahim 'U. [..] (both interviewed by Na'ama Ben Ze'ev, Ramih, 8 December 2006, and Kafr Kanna, 23 May 2008, respectively).

[31] *Filastin*, 8 July 1944; *Davar* and *Haaretz*, 7 July, 1944. For similar examples, see *Filastin* and *Davar*, 13 August 1944; *Filastin*, 17 October and *Davar*, 25 October 1944.

[32] *Filastin*, 17 March 1946; *Hamashkif*, 15 March, and *Davar*, 18 March 1946.

[33] For some examples, see *Filastin*, 19 June, 2, 3, 7 July 1935; 7 September 1944; 4 July, 26 September 1947; *al-Difa'*, 4, 31 May 1943; 2 January, 19 April, 14 August, 19 October 1944; 31 March 1946; *al-Ittihad* (Jaffa), 2, 9 November 1947.

European languages attractive mainly to the Jewish public.[34] This duality was most visible when papers selectively announced only some of the events that took place in one location while ignoring the rest of them. Movie halls regularly showed different films at different times of the same week, but newspapers often publicized only those that would suit their respective readers. The phenomenon was common mostly in the Arab press. To pick an example, in July 1944 *'Ein Dor* theater (where Arab and foreign films were alternately shown) ran an Egyptian movie entitled *Nida' al-dam* (*Blood Call*), along with two foreign productions. We learn of the latter two from Hebrew papers, but their Arabic-language counterparts promoted only the Egyptian one.[35] In the following month, likewise, *Filastin* publicized the Egyptian-made *Al-Tariq al-mustaqim* (*The Right Path*) shown in that theater while disregarding two foreign movies featured there at the same time.[36] It seems that theater owners – obviously eager to prop up their business as best they could – saw little sense in trying to lure Jews to Arabic-speaking films or Arabs to foreign-language ones. For whatever consideration – economic, political, or otherwise – they apparently assessed that the potential market in the opposite community was too small to warrant more than perfunctory promotional efforts, and they acted accordingly.

This kind of selectivity is no less telling than the cross-advertising of cultural events by the Arabic and Hebrew media. It seems to have epitomized a prominent feature of Mandatory Haifa's entertainment life: its being a bifurcated scene with two separate sets of leisure patterns and only a limited area of overlapping between them. Why this was so is easy to see. Cinema-going is for pleasure, and the choice of entertainment depended on how comfortable people felt doing so. Their comfort, in turn, was determined by a variety of factors, some of which were cultural. Differences in language and cultural taste would keep European-born Jews away from Arabic-speaking films and many Arabs away from the foreign imported ones. Political factors must also have played a role: the 1940s was a time of increasing tension countrywide, which inevitably spilled over into Haifa. The press selectivity in advertising movies was one mark of this. People were probably less comfortable than before visiting the other group's territory, especially in voluntary activities intended for enjoyment. Whether for cultural or political reasons, and frequently for both, spending

---

[34] Ads for such events appeared in the Hebrew press almost daily from the early 1920s onward.
[35] *Haaretz*, 23 July 1944; *Davar*, 25 July 1944; *Filastin*, 1 July 1944.
[36] *Filastin*, 10, 13 August 1944; *Davar*, 9, 10, 13 August 1944.

one's afternoon or evening in the cinema in a company that was not one's natural element could be disagreeable.

While we cannot assess the real scope of such fun-time sharing, it is obvious that the picture was not idyllic, surely not at all times. More realistically, Haifa's Arab-Jewish cinema experience was a two-sided coin, with attraction on one side, avoidance on the other. The former side, so it seems, shined brighter in the early part of the Mandate; the latter side in its later years.

FOOTBALL: ORGANIZED ENCOUNTERS

Unlike movies – and unlike the beach, the public garden, the café, and other sites where Arabs and Jews met mostly incidentally – sport matches were expressly meant for encounter. Involving players and fans, mainly if not solely from the middle and lower social classes, football implied team spirit, popular symbols and inter-group contest, and hence was sensitive to political circumstances. In this field of leisure activity the oscillation of Arab-Jewish relations reflected clearly.

Before proceeding to the particular case of Haifa, it is worthwhile to give a short survey of the general history of football in Palestine. Palestine's first documented football game between an Arab and a Jewish team was held in Jerusalem in September 1919. As we have seen, football clubs emerged throughout the country in the 1920s and 1930s, including a few in Haifa. Matches between them – both local and intercity – gradually consolidated this activity as a popular form of public recreation. The Palestine Football Association, founded in 1928,[37] ran three leagues on three different levels, comprising at its outset a total of some 70 Arab and Jewish clubs countrywide. The Association soon displayed a pro-Zionist tilt and the Arabs began to boycott its activities. In 1934 a separate Arab Palestinian General Sports Association was formed, and the country's Arab teams all came under its roof. Paralyzed during the stormy period from 1937-1944, the Arab Association was then reorganized to administer all Arab sports activities until 1947. Meanwhile, the old Association continued to thrive, bringing more Jewish and British clubs within its folds.

Arab-Jewish matches took place from the early 1920s to the early 1940s, usually in one of the city's southwestern playing fields. They were infrequent; compared to matches in which both teams were either Arab or Jewish, mixed games were indeed rare. Slightly more common in the

---

[37] See note 15 above.

1920s,[38] they became scarcer in the 1930s and early 1940s,[39] and ceased completely once the Arab Association was revived. This was equally true of Haifa and the country as a whole. Apparently the last Arab-Jewish game to be played in Haifa was during the May 1943 Palestine War Cup series, which pitted *Hapo'el* Haifa vs. *Shabab al-'Arab*.[40]

Press accounts of these infrequent events were markedly laconic. Reports of Arab-Jewish matches in Haifa, like elsewhere in the country, usually tell us little beyond the names of the playing clubs, the date of the match, and the results. We hear nothing about the course of the matches, the general atmosphere around them, the size and composition of the crowds attending, or fans' support for their favorite teams. One 1931 report in *Davar* noted merely that "a big crowd watched the game, including a large number of Arabs"[41] – a flat description, and most standard accounts tell us even less. Such limited interest stood in contrast to the covering by Arabic and Hebrew journals of matches in which both teams were either Arab or Jewish, respectively. Reports on these matches were often detailed and vivid, expanding on the course of the match, the good and weak players, the size of the crowd attending, and the game's broad implications.[42] This slight attention to Arab-Jewish games is somewhat puzzling: one could perhaps expect that, given the country's growing political tension, encounters between Arabs and Jews – even in football – would stir a more passionate public interest. In reality, just the opposite happened: mixed games were played down or disregarded. Such persistent negligence creates the impression that the mixed matches were viewed as inconsequential by both sides. They were important neither as an arena of inter-communal patriotic clashes nor, for that matter, as an occasion of amicable collaboration. Instead, it seems that Arab-Jewish matches were regarded as a necessary price to be paid for organized public sports life, whose main goal was promoting cohesion in each party separately.

---

[38] Reports in *Haaretz*, 6 February, 25 April, 18 June 1923; 24 November, 8 December, 18 December 1924; 9 March 1925; *Hatzafon*, 26 March, 18 June, 8 September, 5 October 1926.
[39] Reports in *Davar*, 30 November 1930; 21 June 1935; 12 April, 14 April 1940; 5 May 1942; *Haaretz*, 1 May, 8 May 1942.
[40] *Palestine Post*, 28 May 1943.
[41] *Davar*, 5 April 1931.
[42] *Davar* had a fairly regular sports section from its outset in 1925. For some colorful accounts of matches between Jewish clubs, see 8 November 1928; 7 March 1929; 17 July 1930; 25 January 1932; 11 February 1936; 22 October 1937; 8 October 1939. *Filastin* at first considered sports only sporadically, but from April 1944 onward it featured a near-daily sports section. By then, however, Arab and Jewish teams no longer played against each other. See Sorek (2000).

Dynamically progressing within each community, football appears to have been one kind of leisure activity in which Arab-Jewish encounters were of marginal importance. Maybe its association with nationalistic values, along with the rising political tension between the two ethno-national groups, relegated the games (whose prescribed rules required collaborative behavior) to irrelevance. As sport contests came to be increasingly imbued with patriotic symbols, Haifa could hardly afford to run a course differently from the rest of the country. And indeed, it did not represent an exception in this regard. Here, as elsewhere in Palestine, Arab-Jewish football matches were a minor public event, not nearly as exciting as a match between Haifa's *Shabab al-'Arab* and an Arab club from Jaffa, or one between Haifa's *Hapo'el* and *Maccabi*. In the city's football scene, then, nothing indicated that the relations between its two communities were any more cordial than in the country as a whole.

PALESTINIAN WOMEN IN SPACES OF CULTURE AND LEISURE

As noted above, the rapid urbanization that marked Haifa's development under British colonial rule was reflected, among other things, in an expansion of urban public spaces. New public institutions were emerging and old ones were expanding. Urbanization and the changes it ushered in transformed social relations; and gender relations were no exception. They were also reflected in the emergence of what Louis Wirth identified as one of the most important and distinctive traits of urbanity: its heterogeneity.[43] In Haifa, heterogeneity was seen in the ethnic and national diversity of the people who shared the same urban space, and the side-by-side existence of various ways of life, tastes, and interests.[44] Such heterogeneity seems to have facilitated the forging of economic, political, social, and cultural ties between Arabs and Jews that were unrelated to the power relations prevailing in the city during the period.

The changes effected by urbanization created new opportunities for Palestinian women of different classes. They resulted in an increased female presence in the city's many public spaces, including spaces of economics, politics, culture, and leisure. They also opened new spheres for feminist writing and feminist discourse.[45] Some of these new opportunities will be discussed below. It is important to bear in mind that, as with the

---

[43] Louis Wirth, "Urbanism as a Way of Life", *American Journal of Sociology* 44(1) (July 1938), pp. 1-24.
[44] Hasan (2009).
[45] Ibid.

matters discussed in the previous section, our ability to reconstruct the lost Palestinian social and cultural urban landscape is limited due to the loss of so much of its human evidence. This is even truer when it comes to the women's presence in Haifa's spaces of culture and leisure.

Scouting was a voluntary pursuit that may be regarded as a form of leisure activity. During the Mandate, scouting troops for girls were established throughout the country, with hundreds of troop-leaders.[46] Press reports from the 1930s indicate that girls who took part in these activities also participated in nationalist demonstrations.[47] In the early 1930s, members of female scout troops joined women activists and boy scouts in the Arab Flower Day, on which volunteers collected from passersby donations for national purposes, pinning white flowers to the donors' shirts.[48] Female scouts went out on trips in and out of the country and attended camps set up on the outskirts of Palestinian cities. Sonya Habash, formerly of Ramla, recalled that her aunts belonged to a scouting organization: "My aunts Rose and Kafa' were scouts in Jaffa. They took many trips, sometimes to Lebanon and sometimes to Egypt. They traveled to Egypt in the days of Huda Sha'arawi. They went with the scouts."[49]

In an article entitled "The Arabs of Haifa during the Period of the British Mandate," historian Johnny Mansour discusses female participation in the city's scout movement: "It is important to note that the scout movement began to attract girls and young women only in the mid-1940s," he writes. "This was so because scouts movements were regarded as the domain of boys and men, and entailed extended stays outside their homes."[50] However, the sources at our disposal tell a somewhat different story. Oral testimonies and press reports indicate that female youth from cities and towns around the country, including Haifa, began joining scout

---

[46] Photographs of female scout troops appear in different sources. One example is an undated picture showing a group from the Orthodox College for Girls in Jaffa, with one of the girls wearing what appears to be a Palestinian flag; Hanna Malak, *Al-Judhur al-Yafiyya* (1996), p. 77. Another photograph, from 1947, features female scouts of the *al-Zahra* school (ibid.), and a third, from the same year, shows a group of scout leaders of *Kawkab al-Ihsan*, which belonged to the Orthodox College for Girls. This last picture was taken when the group was distributing food and dispensing first aid; on their arms, the leaders are wearing what appears to be a first-aid insignia, with a cross and a crescent and an undecipherable text (ibid., p. 92).
[47] *Filastin*, 7 May 1936.
[48] For example, see *Filastin*, 3 and 4 November 1931.
[49] Interview with Sonya Habash, Amman (Jordan), 30 August 2005.
[50] Mansour (2006), pp. 269-270.

troops already in the early 1930s.[51] Moreover, press reports indicate that young females were certainly being drawn "outside the home" during this period. They suggest that the urbanization process underway in Palestine shaped public spaces and their social architecture so as to increase women's opportunities and weakened male supervision over them.

One such report, from 1933, relates: "A group of female leaders from *Haifa and Nazareth* [emphasis added] held a camp from 7-12 April on the grounds of Safad College and took hikes through the mountains and fields."[52] The groups from the two towns met in Safad, the one from Haifa reaching there first, to be followed by the group from Nazareth: "At seven-thirty [PM] we were welcomed by the leaders from Haifa, who walked ahead to the camp," related a scout-leader from Nazareth, in an article published in *Filastin*.[53] At dawn, after having slept the night in the camp – on their own, outside the home, and with no male escort – the young women began regular camp activities: "one making breakfast, another collecting campfire wood, a third fetching water, and so on." The first hike the women took was through the surrounding hills and valleys, after which they proceeded into town. "At eight o'clock in the evening," the account continues, "we sat around the campfire, talked about what we had seen, sang our songs, and told literary stories. At 10 o'clock we went to sleep." On the next day, after visiting the town's churches and mosques, such as the *al-Ahmar* Mosque and its school, and after eating lunch, they continued to Mount Kan'an, accompanied by Hayfa Shihadih and Hilana Haddad, who provided assistance and guidance during the hike. On the third day, the group climbed up *Jabal Jarmaq*, taking their afternoon break near the fortress and then proceeding to the summit. The following day, a group of women from Safad, accompanied by a troop of girl scouts from there came to visit them. At the camp, the girls played games, sang nationalist songs, drank tea, and bid farewell to each other. On the last day of the camp, the group visited the home of the wife of Dr. Sebasi, who had invited them over for breakfast.

Visiting the public parks of Haifa was another type of leisure activity. Widad Rizq recounted her many visits to one of the city's public parks, which she frequented with her grandmother during her childhood in the 1930s and with her classmates in later years:

---

[51] E.g., *Filastin*, 9 March 1933, 2 April 1933, and 7 May 1933.
[52] *Filastin*, 20 April 1933.
[53] *Filastin*, 7 May 1933.

> The best known public park in the city ... was in Hadar, at the end of Nordau Street ['Gan Binyamin']. We used to call it 'the garden.' That's what everyone called it.... On Sundays and holidays all the Arabs would be there. The garden was so beautiful, with benches and trees, benches and trees.... Many families would visit too, as well as school girls and groups of girl friends. I remember that, when I was little, my grandmother on my mother's side had a friend and that they were extremely cute together: they were two old ladies who stuck together all the time. When not visiting other friends they would go there, to the garden. When I was little, my grandmother used to take me with her. Sometimes we would go and sit on a bench. The two of them would talk; I would sit [and listen]. Her friend, an old woman at the time, was called Jamila Jahshan. She had once worked as a nursemaid for a family that had gone on a trip to Portugal and had taken her with them for a month, or something like that. I'm not sure exactly how long it was.... From the moment we sat down on the bench until we went home, the woman would tell us about Portugal and the wondrous things she saw there. We would just sit and listen. 'Oh, Umm Anis,' she would say to my grandmother, 'In Portugal I saw this and that, and the people there are such and such...' [54]

Haifa beaches and the cafés alongside them also served as spaces of leisure for female Palestinian residents of the city. A popular one, which attracted many visitors, including women, during the summer was *al-Khayyat* Beach, also known as *al-'Aziziyya* (see picture). It was named after its owner, 'Aziz al-Khayyat, one of Haifa's wealthy men.

Press accounts from those years and memoirs of Haifa residents tell us about the beach and its urban setting. Thus, the daily *Filastin* of 20 May 1932 reported the festive opening, a few days earlier, of the bathing season: "Throngs of residents of Haifa and the north attended the celebration, with the British military orchestra playing.... The Casino management has decided to hold dance parties every Saturday evening and concerts with the same orchestra every Sunday afternoon."[55] In his memoirs, 'Abd al-Latif Kanafani provides more information on the site, which he calls "*al-'Aziziyya* resort." This "resort", he reminisces, had a bathing beach, a playground, and a first-class restaurant. *Al-'Aziziyya* was

> the favorite destination of travelers due to its high level, unmatched anywhere in the country. The food and drinks, which were of the highest quality, were served by a Nubian waiter wearing a fez and a garment that was so white, it sparkled. He wore a red cloak around his waist, like the palace servants that filled the Egyptian films. The original jazz orchestra played dance melodies

---

[54] Interview with Widad Rizq, Haifa, 23 March 2007.
[55] *Filastin*, 20 May 1932.

hour after hour in a cheerful, gay atmosphere and, with the Mediterranean water always shining in the sunlit days and the moonlit nights.[56]

Fig. 1: Al-'Aziziyya or al-Khayyat Beach, Haifa 1940s. Unknown photographer

Filastin of 6 September 1933 reported the inauguration of another bathing beach in Haifa, the East Beach, which was also frequented by women. The East Beach opened under the management of "Mr. Abu Nassur, who runs it with great energy and resolve that has won him the praise of many." It attracted "a steady flow of swimmers." The paper advised the police to appoint a special officer to secure and supervise the site for the summer season, especially to prevent what the paper termed "instances of moral violations, mainly on Saturdays and Sundays, when women presence there increases."[57] In her youth, Widad Rizq used to go to Abu Nassur's Beach along with her sisters, friends, and members of her family,

> as well as to Tall Emile Beach (now known today as Dado Beach), which was owned by a wealthy man from al-Butaji family,... a Protestant from our congregation called Emile. He would invite the entire congregation.... But

---

[56] Kanafani (1996).
[57] *Filastin*, 6 September 1933.

most of the time we went to Abu Nassur's. We would go to the beach, take walks, and play in the sand.... We did not swim because my father was very conservative, which was a pity.... But some women wore bathing suits and swam. My friend Wanda, Butaji's daughter, was one example. She was so free, you know. She would invite us to the beach quite often. We would take provisions and sandwiches and go. We would sit on the beach, and she would go down to swim.[58]

Widad had another "very good" friend, "the best friend I had," who used to visit her at home and go with her on trips and picnics. Her name was Najah al-Tamimi and she was from an "aristocratic Muslim family,"

The kind that had a telephone at home and a car, whose [economic] status was something else. We actually went to Najah's house a lot, because unlike our family which lived in two or three rooms, their house had two stories ... it was a beautiful, spacious villa. We were three friends, but we liked going to Najah's house the most, because their house was something else. We would enter the parlor, which was only ours with no one else coming or going, not even her mother or father. There, we felt different.... There was another parlor, and yet another parlor on the second floor, and more.... Najah used to dress so nice and so modern. It was something.... When we went on trips and had picnics, Najah was one of the girls who wore a bathing suit and went down to swim.[59]

In her youth prior to 1948, Maggie Karkabi also frequented Abu Nassur's Beach, as well as *al-'Aziziyya* and *al-Butaji*:

The al-Butaji family was good friends with my uncle's family on my mother's side. They used to invite them [there] and we would go with them to swim and spend the day.... I still have photographs of myself in a bathing suit. My sister, who was married and who used to come with us and with Uncle Adib to 'Atlit, also still has photographs [in a bathing suit].[60]

These were not the only summer recreation places that Karkabi used to visit. She also frequented the Bat-Galim swimming pool built next to the Casino:

We usually went there with my female cousins. There were a lot of girls [in the family].... We were many, [hence] we usually went [only] girls.... We would come to watch those who jumped [off the high-dive] ... and also to swim. We all wore bathing suits [and swam].[61]

---

[58] Interview with Widad Rizq, Haifa, 23 March 2007.
[59] Ibid.
[60] Interview with Maggie Karkabi, Haifa, 24 June 2010.
[61] Ibid.

Cafés were another recreational space for women. Haifa's favorite café for Widad and her friends was Café *Samir*, located "across from the ascent to Balfour [Street]. Later, they expanded the café a great deal, and it became very upscale. *Samir* was expensive but also high quality, so we liked to go and sit there."[62] Also in the neighborhood of Hadar, not far from Café *Samir*, was another café that was also visited by women and men, as one can tell from its advert: *Vienna* Café – the Family Café. *Vienna* was advertised as a "luxurious café with quick service … in which everything is clean and professional." The ad also portrayed it as a meeting place for male and female friends: "When you make plans with a friend," it read, "plan to meet them here."[63]

Women were likewise present in the leisure spaces of various restaurants in Haifa.[64] This is reflected in an advertisement that appeared in the 11 August 1933 issue of *Filastin*, which announced the opening of *mat'am al-marfa'* (wharf restaurant), a garden restaurant owned by Nasrallah Haddad. It was opened near the main postal building on *al-Marfa'* Street, and its ad promised visitors "a spacious garden, beautiful flowers, a natural, breathtaking landscape, quick professional service, piano playing, music, and singing" – a "wonderful [place] for families."[65] But the restaurant of which Widad Rizq has the liveliest memory from that period in Haifa was *Pross*, a Greek restaurant located at the corner of *al-Karmil* Street (today Ben-Gurion Boulevard):

> If you fancied dishes that could not be found in other restaurants, you would go to *Pross*. Of course, we did not go there every day, because it was a 'treat' [English in original]. We would go there with relatives who came to visit us in Haifa. My uncle, who lived on an extremely high standard, would sometimes take us out to eat there, and I also went there with girl-friends occasionally, especially with those who came to Haifa [from out of town]. I would take them out there. When I started traveling and meeting foreign [European] friends, we would take them out to *Pross* when they came to visit.[66]

A favorite leisure activity of many females from different social classes in Haifa was going to the movies. Females went to the movies in groups, with sisters and other family members, or in mixed groups of

---

[62] Interview with Widad Rizq, Haifa, 23 March 2007.
[63] *Filastin*, 13 November 1932.
[64] Hasan (2009).
[65] *Filastin*, 11 August 1933.
[66] Interview with Widad Rizq, Haifa, 23 March 2007.

young males and females.⁶⁷ Simon Abi Nadir from Haifa used to go to the movies with her girl-friends:

> With our group (*shilla*) we went to see a lot of movies in theatres back then. We went almost every week. We would plan to meet up somewhere and then would go to watch an Arabic movie or a foreign movie, depending [on what was playing]. Sometimes my father would drive us, as he had a car, and sometimes we would take the bus just by ourselves. We always came home by bus.⁶⁸

Maggie Karkabi also remembers many, mostly foreign films that she used to see in the theaters, usually with her sister and fiancé:

> We would take the bus ... to the Carmel ... to the Moriya movie theatre, where they used to show foreign films.... In addition, before we got to the theatre, there was this nice café on the Carmel where we used to sit and have coffee and cake.⁶⁹

Women along with men would also watch movies in fundraising and charity parties organized by women's groups, as we learn from numerous announcements in the Palestinian press. An example is a fundraising event organized by the General Philanthropy Association of Arab Women in Haifa (*jam'iyyat al-ihsan al-'amm lil-sayyidat al-'arabiyyat fi Haifa*). The event was well attended and included "the screening of a movie, the proceeds from which were distributed to the city's poor."⁷⁰

A rainbow of clubs – ethnic, religious, athletic and more – were prominent in the urban public sphere and leisure spaces of Palestinian cities, Haifa included. In his 1947 book, *The Arabs in Eretz Israel*, Yosef Vashitz noted that "the educated have ... hundreds of clubs throughout the country: Muslim and Christian, family-based and local, literary and athletic ... in Haifa alone there are 40 clubs."⁷¹ This phenomenon mirrored the changes in social relations, particularly in gender relations, as many clubs opened their cultural and leisure spaces to women as well, as rank and file members, participants in various activities, athletes, musicians, and so forth. Testimonies point to a growing presence of women, particularly of the educated middle class, in the public spaces of the city clubs. This presence assumed different forms: women attended lectures on social,

---

[67] Hasan (2009).
[68] Interview with Simon Abi Nadir-Swidan, Haifa, 17 April 2007.
[69] Interview with Maggie Karkabi, Haifa, 24 June 2010.
[70] *Filastin*, 22 October 1931.
[71] Yosef Vashitz, *Ha-'Aravim be-Eretz Israel: Kalkala ve-Hevra, Tarbut u-Mediniyut* (1947), p. 195.

cultural, economic, literary, and other subjects, and listened to concerts and operas featured by some of the clubs. They also came for the balls and parties that the clubs organized. Some appeared as lecturers, addressing issues such as the status of women, and others performed as singers and musicians in concerts and as actresses in the theatrical productions of clubs. Women also attended classes in clubs, such as painting and foreign languages, borrowed books from their libraries, or simply came to read for pleasure over a cup of coffee.[72]

Cultural clubs also served as arenas for struggle over gender relations, which led to changes in this realm, especially in the country's interior cities, where such changes were late in coming. There, and in the press – another urban tool and an integral segment of the public sphere – women waged a battle for their right to be present in, and to make use of, the spaces provided by the clubs (as was the case in Nazareth and Ramla). These efforts scored some impressive victories.[73] Some clubs had "women's committees" that organized activities – including leisure activities – for women. Thus, for example, a notice in *Filastin* on 16 February 1945 indicated that "the women's committee of the Orthodox Club in Haifa will hold its annual festival at the club beginning at 3:30 p.m. on Sunday, the 18th. [The festival] will be conducted under the auspices of Hanna Salamih, head of the Union of Arab Orthodox Clubs." According to this notice, the festival included handicraft displays, theater plays, games, music, and "various [other] kinds of amusement and entertainment."[74]

Women also took part in club activities as lecturers. Scholar Najwa Ka'war from Nazareth was invited to speak at an evening conference organized by the Arab Orthodox Club in Haifa, on 10 February 1946. Ka'war delivered a talk entitled "A Society that Besieges its Women," in which she discussed "the torrent of Western civilization sweeping through the Arab countries." This flood, she argued, was forcing Arab societies into "a transition period too short to assimilate that civilization and the new modes of organization [needed to absorb it]." In Ka'war's view, this situation was the result of "errors and failures" during the short transitional period itself, in which attempts were being made at once to start "a new life" and to retain "the distant past." It resulted in inconsistencies and contradictions that turned into "confusion and chaos." This situation brought to mind "the case of the king described by Jonathan Swift in his

---

[72] Hasan (2009).
[73] Ibid.
[74] *Filastin*, 16 February 1945.

allegorical novel *Gulliver's Travels*, who wore a pair of boots with a high right heel and a low left heel, causing his walk to look unbalanced and unharmonious." Such disharmony, she maintained, illustrated "all aspects of our life." One manifestation of this was the fact that some young adults had academic education and advanced degrees while others still thought that "the alphabet is a kind of witchcraft." Another, Ka'war suggested, was the fact that some people had "cars and houses [equipped] with the most modern devices, in contrast to other [village] inhabitants still using pulleys to pump water, as did the Egyptians six thousand years ago. These villages," she asserted, "have no relation to the 20th century...." Yet another mark of these incongruities was the fact that some girls followed the norms of Western culture and civilization, which permitted them "to frequent movie theatres and dance halls regularly," while others were "still confined to their homes, dominated by ignorant and oppressive fathers, mothers whose heads were full of nonsense, and fanatic brothers who would not let them leave the home."[75]

Another discussion, held in 1933 at the Young Women's Christian Association in Haifa and attended by "many families and journalists," focused on the right of women to study and work. The debate pitted two groups against each other. One was represented by Sadhij Nassar, a feminist and activist in women's organizations, and Jiryis Khury, the Haifa District Commissioner, who insisted on "a woman's need to study and acquire a profession so she can support herself and her family." The other group was represented by Rashid Khury and teacher Asma' Faris, who underscored a girl's need "to learn how to run a home, [since] she was born for the home and housewifery, not for a job or profession." Each group backed its arguments and theory with weighty evidence. At the end of the debate the audience was asked to voice its views, and most of those present opined that "girls should learn how to run a home, not acquire a profession."[76] Evidently, while new opportunities were opening to women in the cities, the road they traveled was still not lined with roses.

Women from neighboring Arab countries also delivered lectures in the clubs and cultural societies of Haifa. One of them was Damascene poet, author, teacher, journalist, and feminist activist Mary 'Ajami. Born in 1888, 'Ajami was among the founders of the Women's Literary Club in Damascus in 1920 and of the *Nur al-Fayha'* society and its club there. She was also the founder and editor of one of the region's earliest feminist

---

[75] *Al-Mihmaz*, 10 February 1946.
[76] *Filastin*, 5 April 1933.

newspapers, *al-'Arus* (the bride), first published in 1910, during the tenure of Ottoman Governor Jamal Pasha ("the butcher", as he was named by the Arab intelligentsia at the time).[77] Besides addressing feminist, social, and literary subjects in her own and many other publications, 'Ajami attacked the Ottoman government for oppressing its critics, especially after the hanging in 1915 of her beloved fiancé, Petro Pauli, who was executed along with other intellectuals and freedom fighters. She continued her critical writing and nationalist struggle under French colonial rule; an attempt by the Mandate government to lure her with a high monthly salary in order to make use of her newspaper "to applaud France ... and expound on the reforms brought to us by the Mandate", failed.[78] Despite the closing of her newspaper in 1926, 'Ajami continued to write, act and deliver public lectures.

In 1928 'Ajami was invited by the Young Christian Society in Jaffa to attend its annual celebration. Her talk, entitled "Self Deception," was delivered at the National Orthodox School in the city to an audience of male and female guests. The press reported her trip by train from Haifa to Jaffa, describing 'Ajami as "an outstanding scholar ... renowned for her broad knowledge and contribution to the revival of women."[79] Several days later, *Filastin*'s regular opinion column, "The Observer" (*mushahid*), rebuked Haifa's educated circles for overlooking the prominent visitor. This lack of regard for Mary 'Ajami, the column maintained, reflected Haifa's backwardness compared to other cities regarding the education and cultural movements. According to "The Observer":

> 'Ajami, a distinguished Syrian scholar visiting Palestine, chose Haifa, of all places, as her point of residence. However, according to Haifa's newspapers, the city failed to show proper respect for culture. But when she arrived in Jaffa at the invitation of the Young Christian Society, the local cultural clubs 'hunted' her down.[80]

The Jaffa Orthodox Club threw a party in her honor, and the Islamic Sports Club followed suit by holding a "spectacular getting-acquainted party [for her]." Such enthusiasm in Jaffa was not accidental, "The Observer" suggested, but rather the natural product of "the political and cultural awakening of which Jaffans and non-Jaffans alike are aware."

---

[77] Michelle Joha, *Mary Ajami* (2001).
[78] Ibid. *Al-'Arus* was published until 1914, unfolded during World War I, and reappeared in 1918. It appeared regularly until 1926, when it ceased publication for good.
[79] *Filastin*, 1 May and 4 May 1928.
[80] *Filastin*, 11 May 1928.

The existence of free political parties in Jaffa placed it at the forefront of the country's political movement, just as the presence of cultural clubs and societies placed it at the head of the cultural movement. Voicing his delight at seeing Jaffa at the vanguard of the country's cities, "The Observer" noted he was not at all "pleased to see Haifa ... once the cradle of culture, placed at their rear." It was only appropriate for Haifa to have a vibrant political and cultural life, and especially important too, since it was "Palestine's port city ... where visitors to Palestine pass first.... If a diplomat or other man of culture arrives in the country and reads about its situation through the headlines, he should be able to read it correctly."[81]

Another report in *Filastin* indicated that cultural clubs and societies opened spaces for women that allowed them to demonstrate their artistic and other skills, such as drama. Reviewing the play *The Sacrifices (al-dhaba'ih)*, which the Jaffa Islamic Sports Club drama team put on at the Zion Theater in Jerusalem, the report noted that until 13 December 1928, Palestinian women had never performed on the theatrical stage, female roles having been played by men. *The Sacrifices* marked a turning-point, and for the first time Palestinian women acted on the stage.[82] Henceforth, women appeared in theatrical productions organized by different forums, such as athletic and cultural clubs and societies, schools, and women's associations.

One instance of this kind of production was the Haifa Drama Club's play, *The Crime of Lucy Tyron – The Important Crime Perpetrated (for the Sake of Humanity)* [parentheses in original], in July 1932. The cast comprised instructors and students from *al-Najah* National School for Girls in Haifa. The club invited the public to attend, urging it "to hasten and see the play, and thereby show support for national educational institutions and projects."[83] Females appeared on the theater stage in other Palestinian cities as well, particularly the larger ones. The many similarities among Palestine's three major cities, pointed up by existing research,[84] allow us to use findings relating to one of them to infer about the others. Thus, for example, the drama team of the Educational Athletic Club (*al-nadi al-riyadi al-tahdhibi*) in Jerusalem offered women a stage for demonstrating their dramatic skills with its production of *'Abd al-Rahman al-Nasir, King of Andalus*. Performed in December 1929 at Zion Theater, the play featured

---

[81] *Filastin*, 8 May 1928.
[82] *Filastin*, 24 December 1928. *The Sacrifices* was originally written for the Egyptian Ramses theater troupe and was 'adopted' by the Palestinian theater.
[83] *Filastin*, 2 July 1932.
[84] Hasan (2009).

50 actors and actresses.[85] It seems to have represented a trend that was expanding throughout the country.

The dance floors of Haifa's cultural clubs, night clubs, and the Casino offered another type of public leisure space in the city. By the 1920s, the increasing number of dance floors in Haifa reflected the spread of what newspapers called the "fashion" of mixed male-female dancing. This phenomenon elicited much opposition in conservative circles; one critic even attributed the earthquake that shook the country in 1927[86] to this new habit.[87] The growing popularity of this "fashion" was seen in the appearance of an Arabic-language guidebook entitled Learning Modern Dances, by Na'im 'Azar, published in 1928 by the Modern Press of Palestine (*matba'at filastin al-haditha*). 'Azar was a dance teacher who had studied in France and was a member of the Dance Teachers' Union there. The 111-page guide featured photographs illustrating different dancing moves, along with up-to-date instructions for learning the Tango, the Charleston, the Boston, and more. It discussed "proper behavior on the dance floor, hand and foot positions and movements, types of steps ... explained dance [floor] etiquette and carried comments on attire."[88]

In addition to the mixed dance floors, professional male and female dancers also performed in certain leisure spaces that served as night clubs and cabarets. One such venue was the *Bat Galim* "Casino," built in 1934 by a Jewish entrepreneur, Pesach Bonshtein. "Despite the name 'Casino', it was never used for gambling but rather operated as a cabaret and a fancy nightclub with a fancy gourmet restaurant."[89] The Casino's clientele was heterogeneous both in gender and national/ethnic identity. In the 1940s it was frequented by Maggie Karkabi, her sister, and her sister's fiancé. According to Karkabi, the Casino attracted women and men,

> Arabs and Jews; but to tell you [the truth], most were Arabs…. It was not really a casino, and there was no gambling there. It was a café with a show. A woman named Carmen Pidy would perform there, always dancing and singing. She was a pretty woman, Carmen Pidy. We would always see there

---

[85] *Filastin*, 25 December 1929.
[86] The earthquake occurred on Monday, 11 July 1927 at 3:07 p.m. *Filastin*, 15 July 1927.
[87] *Filastin*, 13 July 1928. "The Observer" columnist who reported this theory derided its author: "what a pity that I was not present to hear this interpretation. I would have asked the honorable gentleman: 'what in your opinion caused previous earthquakes, before men and women began dancing together?'"
[88] *Filastin*, 26 June 1928.
[89] See http://www.tapuz.co.il/blog/ViewEntry.asp?EntryId=1297668.

Hanna Zarubi, the manager of Ottoman Bank, who would come for Carmen Pidy.... She was his girlfriend, but that was before he got married.[90]

ARAB AND JEWISH WOMEN IN LEISURE SPACES

Did the dance floors and other leisure places of Haifa also facilitate encounters between Palestinian-Arab and Jewish women? While the evidence suggests the presence of women from both ethno-national groups in the city's leisure places – its movie theaters, cafés, nightclubs, public parks, bathing beaches – encounters between women of the two groups appear to have been limited to a shared use of the same space but without forging social relations.

Women who had resided in Mandate Haifa testify to this kind of common presence in public spaces which yielded no social relations. Recounting her many visits to "the garden" with her grandmother and grandmother's girl-friend, Widad Rizq "obviously" remembered having "seen Jewish women"; but she never saw her grandmother actually meeting with them there.[91] "On the whole," she added,

> relations between us and Jewish women were very, very, very meager [and occurred] only in exceptional situations.... Even in our school (English High School), which a few Jewish female students also attended, the ties were very superficial.[92] By then we already felt ... learned from our parents and read in the papers ... that they were beginning to penetrate [the country]. But we were not their enemies, no. We exchanged words [in the classroom]; but during the breaks, Arab girls stood apart from the Jewish ones. Out of the school there were rare instances of relations between Arab and Jewish women. For example, Juliet Zakka, who lived across the street and who was murdered[93]... her best friend was a Jewish girl called Mazal Gershon. How come I know her name? Because she would come over (to Juliet) every day. Such friendships were rather 'exceptional' [English in the original]. You see,

---

[90] Interview with Maggie Karkabi, Haifa, 24 June 2010.
[91] Interview with Widad Rizq, Haifa, 5 September 2010.
[92] This took place in the 1940s.
[93] Juliet Zakka attended the Haifa English High School and was Widad Rizq's classmate. Juliet was murdered in 1948 by armed Jewish men near her home on Qisariya Street in Haifa. Along with other girls, she participated in a first-aid program run by the "Red Crescent" in the city. According to Widad Rizq, in 1948 the Jews "fired at a woman. Anyone passing in Qisariya Street would be shot. They would shoot from Hadar.... The woman who was fired at was from the Hamana family, if I am not wrong.... Juliet rushed to treat her and they shot her too. She fell dead on the spot."

going out to meet Jewish girls in a café or restaurant, or going with them to the movies – this did not happen.

According to Simon Abi Nadir-Swidan, a native of Haifa in the late 1920s, the meetings of young women in public places before 1948 in which she participated were overwhelmingly among Palestinian-Arab women only:

> Many Jews and Arabs did go to the movies ... [but] our group [of friends] usually comprised [young] Arab women only.... Only one [Jewish girl] named Shoshana would sometimes join us.... Shoshana was our neighbor, who lived in one of the apartments we rented.... You know, until 1946 we resided on Hillel Street [in upper Hadar], in a house built by my father.... My father had many estates in Haifa ... and in this building [pointing to a map she had drawn] of 4 stories, which he had on 16 Hillel Street, the tenants were Jewish. Shoshana's family was one of them.[94]

Maggie Karkabi has similar memories: unlike the *al-Butaji* Beach, which was private and used only by the owner's friends and community members, "*al-'Aziziya* was an open beach and Jews were [therefore] present there. But to tell you [the truth] – no, no relationship developed between us."[95] Such was also the case with the *Moriya* movie theater on Mount Carmel (a largely Jewish quarter) and the cafés which Karkabi used to frequent there: "Arabs would come there, but no ties were formed between Arabs and Jews. Nothing. Not even a look or a glance."[96]

To a large extent, the reserved attitude described by Karkabi represented a human behavior typical of "the living urban character of the metropolis", in Georg Simmel's definition. According to Simmel, "The mental attitude of metropolis people to one another may be designated formally as one of reserve." Such an attitude is especially characteristic of

---

[94] Interview with Simon Abi Nadir-Swidan, Haifa, 15 September 2010. According to Abi Nadir-Swidan, many homeowners on Hillel Street and on the nearby Tabariyya Street were Palestinians who rented apartments to Jews. In addition to her father, Abi Nadir-Swidan mentioned other homeowners on Hillel Street: members of the Sahyun family, who owned two big buildings; Salih Shabib, her father's business partner, who rented out a house he owned but did not reside in; and a building owned by Ahmad Khalil and his brother. In the adjacent Tabariyya Street she mentioned "a big stone house on the street corner, owned by 'Abdallah al-Lamam. His neighbor was Rafiq Baydun, a Haifa celebrity, a judge or something like that. His house was destroyed and a big concrete bloc[k] was erected instead.... Subhi 'Uwayda too had a stone house [on Tabariyya Street].... Indeed, most homeowners on Tabariyya Street were Arab."
[95] Interview with Maggie Karkabi, Haifa, 24 June 2010.
[96] Ibid.

public spaces that are not work-places (such as the municipality and the refineries) but rather spaces of leisure:

> If the unceasing external contact of numbers of persons in the city should be met by the same number of inner reactions as in the small town [or village, we might add], in which one knows almost every person he meets and to each of whom he has a positive relationship, one would be completely atomized internally, and would fall into an unthinkable mental condition.[97]

Simmel further argues that this typically urban pattern of behavior results partly from these psychological circumstances and partly from our suspicion toward the fleeting and momentary contacts in the big city. This reserve causes us "not [to] know by sight neighbors of years standing and ... permits us to appear to small-town folk so often as cold and uncongenial."[98]

In pre-1948 Haifa, such urban reserve was enhanced by other factors, which further restricted the prospect for social interaction between Jewish and Palestinian women. One of these was the city's special nature, alluded to above; another was the differences between the two ethno-national groups in the status of women in them. The fact that Haifa was a center of Jewish immigration – unlike other cities, such as Jaffa and Tiberias, where older local Jewish communities resided – caused the Arab population to view the city's Jews as "foreign", "European", "Eastern European", or "from the *Haganah*" (that is, potential conquerors). This perception was repeatedly expressed in the oral testimonies of Palestinian women who had lived in Haifa at the time.[99] Unique to Haifa, this situation must have rendered Palestinian-Jewish sociability less likely than in cities with older Jewish communities. The suspicion and alienation Palestinians in Haifa felt toward the Jewish immigrants differed markedly from the attitude to the Jews in Tiberias, for example: according to many interviewees, these were "Jewish Arabs," "Arab Jews," or "Jewish Palestinians" – the same kind of classification they would apply to Palestinians of other religious groups, Muslims, Christians, and Druze.[100]

More generally, the fact that women typically assume the role of demarcating borders between different ethno-national collectives[101]

---

[97] Georg Simmel, "The Metropolis and Mental Life", in Gary Bridge and Sophie Watson (eds.), *The Blackwell City Reader* (2002), p. 15.
[98] Ibid.
[99] Hasan (2009).
[100] Ibid.
[101] For example, see Nira Yuval-Davis and Floy Anthias (eds.), *Women-Nation-State*, "Introduction" (1989), pp. 1-15.

represented another obstacle to sociability between Jewish and Palestinian women in leisure spaces. Combined with the increasingly antagonistic relations between the two communities, this role considerably limited the possibilities for social interaction between Arab and Jewish women.

CONCLUSION: WHAT KIND OF COEXISTENCE?

Arabs and Jews shared Haifa's urban life in many ways, from city administration to public transportation, from common working places to shared shopping areas. But their coexistence and relationships throughout the Mandate were marked by ups-and-downs that were molded by changes in the political reality and other factors. Notably, even in times of tension some level of collaboration was always there, mostly out of necessity. Such vicissitudes also typified the Arab-Jewish male and female presence in the city's public spaces and recreation sites examined in this chapter. However, since leisure is a matter of choice more than of necessity, coexistence in this realm was more susceptible to shifts in the general atmosphere and seems to have been more easily damaged in times of political disquiet.

As we have seen, past individual and group behavior is ever-difficult to recapture, let alone quantify. Hence our findings should be taken as no more than a general impression of these relations. Our impressions – which are quite clear at that – may be summarized by the following two points:

1. Throughout the Mandate period, the cultural and recreational life of the two communities ran in parallel courses, like two rivers flowing side-by-side through the same landscape. Here and there they came closer together; sometimes they even joined courses, projecting an impression of one flow. But facing an obstacle on their path they would split off again, returning to their separate ways. This pattern was seen in leisure activities of Arab and Jewish men and women: their convergence turned out to be a temporary circumstance for the two distinct streams that flew independently.

2. The closer we get to the end of the Mandate, the more distant and alienated these relations become. Arab and Jewish men and women were more interested in each other and spent more time together in the 1920s than in the 1940s. Toward the end of the period, whatever social and cultural relations between Arabs and Jews were still there, their significance was becoming marginal, even negligible in view of the major confrontation that palpably lay ahead. "We no longer had faith in them," Widad Rizq recalled,

referring to her Jewish counterparts with whom she had previously shared the city's public spaces, "we realized they wanted to take our country from us."

COMMODITIES AND POWER:
EDIBLE OIL AND SOAP IN THE HISTORY OF
ARAB-JEWISH HAIFA

MUSTAFA ABBASI AND DAVID DE VRIES

The production and trade of edible oil and soap has for long held a significant role in the history of modern Haifa as a mixed town. One reason was the impact of olive oil and soap on the general history of trade in the town itself and in the wider Haifa region. This impact was not only economic, but also social and political, exemplified in the formation of the local oil merchants as one of the leading groups in Haifa's Arab elite. The second reason was the towering presence of the Shemen factory in the town's economy, in the industrialization of Haifa during the period of the British Mandate, and in the economic and social roles that the factory came to play in the development of the Jewish sector and in its relations with Haifa's Arab society. Finally, oil and soap products have always been essential to Haifa because they reflected the presence of the British rule: in the protection the Palestine government gave to the Shemen factory and thereby to the Jewish sector, in the ownership of the factory since 1929 by a British stockholding company (Unilever), and in the direct attempts of the British authorities during World War II to increase the trading potential and exporting capacities of local oil and soap.

Much has been written on these aspects, in particular on their impact on the intertwining economic, social and political significance. Since the early 1920s the demands of the producers and merchants from the colonial regime for economic support filled in mounting correspondence and reporting. The close association of the Shemen factory with the institutions of the Zionist movement (both in London and in Palestine) likewise produced rich textual and analytical materials. The occasional inquiry commissions the British held during the Mandate period to discuss Palestine's economy and politics often referred to Haifa and to Palestine's oil and soap industries. And in the Jewish sector itself – both in its communal and neighborhood institutions and in the organs of the labor movement – the progress and tribulations of the edible oil industry were often on the public agenda. To this was added a rich historiography that has for long described and analyzed the olive oil's historical, economic and symbolical expressions. These varied sources substantiated the association of oil and soap in the Haifa region with the politics of the Mandate period, with the relations of Haifa society with the colonial ruler, as well as with the relations between Haifa's Arabs and Jews.[1]

Despite the richness of sources there is however a clear imbalance in the historiography of Mandate Palestine between the voluminous sources on the Shemen factory in Haifa's Jewish sector on the one hand, and the paucity of sources on edible oil and soap production in Haifa's Arab community on the other. The imbalance is further accentuated by the marked difference between the Arab and Jewish communities in Haifa – the first traditionally concentrating on home-based production, trade and on local consumption, while the latter on industrial production and export. Furthermore, the myriad connections between the main center of oil and soap production in Nablus and the edible oil and soap merchants in Haifa further emphasize the absence in the literature of a wider regional perspective. It is partly for these reasons that the dual character of oil and soap production in Haifa remained understudied, and that the imbalance of sources between the interacting Arab and the Jewish sides of the story made it all the more difficult to provide a fuller perspective that respects mutual economic intersections and related political aspects. The discussion below attempts to start filling in the gap by focusing, from the perspective of Haifa Arab merchants of olive oil products and that of the Shemen factory, on how economic entanglement and duality came about. To answer the question the discussion touches upon the nature of the olive oil and soap production in Haifa and in the Haifa region before World War I, the impact of the Shemen factory on the Arab olive oil and soap merchants, and finally the role the Palestine government played in these relations.[2]

EARLY CONTEXTS

Prior to the 20th century the production of edible oil and olive oil based soap in the Haifa region was relatively small. The branch, based as it was

---

[1] The archival and historiographical richness, partly detailed in the bibliography, stands out also in relation to the histories of other economic branches and consumer products in Mandate Palestine.

[2] Zachary Lockman, *Comrades and Enemies: Arab and Jewish Workers in Palestine, 1906-1948* (1996), pp. 3-9; Jacob Metzer, *The Divided Economy of Mandatory Palestine* (2002); Jacob Metzer, "Economic Growth and External Trade in Mandatory Palestine: A Special Mediterranean Case", in Sevket Pamuk and Jeffrey G. Williamson (eds.), *The Mediterranean Response to Globalization before 1950* (2000), pp. 363-366.

on olive trees and on domestic oil presses, was largely concentrated in Nablus and Jaffa. Haifa and its small population were but another marketing spot for the more established Nabulsi oil and soap. However, three characteristics of olive oil products produced in Nablus prior to World War I bore formative influences on the future development of olive oil trade in Haifa. The first was the high price of the products, and in particular of the virgin oil. The second was its high acidity, relative to the edible oil produced in other Mediterranean countries. The third characteristic was its limited storage life.[3] These characteristics determined the low export capacity of the Palestinian olive oil products, its limited capacity to compete with the products produced in other regions of the Mediterranean (Spain in particular), and its consequent reliance on local consumption and on markets near Palestine, such as Egypt and Anatolia.[4] Moreover, these were also the causes for the small number of oil and soap merchants in the Haifa region in the late 19th century. They also explain the limited productive capacity of the Haifa soap factory ran by the German Templars, and the economic tribulations experienced by Atid, the small Jewish factory established in Haifa in 1906, which produced oil and soap mostly from olives press waste.[5]

These were also the reasons for the focusing of the entire branch in the hands of a few Arab families in the Haifa region whose social and economic status was undergoing a change due to the reorganization of the Ottoman Empire in 1839-1876 and the Tanzimat reforms. This was true in particular in comparison to Acre that suffered deeply from the 1830s

---

[3] Said B. Himadeh, *Economic Organization of Palestine* (1939), pp. 216-217; Beshara Doumani, *Rediscovering Palestine: Merchants and Peasants in Jabal Nablus, 1700-1900* (1995), pp. 14-15.

[4] Himadeh (1939), p. 146; Ramón Ramón-Muñoz, "Specialization in the International Market for Olive Oil before World War II", in Sevket Pamuk and Jeffrey G. Williamson (eds.), *The Mediterranean Response to Globalization before 1950* (2000), pp. 159-198. Acidity determines the extent of the oil's oxygenation. The lower the acidity the better chances of the oil to guard itself from oxygenation and the better the quality of the oil. Still, in some parts of Palestine consumers preferred high-acidity olive oil.

[5] Shmuel Avitsur, "Nahum Wilbusch: From Traditional to New Industries", *Inventors and Adaptors: The Makers of the Revolution in Palestine's Manufacturing* (1985) (in Hebrew), pp. 122-128; Shmuel Avitsur, "The Production of Olive Oil in the Galilee and Its Dimensions at the Beginning of the Century", *Ofakim be-Geografia* 20 (1987) (in Hebrew), pp. 3-16; David Kushner, *Palestine in the Late Ottoman Period* (1986), table 9 on p. 201. In his memoires Nachum Wilbusch told that the Atid attempted to export toilet soap to Egypt, Anatolia and Syria, but without much success. See Zvi Kroll (ed.), *The Oil Jug: Shemen's Twenty Year Anniversary* (1945) (in Hebrew), p. 62. Olives press waste is *Gefet* in Hebrew and *Jift* in Arabic.

Egyptian occupation of Palestine causing, as it did, the transfer of social and economic gravity points from Acre to Haifa. Economically Haifa saw now the beginning of a modernization phase, a significant enlargement of commercial activity, the multiplication of production factors, the adoption of technological innovations, and a change in the structure of the business sectors. Equally influential on the status of the Arab trading families was the growth in volume and character of consumption, parallel to the improvement in living standards of Haifa's society in general. This was further supported by the emergence of new social forces, e.g. Jews, Templars and others, that further cemented the links between Haifa and the Mediterranean and western economies, and contributed to gradually making Haifa a cosmopolitan entrepôt. These processes have to be further contextualized in a larger demographic process in which Haifa's population increased from 2,000 around 1840 to 24,600 in 1922. Haifa was growing dynamically in the late Ottoman period and it was therefore not accidental that the Ottoman authorities chose the town as the principal seaport of the Hijaz railway system (in operation since 1905). This maritime linkage further secured the expansion of the Haifa economy, and allowed Haifa's merchants to materialize the potentialities of the Arab hinterland in connecting its oil, sesame, wool and corn producers with destinations beyond Haifa and Palestine.[6]

The Catholic Sa'd family was a typical example of this burgeoning prosperity that the Tanzimat reforms initiated. The family, headed by Fu'ad Sa'd, was related by marriage to the Catafago – a family of merchants from Italy led by Salim Bey Catafago (d. 1922) who was Fu'ad Sa'd's grandfather on his mother side. The two families ran a prosperous land and trading businesses in Acre, Kufur 'Inan, Mughar, Sajur and Ramih in the late 19th and early 20th centuries. And on Acre's economic decline they moved their operations to Haifa – the town has now gained the region's economic supremacy. The Salname (the Ottoman yearbooks) of the Syrian and Beirut provinces tell that Jubran, Fu'ad Sa'd's father, was a prominent

---

[6] Mahmoud Yazbak, *Haifa in the Late Ottoman Period, 1864-1914: A Muslim Town in Transition* (1998), p. 16; Yehoshua Ben Arieh, "The Population of Large Towns in Palestine during the Eighty Years of the Nineteenth Century According to Western Sources", in Moshe Ma'oz (ed.), *Studies on Palestine During the Ottoman Period* (1975), pp. 49-69; Government of Palestine, Palestine Report and General Abstracts of the Census of 1922, edited by John. B. Barron (1922); Alexander Scholch, *Palestine in Transformation 1856-1882* (1993), pp. 19-46; Yosef Vashitz, "Social Changes in Arab Society during the British Mandate: Merchants, Entrepreneurs and Others", in Nachum Karlinsky and Avi Bareli (eds.), *Economy and Society in Mandatory Palestine, 1918-1948* (2003), p. 395.

political figure in the Acre region, at least since his initial membership of the Acre town council in 1875 and his activity in banking.[7] In 1880 he worked also as a translator in the Italian Consulate in the town and his connections with the latter were greatly helped by the Italian Catafago network.[8] During this period the Sa'd family turned into one of the richest feudal families of the region and Fu'd Sa'd was already exporting edible oil from the port of Acre.[9] By 1885 he sat on the district agricultural board, and by 1901 he was a member of the town's trade and agriculture board. Similar to Jubran, Salim Catafago reached also public prominence as a member of the highly influential district administrative council.[10]

These positions demonstrated the high status of both families in the late Ottoman period, and they clearly assisted Fu'ad Sa'd when he transferred the gravity center of his commercial and land activities to Haifa. Though the move hardly challenged the hegemony of Nablus in the production of edible oil and soap, it laid in Haifa a new commercial infrastructure – exemplified by the establishment of an edible oil factory in the *al-hara al-gharbiyya* (the Western neighborhood). It even caused the Nabulsi family to later relocate some of their marketing of oil and soap to Haifa. Furthermore, the association of the Sa'd family with local politics, and the centrality of Jubran and Fu'ad Sa'd in the establishment of the 'Catholic Society' in Haifa, demonstrated the making of a new Arab bourgeoisie in the town – based as it was on land ownership, trading and marketing networks, and, no less significantly, on social notability.[11]

---

[7] Salname of Syria Province (Istanbul, 1875), p. 99; on the Catafago family see also Thomas Philipp, *Acre: The Rise and Fall of a Palestinian City, 1730-1831* (2001).
[8] Salname of Syria Province (Istanbul, 1880), p. 196.
[9] Mustafa Abbasi interviews with Ghattas Yusif Ghattas and Hasan Ahmad Mansur, Ramih, 7 September 2010.
[10] Salname of Syria Province (Istanbul, 1885), p. 136; Salname of Beirut Province (Istanbul, 1901), pp. 140-142. Fu'ad Sad also bought land in the Zichron Yaakov area, established an ice factory in Haifa and worked as a translator for the German Consulate in Haifa. For Sa'd's later land activities see CZA J/15 5134 and J/15 2094. His oil press in Ramih in the late 1920s was known to have developed modern technology. See *al-Karmil*, 6 February 1928.
[11] Salname of Beirut Province (1908), p. 278; *al-Karmil*, 18 February 1934; May Seikaly, *Haifa: Transformation of an Arab Society, 1918-1939* (2002), p. 110; Kenneth W. Stein, *The Land Question in Palestine, 1917-1939* (1984), pp. 26 and 223; Shmuel Avitsur, *Apparatuses in Landscapes: Chapters in Palestine's Industrial Archeology* (1994) (in Hebrew), p. 95; Johnny Mansour, "The Hijaz-Palestine Railway and the Development of Haifa", *Jerusalem Quarterly* 28 (1983), pp. 5-21; Itzhak Klein, "The Arabs in Haifa under the British Mandate: A Political, Economic and Social Survey", *Occasional Papers on the Middle East* (1987), New Series, No. 5 (in Hebrew).

INCIPIENT CHANGE

The acceleration of the economic and demographic development of Haifa form 1890-1910, which made the above mentioned social process possible was, however, curtailed by World War I. Similar to other economic branches a crisis in the development of local oil and soap production and commerce ensued, and it was not until the conquest of Palestine by the British in 1917/1918 that another substantial change took place.[12] The impact of the British conquest is all too known in Palestine's and Haifa's historiographies. The British support of a National Home for the Jews, the Jewish immigration that followed, and the administrative infrastructure that the British began establishing in the Haifa district, triggered a chain of economic and social processes that deeply influenced the edible oil and soap industry. Particularly affected was the main process under discussion here – the splitting of the branch into two separate routes of production and trade.[13]

An examination of the establishment of the Shemen factory in 1919-1924 reflected the onset of that splitting. After the Atid factory collapsed early in World War I the engineer and architect Gedalia Wilbushewitz (1865-1943) started a company that aimed to produce oil-related products. The Zionist Wilbushewitz, himself a veteran founder of Atid, was for many years engaged in surveying areas in Palestine for water extraction and edible oil production; and after the war he led the industry department at the Delegates Committee (Vaad Hatzirim), the committee under Chaim Weizmann's leadership that in 1918-1921 represented the Jewish society in Palestine and handled its postwar recovery. Wilbushewitz linked Russian Jewish capital owners (among them the oil magnate Ilia Eliyahu Paenson) with his brothers, Moshe and Nachum Wilbushewitz, who were engaged in Russia and Switzerland in food engineering and renovations in oil production, and in 1919 they established together The Palestine Oil Industries (Shemen) Ltd. in London. After two years of failed attempts to start an industrial plant in Caesarea (and to convince the British to declare the Caesarea port as a free trade zone), the entrepreneurs decided to move to Haifa. Here they joined in the Agolin company, that produced

---

[12] Alex Carmel, *The History of Haifa under Turkish Rule* (1977) (in Hebrew); Yazbak (1998), Chapter 6. It should be noted that soap production continued to function despite Atid's collapse. This continuity was essential when Shemen began to operate in 1924. See also Seikaly (2002), p. 36.

[13] Splitting and dualization are used in this chapter interchangeably so as to simplify a much needed problematization of the two concepts.

oil in Alexandria (owned by Paenson himself and Barki, a Sephardic Jew), and established a factory close to Haifa's coast, at the location of the ruined Atid.[14]

The reason for the passage from Caesarea to Haifa was twofold. First, the older image of Haifa as the 'city of the future' of industrial development in Palestine – an image strengthened after the war because of the town's importance for the British and its attraction for Jewish industrial entrepreneurs. The second reason stemmed from Haifa's advantageous position as a port town, an entrepôt of land crossroads, and an essential point of entry for immigrants, capital and machinery. It was against this background that Shemen's early association with the Zionist project has to be understood – through the acquisition of land for the industrial plant, its role in the economic infrastructure of the Jewish settlement in Haifa (which grew during the 1920s into a third of the town's population), ending with the exclusive employment of Jewish immigrants and workers in building the factory and in production. Similar to the many other forces that shaped the dualization of both the Palestine and the Haifa economies, the establishment of Shemen too, and the start of its operations in December 1924, was the end result of a mix of forces, of external capital and local initiative, exogenous know-how and initiative and endogenous political forces. The mix of economy, politics and national ideology was essential in the progress of Shemen factory in the latter part of the 1920s, and in its positioning on a separate route from the older Palestinian oil and soap industries and commerce.[15]

---

[14] The capital invested at the establishment of the factory was ca. LP 250,000. The construction of the factory, the purchasing of the machinery and the initial labor costs increased the invested capital with at least LP 100,000. See also "From the History of Jewish Industry in Palestine", *Davar*, 26 April 1934.

[15] Correspondence and minutes of protocols of Shemen in Central Zionist Archive, A/112, files 134-137; Shemen's correspondence with the executive of the Histadrut (General Federation of Jewish Labor) in the early 1920s, in the Labor movement archive, Lavon Institute, IV-208-1-3-1b; Kroll (1945), pp. 64-67; Nachum Gross, "Haifa at the Beginning of Jewish Industrialization in Palestine", *Riv'on Le-Kalkala* (September 1980), pp. 308-319 (in Hebrew).

Fig. 1: Shemen Oil Works, Haifa, March 1939
Source: Photo Department, American Colony, Jerusalem

AN ECONOMIC-POLITICAL COMPLEX

To clarify the process three problems which the new factory in Haifa had to face have to be borne in mind. The first was the conflict between the aspirations of the factory's owners for continuous and industrially-punctuated production on the one hand, and the shortage in raw material caused by the one-time yield of crops that olive groves gave in a year on the other. The implication of that shortage was the total dependence of Shemen on importing raw materials (mainly sesame seeds and coconuts) from outside of Palestine, and the need of the owners to pay high customs on that import. The problem turned all the more acute because of the intention of Shemen to extend its production beyond edible oil and soap, mainly to cosmetics for which coconut oil was essential.

The second problem Shemen faced at the onset of its operation was competition with relatively cheaper edible oil and soap products which were produced outside of Palestine – in particular the cottonseed oil imported into Palestine from Egypt, and soap imported from Marseilles (Savon de Marseilles, which was made of vegetable oil). Significantly, the customs on the import of these items into Palestine was lower than those levied on the raw materials Shemen so direly needed. Thirdly, Shemen entered a well established market in Palestine which, as has been mentioned earlier, was dominated by Nablus producers, and in which it had to compete with oil and soap merchants in Haifa itself and the northern region in general. These products – marketed as they were in Haifa and the rest of Palestine – were expensive, but still cheaper than the costs the Shemen factory had to pay for the import of the raw materials it was interested in.[16]

These problems – relatively high import costs, exogenous competition and local competition – became closely interrelated by the presence of the British authorities: all the actors were dependent on British customs policies and on the British preference (indeed, from the start of their rule) to lend support to any sector that would improve the balance of its expenses on governing Palestine. As the economic historiography of Mandate Palestine has already demonstrated this preference for a "strong economic sector" meant mainly support of Jewish capital and the Zionist project. It thus implied a formative British impact on the making of the dual economy.[17]

Shemen's first problem began to be resolved in late 1925 upon the British decision to cancel customs on the import of the raw materials that the factory aspired for. The cancellation meant a significant reduction in Shemen's overall expenses on customs. It allowed the factory to increase the import of raw materials and to begin competing with externally and locally produced products. This was true not only with regard to edible oil itself, but also in relation to soap which Shemen now produced from imported coconuts. Syria, the United States and England itself would become now Shemen's main exporting destinations. Moreover, the change in customs costs also allowed manufacturing variegation, namely, the production of coconut oil and flaxseed oil for dies (extracted from linseeds). Finally, the change in customs enabled Shemen to start producing sunflower oil (used both in cooking and in cosmetic emollients for skin softening). The sunflower oil also allowed Shemen to tackle a forgery problem – the marketing of Egyptian cotton oil in Shemen's cans. Product variation and sophistication of marketing and advertisements naturally increased Shemen's revenues, and explained why industrial relations in the

---

[16] For a contemporary reference to these problems see Kroll (1945. See also Deborah S. Bernstein, *Constructing Boundaries: Jewish and Arab Workers in Mandatory Palestine* (2000), pp. 117-122. Coconut oil in Hebrew is Shemen Kokus and in Arabic *Zayt Juz al-Hind*. Cottonseed oil in Hebrew is *Shemen Kutna*, and *Zayt Budhur al-Qutun* in Arabic.

[17] Central Zionist Archive, S8/1152/2; "The Manufacture of Oil and Soap in Palestine", *Palestine and Near East Economic Magazine*, 25 November 1926; Seikaly (2002), Chapter 8; Roza I.M. El-Eini, *Mandated Landscape: British Imperial Rule in Palestine, 1929-1948* (2006).

factory were quiet, relatively to Haifa's turbulent labor disputes and strikes.[18]

All in all British policy in protecting Shemen stemmed from the economic interests of the British Empire, and in particular from the need to reduce the Empire's financial burden, through increasing local competitive capacities and through encouraging export.[19] However, the protection, protested against by the Arabs, could not be dissociated from political issues. And in particular from the pressures exerted by the Zionist movement – in themselves originating from the thorny problems the Jewish settlement in Haifa and Palestine as a whole were faced with during and following the massive mid-1920s immigration wave of Jews.

Furthermore, the overwhelming backing Shemen was given by both the Zionist movement and the British could not be understood without the novel technological and managerial message the factory carried, and the lowering of costs it allowed. The novelty lay first in the joining under one roof of all the phases of pressing and production of oil and soap. In the traditional way olive oil was extracted by pressure and sold as virgin oil (that is using physical means and no chemical treatment). It had a limited storage life (the raw material could be kept only for a few days after the autumn harvest), and it contained many impurities. Storage could be prolonged only if the pressed oil was chemically refined (by heating and extraction), and it was usually done by a separate firm. What Shemen did was to apply vertical integration – combining the extraction and the refinement at one plant, thus allowing a year round operation and overcoming the short seasonal nature of traditional production. To this Shemen added industrial production of soap and later also cosmetics, some of which was produced from imported raw materials such as oilseeds. The second aspect of the novelty was the variety of products forwarded now to the local market, and increasingly to export. It was this association of the political perceptions of technological and managerial advantages with customs policies that explained Shemen's growing competitive capacity.

---

[18] Central Zionist Archive, S8/1152/2; Haifa Labor Council, *The Histadrut in Haifa, 1933-1939* (1939), pp. 66-70; David De Vries, *Idealism and Bureaucracy in 1920s Palestine: The Origins of 'Red Haifa'* (1999) (in Hebrew). Linseeds in Hebrew are *Zirei Pishtan*, and *Zayt 'Abbad al-Shams* in Arabic. Sunflower oil in Arabic is *Zayt al-Nakhil* and *Shemen Hamaniot* in Hebrew.

[19] Barbara Smith, *The Roots of Separatism in Palestine: British Economic Policy, 1920-1929* (1993), pp. 335-340; Seikaly (2002), pp. 101-107; Yosef Vashitz, *Social Changes in Haifa's Arab Society under the British Mandate*, PhD (1993) (in Hebrew), p. 404.

For these reasons the impact of Shemen's emergence in the edible oil and soap market of Haifa and of the wider region was not only economic.[20]

DUALITY

Shemen's impact on Haifa's economy was clearly felt in the Jewish sector. The economic absorptive capacity of Jewish immigrants increased, and the spatial and economic presence of the Jewish sector widened. The Jewish owners and the managers of the factory (among them the brothers Wilbushewitz, Shmuel Slitzan and Menashe Erman) added to the strengthened presence of local Jewish industrial and managerial elite, and challenged the Haifa Labor Council (the local representative of the *Histadrut* – Jewish Labor Organization) to new challenges and contests in industrial relations. Though in its first two years of operation the factory's accumulation of capital was moderate, its economic and social impact was wider, because it linked with a wider industrialization process that the Zionist movement and private capital led in the 1920s and 1930s in the town.[21]

For these reasons the impact of Shemen's emergence on Haifa's Arabs was Janus-faced. In the slow recovery of the Haifa economy after World War I the establishment of Shemen reflected a larger split between small size enterprises that characterized the town's Arab sector, and the larger enterprises in the Jewish one. The building of the factory was assigned mostly to Jews, and many of the builders remained later as the factory's oil and soap workers. The few Arabs who were employed in the building of the factory did not. This added to the Zionist policy of the factory on Jewish-only employment, and was in line with the principle of "Hebrew Labor" advanced by the Labor movement and the *Histadrut* and which was followed by some of the Jewish industrialists in Palestine. The employment pattern further reflected the gradual "dualization" of the local economy and the segregationist nature of the incipient Zionist presence in the mixed town.[22]

---

[20] Rafael N. Rosenzweig, *The Economic Consequences of Zionism* (1989), pp. 41-43; Seikaly (2002), pp. 87-89. On the industrial development of Haifa's Jewish sector see Arnon Sofer, *Industrial Location in Haifa Bay Area*, PhD (1971) (in Hebrew), and Shimon Stern, *The Development of Haifa's Urban Network, 1918-1947*, PhD (1971) (in Hebrew).
[21] Gross (1980), pp. 308-319.
[22] On Shemen's association with Zionism see Kroll (1945); Itzhak Roll and Yaakov Yasuur, "Shemen and the Development of Jewish Haifa", in *Haifa-1954: Municipality Book* (1955), pp. 270-273 (in Hebrew); Ariella Bat-Zvi, "On the Nature of a Pioneering Enterprise",
(continued)

Shemen's competition with Arab edible oil merchants, and the support the factory was given by the Zionist movement and the British were certainly part of the process. At the same time however the variety of Shemen's products quickly placed the product on a totally different route of production and marketing than that of the Arab merchants and retailers – to the point that direct competition gradually became insignificant. Moreover, Arab consumption of the relatively cheaper products of Shemen gradually widened, and by the early 1930s the spread of Jewish oil products among Arab consumers meant less demand for traditional Arab produce. This was apparently expressed in increasing Arab consumption of Shemen's edible oil, adding to the customary Arab cooking fat. Furthermore, it was also reflected even in the widening of Arab consumption of the various Shemen products in other mixed towns as well. The spatial aspect of that consumption reflected not only the factory's emphasis placed on marketing and bi-lingual advertisement in the Palestine press, but also Shemen's capacity to compete with edible oil factories in the Tel Aviv area.[23]

It took however a few years for the more dramatic impact of Shemen to become explicit. Despite Haifa's economic attraction, industrialization in the 1920s was gradual, and the group of entrepreneurs and industrialists was still small relative to craftsmen and manufacturers. The town's Arabs (among them merchant families who moved from Nablus to Haifa following the 1927 earthquake), saw with suspicion the link between the emergence of the Shemen industrial plant and its openness to the employment of Jews only. Still, as can be gauged from the sources, not many merchants internalized Shemen's aspirations for a wide variety of products and such a variety of exporting destinations (that is, beyond Egypt, Syria and some other Mediterranean countries).[24]

The gap between the factory's economic infrastructure and the awareness of a looming change it was about to cause in Haifa's economy (indeed, in Palestine as a whole) characterized also the presence of the Nesher factory near Haifa, that would turn from 1926 onwards into the largest factory in the Mediterranean for cement. It characterized also the Grands Moulins des Palastine that industrialized in Haifa the wheat economy and the making of flour. Haifa's Arab press (*al-Karmil* in particular) was aware of Shemen's competitiveness, and harshly criticized

---

Davar, 5 January 1961. At the end of the decade Shemen reported that at least 40% of its produce was purchased by Haifa's Arabs. See also Bernstein (2000), pp. 117-122.
[23] Seikaly (2002), pp. 82-97 and p. 107. Reliable quantitative sources on these changes in consumption were not found.
[24] Seikaly (2002), p. 107

the British policy of reducing customs on imported edible oil, the import of sesame seeds (that have greatly assisted Jewish industry), and the absence of protection on local oil and soap production. But this criticism hardly provoked the Arab merchants who pointed their protest more against the British and much less against Shemen itself.[25]

Fig. 2: Hajj Nimr al-Nabulsi 1870-1940

Among them were Palestine's leading oil and soap producers prior to World War I Hajj Hasan Nabulsi and his sons, of whom Hajj Nimr Nabulsi who owned two big soap factories in Nablus was prominent. While focusing their activity in Nablus, this family moved many of their commercial operations to Haifa. This was the main link between the basis of the Arab oil and soap industry in Nablus and the new commercial developments in the Haifa region, and it was clearly influenced by the

---

[25] *Al-Karmil*, 7 February 1926 and 14 March 1926; for earlier examples of mechanization modifying traditional oil production see also Massimo Mazzotti, "Enlightened Mills: Mechanizing Olive Oil Production in Mediterranean Europe", *Technology & Culture* 45/2 (2004), pp. 277-304.

demographic growth of Haifa and the growing demand for edible oil and soap.[26]

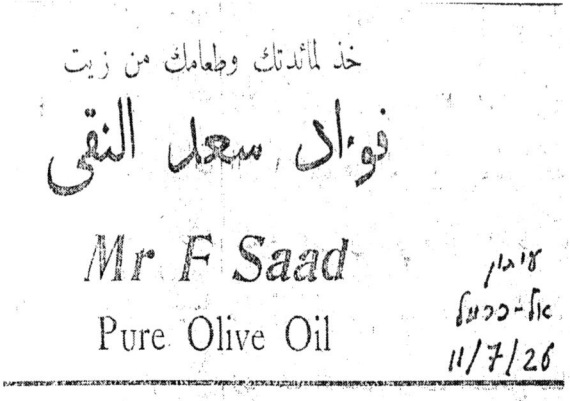

Fig. 3: Fu'ad Sa'd advertisement, al-Karmil, 11 July 1926

Another merchant who moved part of his operations from Nablus to Haifa was Hajj 'Abdul-Rahim Efandi al-Nabulsi who was connected to the former family. 'Abdul-Rahim not only marketed his soap in Haifa but elaborated an advertisement campaign increasingly appearing in the press from the 1930s onwards. The advertisements testified to the link of the merchants with Najib Nassar, the editor of *al-Karmil*, and the involvement of the editor in the marketing of the soap from his own newspaper office and to the fact that he enjoyed part of the income. These links would become even more apparent later when 'Abdul-Rahim was elected as member of the committee on olive oil that the British established in 1941.[27]

In practice the gap began to close in the late 1920s only when the Arab economic elite of Haifa grasped the full significance of the association between the British plan to build a modern port in Haifa on the

---

[26] 'Izzat Muhammad Darwazza, *One Hundred Palestinian Years*, Vol. I (1984) (in Arabic).
(1984), pp. 77-81. Hajj Nimr al-Nabulsi was born in Nablus in 1870. He was educated in Nablus and studied at al-Azhar University in Cairo. He returned to Palestine where he inherited his father's wealth and became well known in the soap trade in Palestine and Egypt. In 1934 he was one of the founders of the Palestinian Defense Party and active in charity during the strike of 1936. He kept a rich library which is a reference for old manuscripts; built a mosque in Nablus and donated his personal library to it; the mosque and a soap factory in Nablus still carry his name; Hajj Nimr al-Nabulsi died in 1940. See http://www.passia.org/palestine_facts/personalities/alpha_n.htm.

[27] *Al-Karmil*, 23 March 1932.

one hand and the support they gave to Jewish industry on the other. Nevertheless, when this awareness also trickled to the stratum of Arab merchants that marketed oil and soap in Haifa and the Galilee the gap and the splitting of the oil economy turned a full-fledged reality.

The dualization of the oil economy had also an indirect impact: it forced the Arab merchant to reduce the prices he demanded for his oil and soap products. The merchant's capacity to variegate the products he marketed and to leverage (like Shemen) a sophisticated marketing system was limited. The few that could, such as Hajj Nimr al-Nabulsi mentioned above, narrowed themselves to creating new types of body soaps and oral hygiene products. And as industrial efficiency was irrelevant to the merchants' operations the main option left for the marketers of oil and soap (and for those who cultivated olive groves and sesame plants in the Haifa region) was to reduce prices and narrow down labor costs.[28] However, these options were usually possible only with government assistance and encouragement, through customs policy in particular, given mainly to the Jewish sector.[29]

This was further clarified by the growing external competition of the Haifa merchants in the 1930s. The 1929 customs agreement enabled Syria to export to Palestine customs-free olive oil which was cheaper than that marketed in Haifa.[30] To this was added the change in the production of laundry soap. If the latter depended until 1928 entirely on olive oil from that year on it was replaced with acid oil which was also used at Shemen's in the production of margarine. The replacement of olive oil soap with acid soap was instrumental in the increase in Shemen's exports, and thus in the hardships of the Arab oil industry and in deepening the split in the branch.

---

[28] In 1931 *al-Karmil* reported on a sharp decline in soap production in Nablus and called the soap producers to unite so as to save the branch. See *al-Karmil*, 20 February 1931; see also Seikaly (2002), Chapter 8.

[29] *Al-Karmil*, 8 January 1928. These efforts continued in the following years and demonstrated Shemen's technological influence on the Arab producers as reported by *Al-Karmil*, 4 June 1932 on the soap production of Hajj Nimr al-Nabulsi. These issues were partly dealt with by a government for which see the Johnson-Crosbie Committee Report (1930). See also Y. Ben-Dor, "The Decrees in Favor of the Agriculturalists", *Davar*, 15 August 1930; and M. Dana, "The Soap Industry in Nablus", *Davar*, 26 May 1932.

[30] Syria was a long-standing exporter of olive oil to Palestine and a major factor satisfying local demand. See "The Olive Oil Industry", in Report of the Olive Oil Sub-Committee, 10 November 1941, ISA/672/AG/38/1/2. On the competition with Syria see also an interview with Hajj Nimr al-Nabulsi the owner of a soap factory in Nablus, in "In the Arab Economy", *Davar*, 26 October 1932. On the effect of the agreement see also Nahla Zu'bi, "The Development of Capitalism in Palestine: The Expropriation of the Palestinian Direct Producers", *Journal of Palestine Studies* 13/4 (1984), pp. 88-109.

Furthermore, in 1931 Egypt placed customs on the imports of olive oil soap, directly harming the marketing options of the Palestine merchants. In 1925 Palestine exported to Egypt 5,125 tons, by 1933 it decreased to 1,064 and by 1936 it deteriorated to 792 tons alone.[31]

Fig. 4: Soap factory in Nablus

A clear contrast increasingly yawned in the first half of the 1930s between the capacity of the Haifa merchants to compete and export on the one hand, and the intensive development of Haifa as a port town and industrial entrepôt on the other. This was further clarified at the onset of the Arab Rebellion. While Palestine's export of unrefined edible oil further declined from 309 tons in 1932 to 179 tons in 1937, export of refined oil (produced mainly by Shemen in Haifa and Yitzhar in Ramat Gan) only increased. Further evidence to that, and to the failure of the Arab boycott during the rebellion to advance the Arab oil industry, was provided by the huge increases of imports of both factories of the raw materials they used – decorticated groundnuts, sunflower and copra. The intense economic activity could have hardly been balanced by British assistance to the Haifa

---

[31] Government of Palestine, *Report by His Majesty's Government in the United Kingdom of Great Britain and Northern Ireland to the Council of the League of Nations on the Administration of Palestine and Trans-Jordan for the year 1929* (1930); Himadeh (1939), pp. 266-267; Seikaly (2002), p. 84. Acid oil is *Zayt Ma'mal* in Arabic and *Shemen Dekalim* in Hebrew.

merchants, and in particular without enforcing customs on the import of the raw materials.[32]

THE IMPACT OF WAR

The problem of government presence was all the more significant during World War II, as demonstrated in the case of *Jam'iyyat Ta'awun al-Qura* – the association of village cooperation.[33] The association appealed to the Palestine government already in 1926 regarding the import of oil and sesame, claiming, as *al-Karmil* reported, that

> exempting these two types clearly harms the [Arab] farmers. These farmers expected the government to protect their agricultural production from any external competition so that they could be paid suitable prices for their agricultural product – the farmers who toiled hard to prepare the soil and grow, who were in great difficulty to find a proper market, and all these because of the external competition with the imported oil. This was why we – the association of villages in the Haifa district, who represent the interests of the Fellahin, turn to you in request to reconsider the said step, and place a custom for the protection of local produce.[34]

These appeals were reiterated in the following years but to no avail. Indeed, the assistance came only in 1941-1942 when the needs of the British war economy made imperative food control, making available various food products for the growing number of military forces in the Mediterranean, and the encouragement of the exports from Palestine of oil-related products.[35] The Arab olive oil and soap merchants were central actors in this scheme and in the working of the British-led committee that aimed to put the assistance to export into practice.[36]

---

[32] "Palestine's Oil Industry", *Palestine Post*, 29 July 1936; Gail Hoffman, "Made in Palestine", *Palestine Post*, 1 November 1938; Vashitz (2003), p. 404; Himadeh (1939), p. 146; Metzer (2000), p. 380.

[33] The association was headed by Nayif Al-Madi, son of a wealthy family in Haifa and in nearby Ijzim. See Seikaly (2002), p. 187.

[34] *Al-Karmil*, 21 February 1926.

[35] Shemen's press announcement, "Facts about Soap Shortage", *Palestine Post*, 6 November 1941. Edward Mayow Hastings Lloyd, *Food and Inflation in the Middle East, 1940-45* (1956), pp. 263-265. On food control in wartime Palestine, see Sherene Seikaly, *Meatless Days: Consumption and Capitalism in Wartime Palestine 1939-1948*, PhD (2007).

[36] Shemen to the Food Department of the Government of Palestine, 12 September 1939, Israel State Archive, 5035/16; Government of Palestine, Office of Statistics, Census of Olive Oil Production 1943/44 Season, Israel State Archive, M/17/672 and 18; Uriel Friedland, "Palestine's Oil Industry", *The Palestine Economist Annual* (1948), pp. 102-106; Vashitz (1993), p. 76; El-Eini (2006), pp. 132-133.

The Olive Oil Committee was established on 5 November 1941, and brought together Arab olive oil growers and merchants such as 'Abdul-Rahim Afandi al-Nabulsi, Jewish oil industrialists, and British officials. The committee held six meeting and examined ways to improve production, whereupon the needs of the forces stationed in the region probably impacted its deliberations. The outcome of the deliberations was a government ordinance instituting control over the harvesting and the pressing process of olive oil. Moreover, the committee recommended the improvement of the marketing of the Palestine products in British markets and even the American markets. These recommendations were followed in 1943 by a census of the olive oil industry in Palestine.[37]

Not much is known on the operation of the Arab oil and soap merchants of Haifa after the war ended. The merchants probably enjoyed the better years of the world war and of the improving crops; let alone the attention given to them by export-minded officials of the Palestine government and the imperatives of the war-economy. It seems however that the 1930s limitations on the expansion of their activities have now re-emerged. This was partly expressed by the effect of the competition on the Fua'd family to sell large parts of their lands in the Galilee (in the village of Kufur 'Inan for example) by 1944 to Fallahin who previously owned them. The sale significantly narrowed down the family's olive oil trade.[38] Moreover, in the Shemen anniversary book, *The Oil Jug*, which came out in Hebrew in 1945, and aimed among other things to emphasize the contribution of the factory to Haifa's and Palestine's industrialization, the Arab merchants were not mentioned. The Zionist links of the factory and the latter's role in the Jewish settlement and economic expansion in Haifa were expressed in the book in its exclusivist presence in the Haifa oil and soap scene.[39]

However, despite the wartime increase of income among Arab growers from olive oil products, the scheme to encourage exports was

---

[37] Editor, "Local Olive Oil Production", *Palestine Post*, 18 May 1941; ISA, MEM/18/672; Government of Palestine, Office of Statistics, Census of Olive Oil Production, 1940/41 Season, ISA, 4342/42; Gail Hoffman, "Harvesting Our Oil Crop", *Palestine Post*, 2 November 1942; Government of Palestine, Office of Statistics, Census of Olive Oil Production 1943/44 Season, Israel State Archive, M/17/672; Anglo-American Committee of Inquiry on Jewish Problems in Palestine and Europe, Report (1946), p. 1004; *Davar*, 11 May 1941. On the committee see note 30 above, and Shaul E. Cohen, *The Politics of Planting: Israeli-Palestinian Competition for Control of Land in the Jerusalem Periphery* (1993), pp. 51-53.
[38] Interview with Hasan Ahmad Mansur, 7 September 2010.
[39] Kroll (1945); Friedland (1948), pp. 102-106.

largely ineffective. This was made clear by a petition forwarded to the High Commissioner of Palestine written in August 1945 by olive farmers in the Acre and Haifa regions:

> His Honor the High Commissioner knows only too well that the two main economic branches in Palestine are citrus and olive oil. The agreement between the government and the Jewish companies pertained to edible and salad oil which are produced from plants with a small addition of the famous Palestinian olive oil, and its marketing in all Palestine's markets in cheap prices, backed by the Mandate government that imports the seeds for oil production from abroad. These impact the produce of Palestine and serve a severe blow to local produce, causing stoppage in the sale of Palestinian oil from the day that the new salad oil has began to be marketed. This brought about a severe financial crisis in the sector of Arab oil producers. We demand to decree the cessation of the sale of salad oil and the support of the marketing of local olive oil.[40]

The ineffectiveness of government assistance was further aggravated by the ending of the war, the termination of emergency conditions and the olive tree crop failures of 1946-1947. Evidently, the Haifa Arab merchants, mainly the Sa'd and the al-Nabulsi families, who initially pressed to convene the committee, and after the war tried to improve the technology of their soap production in order to compete with the local marketing of Marseille soap, could now achieve only little governmental attention, and consequently the branch in the Arab sector of the town further deteriorated.[41] The nearing withdrawal of the British from Palestine and the 1948 war would be now crucial in sealing off the process. Both the Sa'd and the al-Nabulsi families were turned into refugees, their commercial and marketing establishments were shut down, and the economic operations which they started a few decades earlier in Palestine's north and in the Haifa area in particular came now to an end. The impact of the war on the two families thus accentuated the human and political aspects of this economically-focused history.[42]

---

[40] Petition of the olive oil growers, 16 August 1945, ISA 22/4305; see also Amos Nadan, *The Palestinian Peasant Economy under the Mandate: A Story of Colonial Bungling* (2006), p. 89.

[41] On the consequent sale of lands in the Sajur village by the Sa'd family, lands which after 1948 were defined as absentee, see interview with Ghattas Yusif Ghattas, 7 September 2010.

[42] On technological innovation by the Nabulsi soap industry in 1944-1945, see in the Yosef Vashitz papers, Yad Yaari Archive, file 35-95.7(3). On Shemen at the end of the Mandate period, see Friedland (1948), pp. 102-106. The report ignores the Arab oil and soap merchants.

In the final analysis the Haifa Arab trade in edible oil and soap could little develop before the war beyond the confines of the local Palestine market, and already by the end of the 1930s Shemen alone provided half of the entire edible oil consumption of the country. Arab merchants, some of whom also even marketed Shemen products, could hardly withstand the competition, or exert pressure on the government to balance the structural change and strong competitiveness that Shemen put forth. This is made clear by the mix of factors that shaped this change since the Shemen's emergence in Haifa in the mid-1920s: its technological and marketing advance, the backing it received from the Zionist movement, the protection of the Palestine government, the Egyptian customs policy, and last but not least the competition stemming from regional specialization.

Haifa society may have developed a form of commercial bi-nationalism: with Shemen purchasing raw materials from Arab farmers, Shemen exporting to Trans-Jordan, Syria and Lebanon, Arab merchants selling Shemen products, and the Arab and Jewish communities consuming to a certain degree products produced by both of them. However, this economic exchange and reciprocity was overshadowed by the splitting and dualization in which both political and economic forces played a role, and which increasingly shaped the branch's fate. It is for these reasons that production and marketing of oil and soap in Mandate Haifa, and the fate of the Arab role in them in particular, shed light on what the Arab economy and society faced at the advance of the British-backed Jewish sector, and of the complex transformation of such a historically symbolic branch as olive oil.

HISTORICIZING CLIMATE:
HAYFAWIS AND *HAIFO'IM*
REMEMBERING THE WINTER OF 1950

DAN RABINOWITZ AND JOHNNY MANSOUR[1]

INTRODUCTION

Gharib 'Asqalani's short story *The Rain*[2] begins on a freezing night in early 1950 in a refugee camp in Gaza, with a young Palestinian man taking off his clothes and standing stark naked in the presence of others. He was not a lunatic. He used his clothes – the only ones he owned – to cover and protect his newborn son, whose birth coincided with the coldest night in living Palestinian memory.

It soon transpired that the newborn was impaired: he was left handed – something traditional Arab culture sees as an aberration – and had a tremble in his teeth and lips. His father took these imperfections philosophically, seeing them as the 'inheritance' of *Sanat al-Thaljih* (The Year of the Snow). He also nurtured the belief that if the boy would be warmed by a fire fed by branches of an olive tree rooted in the soil of Majdal 'Asqalan, the family's *alma mater* which fell in Israeli hands in 1948 and was subsequently destroyed,[3] his bodily impairment would disappear.

In June 1967 Israel occupied Gaza. As a consequence, those living in the Gaza Strip could access Israel again, for the first time in almost twenty years. That winter the father took his 18 year old son to Majdal

---

[1] The authors wish to thank Benny and Galia Nachshon, the 'Ifara family, Zahi Karkabi, Erica Zohar, Abbas Shiblak, Miriam Gubernik, Ra'ifa Sa'id, Munir Sharqawi, Gershon Levi, Fatima and Ahmad Abu-Qtanah, Layla 'Atallah and Kalman Greidinger, for their generous willingness to share their memories of the winter of 1950 with us as part of this project.
[2] Gharib 'Asqalani, *The Rain* (2009), www.daralkashkol.com.
[3] Majdal 'Asqalan's location is today incorporated within the Israeli town of Ashkelon, established in the 1950s.

'Asqalan and brought him into the compound of an ancient Palestinian shrine that had been kept intact. The man, who had collected branches from a nearby olive tree, set them alight and told the boy to strip off naked and stand by the fire. The youngster did as he was told, but the moment was short lived. An Israeli patrol passing by noticed the unusual proceedings and apprehended the father and the son for questioning. The soldiers soon let them go, but the ritual could not be rekindled. Its coveted remedial impact would never be put fully to the test again.

Fig. 1: Refugee Camp in Lebanon, ca. 1950
Source: UNRWA website

Climate, detached from human will and perfectly immune from intervention on the part of mortals, is usually construed as external to historical trajectories and political developments, and thus mostly excluded from socio-cultural analyses.[4] When it does make an appearance in the social sciences, it tends to be akin to the weatherman's performance following the main part of the news show: a neutral and detached figure, bringing ephemeral information whose significance for the essential matters of the day is limited most of the time.

Cyclical and repetitious, climate features in many languages in ways denoting stable, unrelenting regularity. For the English, if something is predictable and proper it is 'right as rain'. In Hebrew and in Arabic a

---

[4] Cf. Dipesh Chakrabarti, "The Climate of History: Four Theses", *Critical Inquiry* (Winter 2009).

plain and simple fact is *Wadih mithl a-shams* (Arabic) and *barur kashemesh* (Hebrew) – clear as the sun. An unexpected event is described by the oxymoron "Thunder on a sunny day", or "out of the blue" (sky). An unusual period standing out as an exception in the course of normal time is sometimes given a dissonant adjective such as "The yellow time" – the label given by one of David Grossman's Palestinian interlocutors in 1987 to the distorted period that began with the Israeli occupation of 1967.[5]

Like gravitation, climate is an omnipresent, concrete, systemic force. Complex but predictable, it impacts reality in ways beyond our comprehension or control – a far cry from the social, economic and cultural realities that shape the power structures and dependencies affecting individual and communal lives.[6]

There are times, however, when Outstanding Climate Events (OCEs) can assume socio-historical significance. Standing tall in individual and collective memory, such events are often reified, becoming benchmarks for temporal denotation,[7] wider cultural sensibilities, and even identity.

The extraordinary cold spell that swept the Middle East in the second week of February 1950 is one such case. This chapter traces the resonance of this event in memory and narrative. Based on archival materials, literary pieces, newspaper articles and interviews conducted in 2009 and 2010 with *Haifo'im* (Israeli residents of Haifa) and Palestinian *Hayfawis*,[8] both residents and refugees in exile, it seeks to comprehend the socio-historic weight that week still carries.

In February 1950 Haifa, then Israel's only industrial center and maritime transportation hub, found itself in the aftermath of the 1948 war and the forced departure of some 70,000 Palestinian residents – roughly half its pre-war population.[9] At the end of the war Israeli bulldozers demolished the old Muslim quarter, and the majority of Palestinian residential properties elsewhere in the town were apprehended by state agencies and made available to Jewish immigrants. Most of the residual

---

[5] David Grossman, *The Yellow Wind* (1988), original title in Hebrew: *Ha-zeman ha-tsahov* (*The Yellow Time*) (1987).
[6] For a significant exception see Jared Diamond, *Collapse: How Societies Chose to Fail or Succeed* (2005).
[7] Johannes Fabian, *Time and the Other* (1983).
[8] For an early usage of *Haifo'im* and *Hayfawis* see Dan Rabinowitz and Khawla Abu-Baker, *Coffins on Our Shoulders: The Experience of the Palestinian Citizens of Israel* (2005).
[9] Benny Morris, *The Origins of the Palestinian Refugee Problem* (1994); Tamir Goren, *Cooperation in the Shadow of Conflict: Arabs and Jews in the Municipal Government of Haifa During the British Mandate* (2008) (in Hebrew).

Hayfawi (Palestinian) population, numbering a few thousands, had been displaced and dispossessed. Holding formal Israeli citizenship, most of them were confined to a small residential enclave downtown, living in much poorer conditions compared to what they had before 1948. A slight majority turned into a negligible minority, the remaining *Hayfawis* found themselves amidst an overwhelmingly modernizing Jewish town with rapid urban reconstruction, bustling industrialization and swift economic growth. Like Palestinian citizens elsewhere in Israel, residual *Hayfawis* were now restricted to the town's municipal boundaries. Trips beyond required formal permission from the office of the military governor.

The proximity to 1948 – a watershed event for *Hayfawis* and *Haifo'im* alike – makes the snowstorm of February 1950 particularly suggestive. The written record we uncovered and the oral evidence collected suggest it had an emblematic significance for the period as a whole. Creating a temporal suspension, it carved out a chunk of time outside conventional time.[10]

I. SANAT AL-THALJIH – HOREF HAMISHIM

Saturday, 4 February 1950 saw severe storms, low temperatures and heavy precipitation across Galilee, the coastal plain of Israel, Jerusalem, the Judean hills and the Negev.[11] The cold spell was not confined to the Holy Land. Reports from Turkey, Lebanon, Jordan, Egypt and North Africa that week cite significant physical damage, with dozens killed and many injured.[12]

---

[10] Cf. Ernst Cassirer, *An Essay on Man*, Chapter 1 (1962); Fabian (1983); Maurice Halbwachs, *On Collective Memory* (1980); Andrew Abbott, "Temporality and Process in Social Life", in Andrew Abbott, *Time Matters* (2001), pp. 209-239.

[11] *Al-Hamishmar*, 5 February 1950, p. 1.

[12] Ibid. *Haaretz*, 5 February 1950, p. 1, *Ma'ariv*, 5 February 1950, p. 1. A report in the Israeli daily *Al-Hamishmar* on Sunday, 5 February in fact includes a passage on a storm in the Atlantic a few days earlier that caused the injury of 53 passengers aboard the British ocean liner Queen Mary, whose arrival in Southampton was delayed by twenty four hours. It also mentions that 32,000 people had been stranded in the USA as a result of storms and flooding related to the self same weather system. These accounts are consistent with reports of a stormier than usual winter on a global scale, with significant outbursts in North America, Europe and East Asia. For North America see
http://www.komonews.com/weather/asksteve/4346981.html (accessed 28 February2009). For an account of US soldiers suffering in the Korean winter see http://www.paulnoll.com/I-Korean-War.html (accessed 28 February 2009). For an account of Influenza outbreak in Japan as a result of extreme cold see http://www.ncbi.nlm.nih.gov/pubmed/14897501

Fig. 2: View of the coastal plain south of Haifa, February 1950
Source: Haifa Historical Association Archive. Photographer unknown

But weather conditions on that Saturday were only a precursor to the onslaught that took place the following day, Sunday, 5 February. All the Israeli dailies that appeared the next day (Monday, 6 February) featured weather related lead stories. *Haaretz* front page headline read "Snow and storms throughout the country". *Davar's* was "Snow and Frost Throughout the Country", *Al-Hamishmar's* had "Snow in Israel from Galilee to Rehovot", while *Ma'ariv* reported a weather related accident involving an El-Al passenger airplane as it attempted to take off from Lod (later renamed Ben-Gurion) airport.[13]

The stories filed under these headlines reported the suspension of school work in Jerusalem, stoppages of train services between Haifa and Tel Aviv, broken tents at various immigrant transition camps (ma'abarot), communities in Galilee stranded with no supplies of food and water,

---

(accessed 1 March 2009). For media stories in the Israeli press on the winter of 1950 see http://www.mezegavir.net/read.php?id=418 (accessed 3 April 2009),
http://www.ynet.co.il/articles/1,7340,L-3350931,00.html (accessed 3 April 2009) and http://www.fresh.co.il/vBulletin/showthread.php?p=3222485&mode=linear (accessed 3 April 2009). For a brief summary of the events in Israel see also the website of Egged, the national bus company http://www.egged.co.il/main.asp?lngCategoryID=2566 (accessed 18 August 2009).

[13] Two passengers were lightly injured. *Ma'ariv*, 6 February 1950, p. 1.

agricultural damage and so on.[14] *'Al-Hamishmar* included a light hearted report on an attempt by Jordanian soldiers in Jerusalem to provoke a snowball confrontation with Israeli troops across the inner-city border, jokingly suggesting this was related to "a new ice age that came as a result of the cold war."[15] *Davar* had detailed accounts of below freezing temperatures in Tel Aviv, heavy snow along the coastal plain, the Negev and even low altitude Tiberias on Lake Galilee.[16]

Temperature and precipitation figures for that week were indeed striking. On 6 February the temperature in Jerusalem plunged to 5° below zero centigrade. Tel Aviv had minus 2°, Tzefat (Safad) minus 9° and Beer-Sheva (Bir al-Sabi') minus 4° [17] – values lower than anything recorded since measurements began in 1860[18] and, in retrospect, to date.[19] Snow cover reached 55 centimeters in coastal Acre, 40 centimeters in Nazareth, 50-70 centimeters in Jerusalem, 10 centimeters at Lod airport and 5 centimeters at 'Auja in the Western Negev.[20] In Jerusalem the last snow finally melted only the following week, on 11 February.[21] It even snowed in Jericho[22] which, situated at 258 meters below sea level, has an average temperature in January of 15° C.[23]

While elevated areas like Jerusalem, Galilee and the Negev mountains see isolated snow events most years,[24] the picture for the coastal plain, including Haifa, is quite different. Haifa, where the average low for February is 8.7° C (50.9° F),[25] and where snow is a very rare occurrence,

---

[14] Ibid.
[15] *'Al-Hamishmar*, 6 February 1950, p. 1.
[16] *Davar*, 6 February 1950, p. 1.
[17] See www.mezegavir.net/read.php?id=418 (accessed 23 February 2009).
[18] See http://www.ynet.co.il/articles/0,7340,L-3350931,00.html (accessed 18 August 2009).
[19] Ibid.
[20] Ibid.
[21] Ibid.
[22] Eugene Makhluf, born 1931, originally from Haifa, was living in East Jerusalem at the time, where he was a student at the College de Freres. In an e-mail communication to us on 7 February 2010 he recounted a trip to Jericho, where his father worked, on the first day following the snow on which travel out of Jerusalem was possible. In his words: "all Jericho area was covered with snow. Can you imagine the Dead Sea area was covered with snow for two days!"
[23] Wikipedia, Jericho, Palestine (accessed 16 February 2010).
[24] Ibid.
[25] Israel Central Bureau of Statistics 2008. Monthly Average of Daily Maximum and Minimum Temperature 1988-2000. The BBC has a slightly higher figure of 10 C. See BBC (2009) Average Conditions–Haifa,Israel. See http://www.bbc.co.uk/weather/world/city_guides/results.shtml?tt=TT002430.

saw temperatures at minus 3° that week, with over 50 centimeters of snow on Mount Carmel and 35 centimeters downtown.[26] Compared with normal occurrences and distributions of snow in the region this was indeed a freak week.[27]

Fig. 3: View north of the Technion courtyard in Hadar ha-Carmel, Haifa
Source: Benny Nachshon personal archive

The snowstorm and the damages it inflicted dominated the printed media for the rest of the week. Tuesday, 7 February had all newspapers reporting somberly of disruptions, physical damage and casualties, including deaths. Four Jewish immigrants, recent arrivals from Yemen, were buried under the roof of the dining room of Ein Shemer transition camp which collapsed under the weight of snow. An adjacent transition camp had to be evacuated by the army, its occupants transferred to a safer location.[28]

The extraordinary weather catapulted Haifa to three or four days of considerable difficulty. Situated on the slopes of the Carmel ridge, many of its streets are steep. As the snow began accumulating on the night of Sunday, 5 February and through the morning hours of Monday, 6 February, many routes were deemed too dangerous for traffic and were closed off.

---

[26] See www.mezegavir.net/read.php?id=418 (accessed 23 February 2009).
[27] A. Bitan and P. Ben-Rubi, "The Distribution of Snow in Israel", *Geojournal* 2/6 (1978), pp. 557-567.
[28] *'Al-Hamishmar*, 7 February 1950, p. 1.

Most bus services were suspended, as was work in the port, Israel's only international marine gateway at the time. By Monday afternoon many, particularly those living in the upper streets of Hadar and on Mount Carmel, were forced to walk home, sometimes wading in knee-deep snow.

Davar (7 February) had this report on Haifa:

> Haifa carried on its back the weight of the snow that fell all day and all night, with short intervals. Transportation was paralyzed and supply was interrupted. Residents descended on shops to store whatever provisions they could. In the parks and private gardens many trees broke due to the heavy load of snow. Road traffic moved with difficulty, and 'Shahar'[29] served only the areas near the center, Haifa Bay and Acre. Contact to Mount Carmel was only intermittent.
>
> The port stopped working, the train did not leave, and only a fraction of Egged buses operated.[30] Contact with the (Jezrael) Valley and Nazareth was broken, and the traffic police, in conjunction with Haifa municipality, had 150 extra workers out to clear the snow. The municipality turned to Solel Boneh[31] and asked for a bulldozer, to help clear snow in the most difficult areas.[32]
>
> Many cars, including emergency vehicles and ambulances, were stuck and broken. Many telephones were not working, and there was no contact with other cities all day Monday. Most schools let students off for the day. Yesterday evening traffic was stopped again, as snow kept coming down with intervals. The public adhered to the calls by the municipality to take off snow from the roofs, and all day people could be seen on roofs, shoveling snow away. Walking the streets is very difficult. Many electricity and telephone lines were cut off, and power cuts paralyzed work in factories and in several bakeries.
>
> All day yesterday there was shortage of bread, especially on Mount Carmel which was cut-off. Towards the evening long lines could be seen next to the bakeries, that resumed work in the late afternoon. Power cuts caused failure of the water system in many parts of town. In the afternoon many of the electricity and telephone lines were being repaired. Many offices [...] downtown were closed off yesterday.[33]

Elsewhere on the same edition the paper reported that

---

[29] The bus company serving Haifa at the time.
[30] Egged is Israel's main intercity bus company.
[31] Israel's main publicly owned construction company at the time.
[32] *Davar*, 7 February 1950, p. 1.
[33] "The Snow Disrupted the Course of Life Throughout the Country", *Davar*, 7 February 1950, p. 1.

Movement of cars from the (Jezrael) Valley to Haifa and to Tel Aviv does not exist, nor is there telephone connection. An Egged bus that left Haifa Monday morning towards Afula took six hours to reach its destiny.[34] Cars went off roads into ditches and were even turned over, but there are no reports of casualties.[35]

Fig. 4: A stationary Egged Bus after days of snow, Kibbutz Galuyot (formerly Iraq) Street, Downtown Haifa
Source: Egged Archives, Photographer unknown

Fig. 5: Hospital Courtyard

---

[34] A distance of 45 kilometers
[35] "The Valley and Galilee are Cut Off", *Davar*, 7 February 1950, p. 1.

Source: www.haifa.org.il/gallery.aspx

*Fig. 6: Shoveling snow off a roof at Hadar, Haifa, February 1950. The public was called upon by the Municipal council to clear roofs.
Photograph courtesy of Benny and Galia Nachshon*

II.

Unfortunately, Arabic language newspaper reports of the OCE of February 1950 in Haifa are difficult to come by.[36] Our search did come up however with a number of more general references to the event in Palestinian novels and short stories such as the one by 'Asqalani cited earlier.

---

[36] One of the consequences of the abrupt truncation in 1948 of most Palestinian urban and cultural institutions in the territory that became subsumed within the State of Israel was the sharp decline of Arabic language journalism, including in Haifa. In February 1950 only two Arabic newspaper – *al-Ittihad* (established in 1944 by the Communist Party) and *al-Yawm* (published by the *Histadrut*, the Jewish Labor Organization), both weeklies, were in regular print in Israel. Printed in Haifa, *al-Ittihad*'s archive was lost in July 2006 when a missile fired from Lebanon during the armed conflict between Israel and Hizbullah hit *al-Hariri* building where the editorial offices were housed. For an account of the destruction of the building and the archive see http://www.haaretz.com/culture/arts-leisure/the-rocket-hit-the-struggle-for-peace-1.194653.

Yahya Yakhluf's novel *Water from the Sky*,[37] tells the story of Palestinian refugees in a camp near Irbid in Jordan, home to many displaced *Hayfawis*. In the early days of the camp most of its inhabitants lived in tents.[38] By 1950, however, many had been replaced by corrugated iron shacks.[39] Yakhluf describes the bitter cold and raging snowstorms that hit the camp, situated at 800 meters (2500 ft.) above sea level, as "hellish" (*Jahim*) for the poor refugees.[40] So much so, he says, that *Sanat al-Thaljih* (The Year of the Snow) was etched, alongside other years marked by outstanding events,[41] as a significant temporal reference point:

> For many years, people continued to use the event as a chronological mark (Ishara Zamaniyya') in the history of the camp. A man would tell another that he had built his new house in *Sanat al-thaljih*. A woman would tell a neighbor that she was married 'two winters' after *Sanat al-Thaljih*. Someone else would say he made the Hajj pilgrimage two years before it, and so on.[42]

'Asqalani's story[43] likewise describes heavy snow and unrelenting winds which broke tents and uprooted them, causing death amongst babies and toddlers. With official registration of newborns somewhat of a luxury at the time, 'Asqalani says, some people used *Sanat al-Thaljih* as an index point to mark births and other significant events.[44]

Ilyas Jabbur, who was born in 1935 in Shafa 'Amr (a town some 30 kilometers east of Haifa), recalled in a recent interview that "the year of the snow began to gain a prominent place in the way people referred to significant events, particularly births. You sometimes come across people saying they were born on Sanat al Thaljah".[45]

In 2007 a writer called Ibn Al-Quds, writing a biographical note about one 'Adnan Al-Ghul, describes how 'Adnan's family that in 1948 had been displaced from a village in the southern coastal southern plain, settled in Rafah, where it encountered *Sanat al-Thaljih*. They experienced

---

[37] Yahya Yakhluf, *Water from the Sky/A Novel* (2008).
[38] Ibid., p. 36.
[39] Ibid., p.72.
[40] Ibid., p. 95.
[41] Other years that likewise became temporal reference points in 20th century Palestinian chronology are *Sanat al-Jarad* (Year of the Locust, 1915-1916), *Sanat al-Hazzah* (Year of the Earthquake, 1927), and *Sanat al-Istihlal* (Year of the [first Israeli] occupation, 1948).
[42] Yakhluf, p. 83.
[43] 'Asqalani (2009).
[44] Ibid.
[45] Johnny Mansour, "Sanat Al-Thaljih: Sixty Years After", *Al Madina* 5 (February 2010), pp. 18-20.

torrential rains, exceptionally strong winds and, most strikingly, heavy snow that fell down from an ominously dark and bleak (dakin) sky.[46]

Some of the accounts of the event we heard in recent interviews with *Hayfawis* likewise echo a sense of a time outside time, creating an aura of a disrupted, eerie period. Khalid, born in Nazareth in 1917, was working at the time in a large food store and depot in Haifa. A resident of Nazareth, he normally commuted into Haifa by bus, but that was interrupted by the storm. In his words:

> I was working at Jad Swidan's shop then, and when the snow started I could not go back to Nazareth. Mr. Swidan offered me to come and stay at his home, and I stayed there for four days. It was difficult. He once sent me down from his home on Mount Carmel to Jaffa road to fetch some items from the store – biscuits, jam, powder milk and, I remember, some imported chestnuts. Going down towards the store was OK. On the way back however I faced a lot of difficulty because of the accumulated snow. I remember climbing up, and being scared of falling down.[47]

Khalid recalled how he saw children playing in the snow near the Greek Catholic church, but said that for him, stranded in Swidan's home, there was no fun. "The only thing to do during those stormy days" he says, "was to sit by the window and watch the ships at Haifa Port".[48]

Al-Ittihad, the (then) weekly published by The Israeli Communist Party (MAKI), was normally delivered to subscribers every Monday, the day of publication. Zahi Karkabi, who worked for the paper in 1950, was responsible for deliveries in the Palestinian neighborhoods of Haifa, including 'Abbas street and Wadi al-Jimal. His wife Maggie tried to prevent him from going out on his round, arguing the snow was heavy and he could slip and get himself injured. Zahi however insisted that completion of his mission was paramount. In an interview with him in January 2010 he asserted that "even as food supplies were missing, essential reading stuff was right on time".[49]

Anwar, a *Hayfawi* born in 1932, was a junior accountant at Haifa municipality in 1950. He remembers that the municipality decided to stop all office work and get all employees to their homes by cars, where they stayed for three days. However,

---

[46] Ibn Al-Quds, *The Qassami Commander 'Adnan Mahmud al Ghul* (2007).
[47] Interview at Al-Banna's home in Nazareth, 17 November 2009.
[48] Ibid.
[49] Interview with Zahi Karkabi in 10 January 2010 in Haifa.

One of the municipal engineers, Mr. Shakib Wadud, insisted on attending work. Returning home in late afternoon, when the snow had already become icy, he slipped on Shabtay Levi street and broke his leg. A relative of mine called Ra'ifa, who was married to Mr. Mu'ayyad Ibrahim, the chief accountant of the municipality, fell too, broke her leg and was treated at the Italian hospital in downtown Haifa.[50]

But things were even worse for *Hayfawi* refugees, many of whom (like many other Palestinians), were still in make-shift tents and wooden shacks in camps across Lebanon, Jordan, the West Bank and the Gaza Strip. According to one AP report, up to 70 Palestinian refugees, many of them children, froze to death in Lebanon and Jordan that week.[51]

The Shiblak family were displaced from Haifa in 1948 and took refuge in the West Bank village of Lubban al-Sharqiyya, south of Nablus. Ra'ifa, who was ten at the time, remembers that the girls were not allowed to go out to the yard, and had to watch from the windows as the boys played in the snow outside.[52] She remembers collecting wood and making a fire inside the house, where the girls and women sat, telling stories and singing as the storm was raging.[53]

Layla, born in 1937, was the third child of the 'Atallah family, a prominent Palestinian family who had owned a tile factory on Jaffa Street in Haifa.[54] In late 1947 the family left Haifa to stay in a village in Lebanon where they had gone for summer holidays before. When the war was over they wanted to return to Haifa, and Layla's father was the first to make the journey back. When he arrived, his wife (Layla's mother), who had stayed in Lebanon with the children, made several trips on foot, taking one child at a time. When Layla's turn came, they walked via Marj 'Uyun, ending up with relatives in Nazareth. It was there that Layla encountered the storm of 1950. In her words:

> We were stuck in Nazareth because the road to Haifa, where we were eventually heading, was blocked by a police checkpoint. And then the snow arrived. I went out to play with children in the neighborhood. There was an icy slope and I remember trying to ascend it and sliding back in the snow. On the second day my mother asked me to walk over to the bakery. I did, only to

---

[50] Interview, 28 November 2009.
[51] AP report, carried by *Al-Hamishmar*, 7 February 1950.
[52] E-mail communication from Ra'ifa Sa'id (na. Shiblak) 8 February 2010.
[53] Ibid.
[54] The house where the factory was located has since been torn down. The space is now (2010) occupied by the Nimni building materials warehouse, on 103 Ha'atzmaut Street.

find that there was no bread, as the bakery did not receive flour due to roads being cut off by the storm. The shortage of food lasted a few days.[55]

Ahmad Abu-Qatnah (born in 1931 in al-Mansi village some 30 kilometers south east of Haifa) had worked in a store owned by relatives in Haifa prior to the war of 1948.[56] When hostilities broke out, he joined his family who fled al-Mansi towards the West Bank and settled temporarily in the village of Birqin, south of Jenin. By February 1950 his family did not have a proper home, so when the snowstorm started the International Red Cross, which was responsible for operating the village school[57] invited families to find protection there. In Ahmad's words:

> The men got wood and lit a fire in the school, and we all huddled around it to warm up. The Red Cross gave us flour, oil, margarine, beans, lentils and dates, but other goods were missing. The villagers took pity on us too, and gave us some supplies. This was a most difficult time, far from our homes.[58]

Ahmad's mother Fatima Abu-Qatnah remembers water shortages, with people boiling snow in pots for drinking water, cooking and washing. She said:

> The snow continued for a week. It was too dark. Nobody could leave the village of Birqin. The cold was severe, and all we had was a single cover and a rug – that was all we got out from our village before it was destroyed in 1948.[59]

Munir Sharqawi (born in Haifa, 1940), who became a refugee in Syria with his family in 1948, remembers:

> The house where we lived at the time had a yard with apple and black mulberry trees that turned all white with the snow. I was ten years old, and my school was only a few minutes walk from where we lived. But there was a steep slope on the way which I had to carefully negotiate. I slipped on the ice that day, fell down almost a hundred meters, and came dangerously close

---

[55] Interview on 29 March 2010 in Haifa.
[56] Abu Qatnah's relatives were Alhajj Farraj, Mrayh Alshar'an, Mustafa Alshar'an and Ahmad al-farraj.
[57] UNRWA had not yet been established.
[58] Interview on 15 June 2009, courtesy of Badil Bethlehem (forwarded to the authors on 13 July 2009).
[59] Interview on 4 May 2009, courtesy of Badil Bethlehem (forwarded to the authors on 13 July 2009).

to the Damascus tramway track. It was only by the mercy of god that my life was saved.[60]

Haifa's residual Palestinian population, like Palestinians everywhere in Israel, was subject to military rule between 1948 and 1966. *Hayfawis* were forbidden to travel out of town unless they had a valid permit from the military governor's office, with checkpoints at all exit points and along the Carmel ridge from Stella Maris, through Central Carmel, *Moriya* Street, *Ahuza* and on towards the villages of *'Isifya* and *Daliyat al-Karmil* some 15 kilometers south east of Haifa.

Emil 'Ifara, a *Hayfawi* born in 1928 whose family ran a car repair shop downtown, owned a truck he had purchased from British military surplus in 1946. On 7 or 8 February 1950, when the town was covered in snow and normal life in it was largely suspended, he and some family and friends went on a trip along the Carmel Mountain ridge. They wanted to go to places they had not visited since 1947. Emil remembers:

> We knew that military checkpoint were in Stella Maris, Central Carmel, the entrance to al-Kababir[61] and in *Ahuza*, up the range. But when the snow fell we thought: what if the guards are gone and the checkpoints are empty? So we got together, 13 young men, and went. And indeed, the road along the ridge was uninterrupted, with none of the checkpoints operating. We would have gone all the way to *'Isifya* if it wasn't for the heavy snow on the *al-Tall* plateau where Haifa University is now located. It was so deep there that the road was blocked and we could not continue.
>
> We stopped there, got out of the truck, played with the snow, and made photographs with the 'Leika' camera my father had given me as a school graduation gift not long before. On our way back we passed Mar Ilyas Monastery in Stella Maris, and saw Father Louigy, Father Valentino and Father Daniel Rufeisen in the monastery yard, enjoying the snow. I knew them of course because during the war of 1948, when my family was forced to leave our home downtown, we took shelter in the monastery, staying there over a year.
>
> Next day we took the truck again and went to the beach. The sand was still covered with snow. There were not many cars: the ice was slippery and people were still worried about slipping on the ice. It took a few more days

---

[60] Munir Sharqawi's letter to Johnny Mansour, 20 June 2009. Sharqawi left Damascus in the 1980s and is currently living in Copenhagen, Denmark.
[61] Ahmadi (Muslim sect) village near Central Carmel, on the western slope of Mount Carmel overlooking the sea.

before the ice was gone, the military governor reinstated the road blocks and life returned to normal.[62]

Fig. 7: The 'Ifara family men with friends on the day of the truck trip in the snow, at the gates of the Baha'i compound on al-Jabal
Photograph courtesy of Emil 'Ifara

The women of the 'Ifara family did not join the truck trip up the mountain. They were, however, at the center of a snow celebration that took place in the yard of the house where the family was living. A life-size kneeling snow camel was built there, complete with ceremonial gear, and served as centerpiece for a rural Palestinian *diwan*.

---

[62] Interview with Emil 'Ifara and his wife, in their home in Haifa, 23 July 2009.

HISTORICIZING CLIMATE: *HAYFAWIS* AND *HAIFO'IM* REMEMBERING

Fig. 8: The 'Ifaras, next to the life-size snow camel at their home in downtown Haifa, February 1950
Photograph courtesy of Emil 'Ifara

Fig. 9: The 'Ifara family (mostly women and girls), next to the life-size snow camel at their home in downtown Haifa, February 1950
Photograph courtesy of Emil 'Ifara

III.

A closer look at Israeli newspapers reporting the weather crisis of February 1950 reveals a number of tropes used by both reporters and editors to frame the event and imbue it with meaning. One is the explicit depiction of the storm and the response it triggered as a continuation of the trials and tribulations the Jewish community had experienced during the war of 1948.

The lead story of *Haaretz* on Tuesday, 6 February uses the idioms of "siege", "isolation" and "cut-off", emphasizing communal resilience, tenacity and ingenuity in the face of adversity:

> The disruption of transportation (in Haifa, D.R. and J.M.) was reminiscent of the days of the siege of two years ago. Traffic to Hadar Hacarmel was redirected through the German Colony, and those attempting to get to Mount Carmel tried [de]tours via Rupin Road and Ahuza. By 7 pm Rupin Road was blocked, and Neve Sha'anan was isolated. The upper neighborhoods in Hadar Hacarmel and Mount Carmel were accessible only on foot and hundreds had no other choice but walk in the snow, having fun on their way. Rothschild hospital was isolated while Elisha and Hacarmel Hospitals were virtually cut-off. Magen David[63] ambulance made extraordinary efforts to reach Elisha Hospital by various [de]tours.[64]

Elsewhere the article says:

> In early evening the bus company ha-Shahar informed the police that its staff were no longer ready to take responsibility over transporting people in the dark, with snow flakes covering their headlights. A vehicle equipped with loudspeakers then took to the streets, announcing the suspension of all bus services at dusk. This too was reminiscent of the days of siege of [the] past.[65]

This allusion to 1948 was not restricted to descriptions of the snow in Haifa. An article published in *Haaretz* that week, under the headline 'Jerusalem was cut-off like in the days of the siege', included the following passage (the sub-headline reads: 'Disconnected from the outside'):

> As temperatures in the Judean region dropped to minus 5° on Sunday evening, all telephone and telegraph lines were disrupted and the town was in fact disconnected from any contact with the outside world – just like the siege of spring 1948. For a few hours even the Voice of Israel Broadcast was silenced and could not be heard anywhere in the city. Newspapers could not

---

[63] The Israeli equivalent of the Red Cross.
[64] *Haaretz*, Tuesday 6 February 1950, p. 1.
[65] *Haaretz*, Tuesday 6 February 1950, p. 2.

be delivered,[66] and even correspondents had no contact with the outside. The only newspaper available in Jerusalem was the *Palestine Post*.[67]

Fig. 10: A street in Hadar ha-Carmel, Haifa, February 1950
Source: Haifa Historical Society Archive
Photographer unknown

Ma'ariv, which in 1950 was the most widely circulating Israeli daily, carried a front page article on Monday, 6 February that included the sub-headline: "Jerusalem is disconnected and under siege due to snowstorms in and around the city for the last 48 hours".[68] The text featured the following assertion:

> For the first time since 1948 we are under siege again joked Jerusalemites. Only instead of lead bullets the air is filled with snowballs, and instead of depression there is an air of amusement and a state of mind of jokes.[69]

---

[66] All major daily newspapers in Israel are printed in Tel Aviv.
[67] *Haaretz*, Wednesday 7 February 1950, p. 4. The *Palestine Post*, later renamed the *Jerusalem Post*, is printed in Jerusalem.
[68] *Ma'ariv*, Tuesday 6 February 1950, p. 1.
[69] Ibid.

שלג במרכז הכרמל חיפה, 1950

Fig. 11: Tractor clearing snow from the road on Mount Carmel, Haifa February 1950 - Source: Haifa Historical Association Archive. Photographer unknown

Two days later the paper had a story headlined "General winter placed Jerusalem under siege", which had the following passage:

> Jerusalem tasted this week once again the taste of siege. Granted, this time it was a mini-siege, as they now say in the context of the Cold War, and rather than a man made siege it is one made by the heavens. Instead of lead bullets we had snowballs flying through the capital's air, and children were building snowmen instead of picking shrapnel's. This fact takes away some of the sting from the unpleasant situation that was created when Jerusalem was cut-off from the rest of the country.[70]

All Israeli newspapers emphasized the good performance of the state and its agencies. Here is an excerpt from an article in *Haaretz* that week:

> The hands of Haifa's traffic police, that had been on alert since 5 a.m., were full of work. Regardless of the snow and the storm, the white sleeved officers were visible in every corner in all parts of town. They patrolled, stopped traffic from approaching danger spots, helped jump start vehicles stuck in snow, redirected traffic and much more. Headquarters used special cars to

---

[70] *Ma'ariv*, Thursday 8 February 1950, p. 3.

reach the men with cans of hot tea and with cups of [b]randy. Members of the public showed sympathy towards officers wading in the snow and mud, giving them sandwiches and [b]randy. Fortunately, there was no loss of life, although some cars were lightly damaged. By night the streets were empty and many coffee houses were shut down. The 'Snow curfew' had most cinema houses half empty too.[71]

A Haifa memorial book, published in 1968 to commemorate the main events in the town since 1948, refers to the snow of February 1950 with the following passage:

> The general impression was 'snow curfew'. Telegraph and electricity lines were covered with snow. The trees in the parks and the streets weighed down under the snow, almost touching the heads of passers by. Branches broke. Mount Carmel was disconnected from all other parts of town, and youths could be seen playing in the snow all day and early evening. These youngsters, who had never witnessed scenes like [these], were not perturbed by the cold and were having a good time. The Fire Brigade and *Magen David Adom* (health emergency service) were called to assist on many occasions, and reached many locations in spite of the extremely difficult conditions. There were no reports of serious accidents.[72]

Fig. 12: Snow covered street in Haifa, February 1950

Source: Haifa Historical Association Archive. Photographer unknown

---

[71] *Haaretz*, Tuesday 6 February 1950, p. 2.
[72] Amos Carmeli, Shlomo Shhori and Ariela Hareuveni (eds.), *Haifa 1948-1968 – Events of 20 Years* (1968), p. 51.

The notion of individuals displaying resilience and courage, and thus contributing to the collective effort of enduring was evident also in testimonies of *Haifo'im* who we interviewed. Zafrira lived near Central Carmel and was employed as an assistant teacher at a nursery school in *Hadar ha-Carmel*, the part of town located on the lower slopes of the mountain. Her daughter, who was four years at the time, attended the same nursery school. In an interview in 2009 Zafrira recalled:

> The snow fell all morning, and was getting heavier. So around midday we decided to close and send the children home. Most children lived near, and their parents came and took them home. But we lived on the mountain, bus services had been suspended and the only option I had was to walk home up the hill with my daughter. I will never forget that day. I was young and strong, but walking in knee-deep snow up the steps connecting Hadar Hacarmel with Central Carmel was trying, to say the least. Sometimes I could not see the next step. But, you know, we managed. That was what we did in those days – tackle difficulties, cope with adversity.[73]

Fig. 13: Poster published by the Haifa Workers' Union, calling for solidarity and material help for children living in transition camps for Jewish immigrants

Miryam, a *Haifo'it* since the late 1930s and mother to a toddler then, recalls:

> We lived on Derekh Hayam, which slopes down from Central Carmel westwards. In those days our house was one of the last houses as you go

---

[73] Interview with Zafrira at her home near Hadera, 24 August 2009.

down. Of course the days of the big snow were fiercely cold, and it was difficult. My son was only two, we had a visitor from England who was taken ill, and it was impossible to keep the house warm since fuel supplies were interrupted – the cars and horse drawn carts delivering kerosene could not get near us in the snow and ice. But we endured. This is what you did in those days.[74]

Kalman Gredinger, a businessman, lived near Central Carmel and used to drive his private car each day down to his office. On the day of the storm, however:

> Towards dusk it became apparent that going up the mountain with my car, in fact in any vehicle, was out of the question. It was icy, slippery, dangerous. I took a room in hotel Zion downtown and stayed there for two or three nights. It was no big deal. We had gone through more trying times in 1948, and in the conflicts that preceded it.[75]

Galia Nachshon, whose parents had immigrated from Russia to Haifa in the 1920s, was 17 in 1950, and has fond memories of the snow week:

> School was suspended so there was general jubilation. Everyone was out on the streets, crowds of youngsters mixing. […] It was really an extraordinary event. I remember a girl who was younger than me, in fact I was her councilor in the scouts, who wanted to give me a photograph of hers as a memento. The one she chose, which I still have, shows her lying in the snow. She wrote something on the back of it – 'a memory for all eternity' or something to that effect. This teaches you something, doesn't it?[76]

Later in the interview Galia recalled snowball fights and snowmen, one of which carried particular significance:

> We threw snow around, and built snow towers and snow effigies. One of the kids who lived near us in Hadar, Amnon Gelfman, was a talented artist who subsequently became a well known architect. And he crafted a snowman, shaping the face most artfully to resemble that of David Ben-Gurion, the venerated prime minister.[77] His creation stood in the yard of ha-Re'ali School, and we all came to see the marvel. Then the press got word and a photograph of it appeared in one of the national newspapers the following day.

---

[74] Interview with Miryam Gubernik, 22 July 2009.
[75] Interview with Kalman Greidinger, 23 July 2009.
[76] Interview with Galia Nachshon (na. Hayam), 21 July 2009.
[77] The founding father of the State of Israel and the incumbent prime minister in 1950.

Fig. 14: Children at Hare'ali School surrounding a snow sculpture of David Ben-Gurion, Haifa February 1950. The sculptor, Amnon Gelfman, is third from the right.
Photograph courtesy of Benny Nachshon

Many accounts of the events highlighted the storm as a 'European' event. *Davar* carried a story on 6 February under the headline 'A Moscowian night in Tel Aviv' that read:

> The Soviet embassy on Rothschild Boulevard had a film showing last night. When it was over, embassy workers came out and were surprised to see the snow descending. They joined the Ambassador in the embassy garden, and together with the children began a snowball battle. One of the Soviet diplomats told our correspondent: 'We felt at home. This was a wonderful surprise for us'. […]. The snowball battle in the garden of the embassy went on for more than an hour, during which the children of the staff were allowed to stay and take part in the joys of 'The Moscowian night in Tel Aviv'.[78]

Two days later a story featured in *Davar* under the headline 'Winter sports on Mount Carmel'. It informed the readership that "with the resumption of transportation to Mount Carmel hundreds of boys and girls ascended there and used the snow for merriment and sport".[79] The following day the front page of the paper had two snow-related photographs on its front page. One featured young men with skis and was captioned: 'Winter sports on Ben Yehouda Street, Jerusalem'. The other had a horse drawn sledge, and had

---

[78] *Davar*, 6 February 1950, p. 1.
[79] *Davar*, 8 February 1950, p. 1.

the caption: 'Members of Moshav Merhavia in a winter horse drawn cart in Afula'.[80]

An article in *Haaretz* that week had a report from Zefat that said:

> Zefat and all the mountains around it were covered in sparking white snow which kept coming down all Saturday night and Sunday. Many of the new immigrants were reminded of snow days in their countries of origin. Some remembered the steppes of Siberia, where they had passed en route.[81]

The next day in *Haaretz* one could read of 'Ski slides':

> Children of new immigrants in Haifa brought out ski sledge[s] and turned al-Khatib alley, which descends from Stanton street towards al-Khamra square, into a sliding arena. Street photographer did well that day, capturing images.

Ma'ariv reported how "On Mount Carmel many residents were seen wearing sportswear and skiing down the steep slopes. Some residents who could not get to work by normal transportation means made their way downhill on skis they had brought with them years ago upon migration from Europe".[82] A photograph on *Ma'ariv* showing a man on skis in Jerusalem that week was captioned: "St. Moritz? No, Jerusalem".[83] And on the same edition, a report of "a rare sigh": five young men who got their skis out of storage and were attempting to navigate King George Street.[84]

Miriam Gubernik, an immigrant from Poland who became *Haifo'it*, remembered that she herself did not bring her skis from Poland, but that other people who did used Derekh Hayam as a perfect ski slope. Erika Zohar, who had arrived from Slovakia, where she used to ski as a youngster prior to the war, had similar recollections. And Galia Nachshon made the following explicit connection to Europe by saying:

> There was an air of happiness. I remember we were laughing all the time. [...] It was so unusual, surreal, like a scene from a movie I had seen. Not a Hollywood type film. More like the Russian films we used to see in 'Armon' cinema house, like 'Flower of the Rock'. Or Swedish films, or something from Lapland. You slipped on the snow and fell, or did not fall – you couldn't care less. There was a shortage of food, but the grocers' shop was just across the street from us, and two days later it was stocked with everything again.

---

[80] *Davar*, 9 February 1950, p. 1.
[81] *Haaretz*, 6 February 1950, p. 2.
[82] *Ma'ariv*, 8 February 1950, p. 1.
[83] *Ma'ariv*, 8 February 1950, p. 2.
[84] *Ma'ariv*, 8 February 1950, p. 4.

Significantly, the sense of jubilation, community resilience and hope instigated by the event that week was not shared by all *Haifo'im*. By 1950 many Jewish immigrants who emigrated from Arab countries were living in downtown Haifa, mostly in houses that had belonged to Palestinians prior to the war of 1948. Many of these properties were managed by government owned housing agencies, and were in poor physical condition. Gershon Levi, born in Morocco in 1939, immigrated to Haifa with his family in 1949. The apartment they lived in Wadi al-Salib was in a house that had been divided up between five families who all shared a single bathroom. The cramped conditions, he remembers, were exacerbated by the snow. The family received some clothes and blankets from the Jewish agency's absorption officers, and the children played together during the snow. But they were cold and hungry, he says, and the municipality did not supply their basic needs. In his words:

> They left us to face the snow alone. I, as a child, was not too bothered. But I remember hearing my father complaining about bread and other shortages of goods.[85]

DISCUSSION: FRAMING AN OUTSTANDING CLIMATE EVENT

The evidence we collected suggests three primary framings of the OCE that hit Haifa in February 1950: the snowstorm as a novelty; as an adversity; and as a test of individual and collective endurance. These framings are evident in real-time media coverage, in short stories and novels and, not least, in retrospective reconstructions conjured up in recent interviews.

A heavy snowstorm in Haifa is a novelty that cannot go unnoticed. An obvious departure from expected patterns, it naturally triggered curiosity, surprise and considerable fun. Not surprisingly, it featured centrally in newspaper reports from Haifa, particularly those published early in the week. Accounts on Monday, 6 February reflected bemusement and a celebratory mood. The storm as novelty was likely present in the tone and content of our interviews with *Haifo'im*, many of whom responded with positive nostalgia, producing accounts of a memorable, benign event.

The sense of *Sanat al-Thaljih* as a novelty was present amongst Palestinian *Hayfawis* too, albeit in a more subdued, restrained manner. Munir Sharqawi begins his account with a placid description of the garden and the trees in his family's house in Damascus, but immediately goes on

---

[85] Interview with Gershon Levi, 27 December 2009.

to tell the tale of a precarious slip he had which almost had him badly injured. The 'Ifara family show pictures of the snow camel they assembled in their yard and of the truck trip to the mountains and the beach, but their story also featured displacement from their original home, Israeli road blocks and the risk associated with their venture out of town. Ra'ifa Shiblak's account of the snow, which caught her *Hayfawi* family in Lubban al-Sharqiyya, is likewise not a simple recollection of a ten year old looking at a snow-covered courtyard through the window. Hers is the story of a child, a female and a refugee, living in other people's home, excluded from the courtyard and the snow by a host of age and gender inequalities. A similar ambiance – an exciting occurrence marred by dire circumstances – comes across in Fatima and Ahmad Abu-Qtanah's account of being taken in by the Red Cross in the Birqin school, and in Layla 'Atallah's memories of being stranded in Nazareth. In all these accounts, the bewilderment at nature and the innocent surprise created by the snow were colored by the predicament of exile.

A second frame discernable in the material is the OCE as an adversity. By Tuesday, 7 February 1950, the second day the storm was prominently covered by the media, the tone of reportage had changed from marvel at the force of nature to concern with the direct and circumstantial damage inflicted by the storm. The four fatalities in the Ein-Shemer camp and the accident at Lod International Airport, along with the temporary closure of Haifa port and of most intercity roads injected a sense of urgency to the reports.

For Palestinians adversity was more severe, often bordering on existential danger. The most vivid embodiment is of course the emblematically impaired infant in 'Asqalani's story. Born on the coldest day in living memory, he and his father (who was pushed to shed his clothes and dignity to save his son) are both reduced to *Homo Sacer* – figures possessing little more than their bare lives, in the most literal sense of the word. The damage the boy suffers from the storm is deep and lasting – an "inheritance", as the father puts it, that would be with the child for life.

Back in Haifa Khalid who is stranded at his employer's home has his daily difficulty of commuting from his home in Nazareth to his work in Haifa under the military rule exacerbated. Likewise, for *Hayfawi* exiles such as the Shiblaks, the Abu-Qatnahs, the 'Atallahs, the Sharqawis and those living in the Irbid camp, who struggle daily for their food and shelter, the wrath of nature complicates a life that is already most precarious.

Third is the OCE as a test of endurance. Texts produced by Israeli journalists in Haifa at the time and narratives that reconstructed the event for us in interviews years later evoke two related tropes: individual endurance and institutional resilience. "We endured" says Miriam Gubernick in 2009 as she describes the difficulties she had at home with a sick guest and a baby, because "this is what you did in those days". And Kalman Gredinger, revisiting that week almost 60 years on says: "we had gone through more trying times in 1948" – a philosophical evocation of the link he takes for granted between personal sacrifice and a communal effort to deal with a trying situation.

In terms of institutional response, as we have seen, media reports appearing later in the week project a growing sense of pride of the performance of the young state and its fledgling agencies. They praise the police, the ambulance service, the hospitals, the army for extending help to immigrants in transition camps, and marvel at Knesset members travelling to Jerusalem within hours of the road opening to get on with the pressing work of legislation.

Accounts of civil infrastructure functioning in spite of the storm and quickly resuming normal service when it was over were carefully conveyed. This, it should be noted, was an era in which numbers of ships docking and immigrants disembarking, amounts of agricultural produce, items of machinery imported and similar data were cheerfully reported by a proud press on a daily basis. The master narrative is of deliverance, American thanksgiving style, with battle metaphors employed to embellish a tale of a young society dynamically saving itself and becoming stronger in the process. Like agricultural and industrial development, civil engineering projects, the absorption of new immigrants or education, coping with the snow was attributed primarily to state institutions. Out of the wrath of nature, as it were, the state emerges as a benign embodiment of communal salvation. It even received a tangible effigy – young Helfman's snow sculpture of David Ben-Gurion, erected in the school yard and immortalized on the pages of *Davar*.

For *Hayfawis*, a residual population in Haifa and a fragmented, depressed and shocked collective in exile, institutional response was not really an option. Significantly, the two accounts we heard in interviews of commendable performance on the part of Palestinian men in official capacity were associated with institutions whereby Palestinians maintained some status and autonomy. Like Haifa's city engineer, one of a handful of Palestinian officials who stayed put and kept their pre-1948 appointments, and who fell during the snow storm and broke his leg. Another was of course the heroic newspaper delivery man, identified with the Communist Party, now mainly representing Palestinian interests and sensibilities.

Finally, a note on the potential of OCEs to shape identity through redefining space. As indicated above, the snowstorm of February 1950 was by no means confined to Israel. In fact many reports in the Israeli press that came out on the first days of the storm contextualized it as a local manifestation of a regional and even global event. Citing freak weather occurrences in the Atlantic, Europe, Turkey, Lebanon, Syria and Jordan, some Israeli newspapers even carried reports originating with news wires about the devastating consequences of the storm for Palestinian refugees. This regional context, however, all but disappeared as the week wore on, and was completely absent from reconstructions we heard in recent interviews with *Haifo'im*. By mid week, the focus of most writers and their editors had shifted to damage inflicted locally, to individual and institutional effort on the part of Israelis to respond and, ultimately, to the return to normal life.

Discursively Israel in general, and Haifa in particular, emerge in this progression as the primary, perhaps the sole location of the OCE. *Horef Hamishim* (the winter of 1950), in other words, was constructed by Israelis as a uniquely Israeli event. Rather than reflecting the fact that all Middle Eastern communities are exposed to the same elements, *Horef Hamishim* became part of a geographical stock-taking project designed primarily to buttress boundaries and underscore them. Anderson[86] has shown how maps, censuses, daily newspapers, novels and national museums help in the project of imagining the nation. For Israelis, it would appear, climate fulfilled a similar function. *Horef Hamishim* and its memory, we argue, accentuated the Zionist belief in the bond between the people and the territory. It did so by merging geography, climate history, and political assertion into a single national entity nurtured by the state.

In a similar vein, the snowstorm was mobilized by Israelis to position Israel as an outpost of European culture and identity. Generally speaking, the *Diaspora* at large and Europe in particular were not objects of legitimate yearning in the young State of Israel. The re-invention of Judaism as the centerpiece of political Zionism was coupled with the re-invention of the new Israelis as a brave new breed. Ostensibly emancipated from the shackles of diasporic life, new Israelis were expected to be disdainful of their diasporic roots and of what these roots were understood to symbolize. The storm created a short moment whereby this imperative was somehow relaxed. For a week, thanks to Mother Nature, European connotations were acceptable again, even desirable. The Soviet ambassador and his staff strolling in the snow inside the embassy compound in Tel

---

[86] Benedict Anderson, *Imagined Communities: Reflections on the Origin and Spread of Nationalism* (1991).

Aviv; people skiing in Derekh Hayam on the slopes of Mount Carmel; snowball fights and snowmen in Hadar and even horse drawn sledges in Afula were now a cause for celebration. The tension inherent in the Zionist imperative between an idealized life in the old-new patria and the repressed yearning for Europe – at once a temple of culture and a mass Jewish graveyard – was temporarily suspended.

The significance of *Sanat al-Thaljih* for Palestinian identity was, again, more subdued, merging into a process of identity formation that focused on the common memory of loss and national calamity of 1948. The war, which had already morphed into unending exile, was fused into a prolonged and dangerous winter of discontent.

"ERASER" AND "ANTI-ERASER"[1]

COMMEMORATION AND MARGINALIZATION ON THE MAIN STREET OF THE GERMAN COLONY:

THE HAIFA CITY MUSEUM AND CAFÉ FATTUSH

SALMAN NATOUR AND AVNER GILADI

INTRODUCTION

This chapter is the product of collaborative work by a Palestinian writer from the village of *Daliyat al-Karmil*, located just outside of Haifa, and a Jewish-Israeli historian of Medieval Islamic culture, who lives in the city itself. Salman, who writes primarily in Arabic and only rarely in Hebrew, was born and raised on Mount Carmel and has a deep, long-term connection with Haifa. Avner, whose native language is Hebrew, was born in a Jewish town outside Tel Aviv. As an "immigrant" to Haifa who has become captivated by its charm over the years, he has become increasingly interested in the history of the city. Due to the different backgrounds and approaches of the co-authors, this chapter incorporates different writing styles and therefore cannot be categorized as belonging to any one specific discipline or genre. The text, rather, is a combination of observation, impression, personal memoir, and analysis of documents and official publications.

The main street of Haifa's German Colony is the artery that physically connects the two institutions that lie at the heart of this chapter: the Haifa City Museum, a municipal educational institution that aspires to foster a local identity in the spirit of the dominant Zionist ideology, and Café *Fattush*, which, with the modest means at its disposal, gives

---

[1] "Anti-Eraser" (*anti-mekhikon*) was the name of a special device installed on color television sets in Israel in the late 1970s. Its purpose was to reverse the effects of the "eraser" method (*mekhikon*) then being used by Israeli television, under government order, to erase the "burst phase" signal of its broadcasts. This ensured that even on color television sets, Israeli broadcasts could be viewed only in black and white. These terms are part of the history of Israeli television and have become idiomatic expressions in the Hebrew language.

expression to the historical account and cultural aspirations of the city's Palestinian minority. Our aim here is to tell the story of these institutions – their development and their relationships with the historical quarter where they are both located. We also hope to shed light on the differences between these two institutions – one an official institution, and the other a spontaneous popular initiative – in substance and purpose, thus revealing a local and typically unnoticed expression of the competition between two historical and cultural narratives.

Fig. 1: General View of the German Colony's Main Road

A COLONY ON THE EDGE OF TOWN

For approximately twenty years, a small group of Israeli women have been holding quiet demonstrations every Friday afternoon at the traffic circle at the top of the German Colony, adjacent to the stairs that ascend the steep hill to the Baha'i Temple. Some twenty or thirty Jewish and Arab participants hold placards bearing slogans against the occupation, in favor of a just peace and the establishment of an independent Palestinian state. Dressed in black, they stand at the circle for an hour, smiling at the drivers who offer encouragement and maintaining their composure when others have nothing but profanities to offer. Sometimes, a beautiful bride wearing a white dress with a silver coronet can be seen strolling around the circle across from the tiled roofs, accompanied by her groom. Their photographer instructs them how to move, when to stop, when to embrace, and when to kiss. At the photographer's command, they smile at each other and then together smile at the camera.

This is a typical scene at the intersection where *ha-Gefen* (Hebrew: The Vine) Street meets Ben-Gurion Boulevard (originally *Shari' al-Karmil*, Arabic for Carmel Street), the main street of the German Colony. The avenues descend in a straight line for about a kilometer, come to an end at the western gate of the port and on their way intersect with the four main streets of lower Haifa: Allenby Street, named for the British general who conquered the city in September 1918; *ha-Maginim* (Hebrew: Defenders) Street, which until 1948 was known as King George Street; *Yafo* (Hebrew: Jaffa) Street; and *ha-'Atzma'ut* (Hebrew: Independence) Street, which until 1948 was known as *Shari' al-Muluk* (Arabic: Kings Street).[2]

These Arabic, Hebrew, and English street names – each with its own ideological baggage and unique role in the struggle over discourse and identity in Haifa – all lose their significance in the presence of the brides, whose beauty transcends national and religious identity, just as the name of the neighborhood – the "German Colony" – transcends time, taking us back to the more distant past, to the days before the Jewish-Arab conflict or, to be more precise, to its very beginnings.

Beginning in the 1920s, the main street of the German Colony served as a multilingual and multicultural meeting place between western culture and eastern culture. Today, like then, cultural diversity finds expression in the tastes and aromas of the neighborhood's cafés and restaurants, with *Taiwan* (Chinese) nestled between *Shish Kabab* and *al-Diyar* (Arabic), *Duzan* (fusion – Oriental-European), *Fattush* (fusion – Arabic-European) and *Garden* (European). The street has flourished over the past decade. Leisure sites that stay open until the early hours of the morning have appeared on both sides of the street, and the appetite for food has stimulated an appetite for culture, primarily Arab culture. The recent development of the neighborhood brings back memories of Haifa during its cultural golden age, before 1948.

Along with the cities of *Yafa* (Jaffa), *al-Quds* (Jerusalem), *'Akka* (Acre) and *Tulkarm*, Haifa was an important center of Arabic culture in Mandate Palestine. It was home to dozens of clubs and cultural centers. In 1946, the city witnessed the establishment of the Union of Arab Clubs,

---

[2] See Johnny Mansour, *Haifa Arab Streets* (1999) (in Arabic).

which consisted of sport clubs and a multiplicity of cultural societies. These organizations joined the city's already existing social and religious societies that served the different communities, a number of *landsmanschaft* associations, established by residents who came from elsewhere in Palestine[3] and two women's organizations.[4] Moreover, between the late 19th century and 1948, Haifa was home to a large number of politically and culturally diverse Arabic language newspapers and journals. Expansion and diversification of cultural activity was particularly marked during periods of economic prosperity and political upheaval. Writers, artists, and intellectuals from other Palestinian towns and from around the Arab world made their way to Haifa. Such "immigrants" to the city included poet 'Abd al-Karim al-Karmi (Abu Salma), who settled in the city in 1948, attorney and intellectual Hanna Naqqara, who lived in Haifa until his death in 1984, poet Wadi' al-Bustani, the writers 'Ajaj Nuwayhid and Musa al-Husayni, and historian Nicola Ziyada. Well known writers from Egypt, such as 'Abd al-Qadir al-Mazni and Amina al-Sa'id, also visited the city and took part in cultural meetings.[5] Popular Egyptian artists – including actor Yusuf Wahbi and the Ramsis Theater Troupe, actors Husayn Husni, 'Abdallah al-Muris, and 'Ali al-Kaasar – performed concerts in the *'Ein Dor*, *Eden*, and *Bustan al-Balad* movie theaters. And the *al-Kawkab* café and theater hosted legendary Egyptian singer Umm Kulthum.[6] Indeed, Haifa was what Ghassan Kanfani described as a bustling city, "a beacon of literature and art."

By 1948, Haifa had not less then 58 cafés, including the well known *al-Sabah, Georges, al-Jreini, Farid, Sankari,* and *Zahir*, which also functioned as cultural centers for the educated population and the general public. On Kings Street, two cafés – *Iskandar Majdalani* and *Edmon* – attracted a clientele consisting primarily of the British soldiers who were stationed at the port or just passing through, and held regular parties and evening musical programs.[7]

This rich cultural life abruptly ceased to exist when Jewish *Haganah* forces conquered and occupied the Arab section of the city on 22 April 1948. Most of the city's Arab artists and intellectuals either fled the city or were expelled, along with approximately 70,000 other Arab inhabitants of the city. The 2,000-3,000 men and women who remained

---

[3] Husayn Ighbariyya, *Haifa – al-Ta'rikh wa l-Dhakira* (2001), pp. 219-221.
[4] Harun Hashim Rashid, *Haifa wa l-Buhayri: Madina wa-Sha'ir* (1975), p. 45.
[5] Hanna Ibrahim (ed.), *Hanna Naqqara: Muhami al-Ard wa l-Sha'b* (1985), pp. 110-111.
[6] Ighbariyya (2001), pp. 389-392.
[7] Interview with Bishara Abu l-'Asal.

were concentrated in the neighborhood of *Wadi al-Nisnas*, where two types of Arab cultural activity emerged, as we will discuss below.

FROM A GERMAN COLONY TO A PALESTINIAN-JEWISH NEIGHBORHOOD IN A HEBREW CITY

The German Colony in Haifa was the first of seven colonies established in Palestine by the Templars, an offshoot of the Evangelical Church whose members consider themselves the representatives of true Christianity – "the people of God." During the 19th century, the Templars attracted followers primarily in the southwestern German state of Württemberg. Against a background of rising messianic expectations that characterized the late 19th century and the conflicts between the Catholic Church and the Greek Orthodox Church in the "Holy Land," the Templars resolved to settle in Palestine, to use their presence to help improve relations between different Christian groups, and to serve as an example for members of other religions. In 1868, a decade after dispatching a delegation to Palestine to assess the feasibility of settlement, the leaders of the sect decided to establish its first colony in Haifa. The difficult living conditions in the crowded city deterred the pioneers, who chose to build their new neighborhood about one and a half kilometers to the west, on land they had purchased outside the city walls. The colony developed rapidly during the decades leading up to World War I. Between 1873 and 1902, it expanded from 245 residents and 31 houses to 517 residents and 92 houses. By 1914, 35 years after the onset of the Templar settlement enterprise in Palestine, the country's German Colonies were home to a total of 2,200 residents, with 750 in Haifa, the largest of the group's colonies.[8]

In contrast to the Carmelites, who since the 17th century had lived within the confines of their monasteries in Haifa (as they still do today), the Templars established a community based on family life and a successful modern economic project that included agriculture, small industry, construction, and projects in transportation and inn-keeping, first within the colony at the foot of Mount Carmel and later in *Carmelheim*, the branch located on the mountain itself (the modern day neighborhood of *Merkaz ha-Carmel*, or Carmel Center).

---

[8] Alex Carmel, *The History of Haifa under Turkish Rule*, 4th ed. (2002), pp. 115-116 (in Hebrew); May Seikaly, *Haifa: Transformation of a Palestinian Arab Society 1918-1939* (1995), p. 23; Mahmoud Yazbak, *Haifa in the Late Ottoman Period, 1864-1914: A Muslim Town in Transition* (1998), pp. 13-16.

The decline in religious fervor among second and third generation Templar settlers in Palestine during the early 20th century and their strained relations with the Ottoman authorities and the Palestinian inhabitants of Haifa, whose roots reached back to the founders of the colony, did not work to the benefit of the Templars. Their situation further deteriorated during the British Mandate. At the end of World War I, during which a few young members of the community served in the German army, the Templars were expelled to Egypt but were allowed to return to Palestine in 1921. In the 1930s, some 30% of the residents of the German Colonies in Palestine joined the Nazi party. In 1939, the Mandate authorities imprisoned in camps those under the age of fifty among the German settlers, and, approximately two years later, expelled some to Australia. Those who remained in Palestine left the country in 1948.[9]

These developments during the British Mandate transformed the composition of the neighborhood's population: the Colony lost its unique German character and began to attract new residents, particularly people of means, such as senior British government employees and wealthy Palestinian and Jewish families.[10] The development of Carmel Street, the Colony's main thoroughfare, was continuously influenced by the changes in social circumstances. In 1933, the Appinger Hotel (established in 1905) underwent renovation and became a luxury hotel, and the Colony's *Pross* restaurant, which opened its doors in 1935, became a meeting place for senior British officials and prominent Jewish and Palestinian figures. The café that opened along the beach just down the street in the summer of 1921 also evolved into a shared place of leisure.[11]

By the eve of the 1948 war, Palestinians already accounted for a majority of the residents of the German Colony,[12] and even after the flight and expulsion of the great majority of the Arab population, 180 Palestinian

---

[9] Yosi Ben-Artsi, *From Germany to the Holy Land: Templar Settlement in Palestine* (1996), p. 12; Alex Carmel, "The Templars' Community House and School in Haifa: The German Settlers in Palestine", in *Between the Mountain and the Sea*, Exhibit Catalogue, Haifa City Museum (2000), pp. 153-155; Motti Golani, *The British Mandate for Palestine, 1948: War and Evacuation* (2009), p. 171 and n. 169.

[10] Tamir Goren, *Cooperation under the Shadow of Confrontation: Arabs and Jews in Local Government in Haifa during the British Mandate* (2008), pp. 40, 46, 127-128, 167 (in Hebrew); Nelly Marcinkowski, *Rain on a Clear Day* (1994), p. 24 (in Hebrew).

[11] Mordechai Ron, *The Haifa of My Youth* (1993), p. 90 (in Hebrew).

[12] Arnon Golan, "The War of Independence in the Mixed Towns of Palestine", in Yair Safran (ed.), *Haifa in 1948: A Collection of Articles, 60 Years of the State of Israel* (2008), p. 7 (in Hebrew); Marcinkowski (1994), p. 110.

families remained in the Colony and the surrounding neighborhoods.[13] Following the war, Jewish families moved into the homes of the Germans who had been expelled by the British authorities during World War II, as well as the Arab homes in the neighborhood that had been abandoned. The German Colony was integrated into the Hebrew city which now became almost completely homogenous in population.

Although the virtual disappearance of Haifa's Palestinian community in 1948 put an end to the inter-communal competition that started at the time of the British Mandate over street naming, it was actually replaced by a mechanism of name-change and erasure – erasure of the memory of the Palestinian past, of the remnants of British rule, and the traces of the German presence in the city. In the latter case, the recent past presented a special challenge. In a letter of 1 September 1949, the local committee of the Jewish neighborhood of *Hadar ha-Carmel* proposed that the Haifa Municipality

> do away with the name German Colony, which conjures up upsetting memories, particularly for the residents of the quarter who are mostly new immigrants who suffered the torture of the Nazi hell. The proposed name Rehavia (from the biblical passage 'the Lord thy God shall enlarge thy border' [Deuteronomy 12:20]) articulates the sense of comfort of the Jewish people, which bore terrifying witness to the tyrannical regime of the Germans.[14]

Regardless of whether or not the committee's formal proposal was actually adopted, the neighborhood's name did not change in the eyes of the public, which continues to refer to it as the "German Colony" without objection, particularly in the wake of the "rehabilitation" of Templar history in official publications and the concomitant renovation of the neighborhood. Nonetheless, the names of two streets in the Colony which are German in origin – Mader and Hoffman – were changed to names symbolizing Jewish resistance and rebellion against Nazi rule in Europe, with the former renamed in memory of the ghetto fighters and the second in memory of Mordechai Anielewicz, the commander of the Warsaw Ghetto Uprising.[15] In 1948, the street where the German hospital was located, which in 1948 bore the Arabic name *al-Mustashfa* (The Hospital), was also re-named in memory of a Zionist leader: Meir Ruttenberg. *Shari' al-Bustan* was

---

[13] Charles Kamen, "After the Disaster: The Arabs in Israel, 1948-1950", *Mahbarot le-Mehkar u-le-Vikoret* 10 (1984), p. 45 (in Hebrew).
[14] Haifa City Archives, HH 00302/9-5895.
[15] Amatzia Peled (ed.), *A Street Guide to Haifa* (2007), pp. 66 and 225 (in Hebrew).

translated into Hebrew, becoming *Rekhov ha-Ganim* (Gardens Street), as was *Shari' al-Karma*, which became *Rekhov ha-Gefen* (see above).

The enterprise of changing and erasing the street names of the German Colony came to a close on a resounding chord: the re-naming of the Colony's main street – Carmel Street, a neutral name which had thus far withstood the winds of change since the Templar period and the first 26 years of Israeli statehood – to Ben-Gurion Boulevard. On 15 September 1974, the municipal Names Committee chose this street to commemorate the first prime minister of Israel, who had passed away the previous year.[16] This decision was highly ironic due to Ben-Gurion's role in the disappearance of the Palestinian old city from the Haifa landscape.[17] Indeed, it was Ben-Gurion himself who in April 1948, shortly after the end of the fighting in Haifa and against the opposition of the city's Jewish leadership, issued an order to destroy the houses of the old Palestinian city, which included remnants of the city built by Dahir al-'Umar some 200 years earlier. Perhaps unintentionally, the change of the name Carmel Street to Ben-Gurion Boulevard symbolically heralded the educational project initiated by the City Museum some thirty years later, which aims to highlight Templar history in general, and their relations with Zionism in particular, while ignoring the Palestinian chapters of the city's history.

THE HAIFA CITY MUSEUM

Stormy Times for the Museum

During the winter of 2007, winds of change began to blow through the Haifa City Museum as Dr. Rona Sela, a well known historian of Israeli and Palestinian photography, assumed the position of curator with a plethora of plans and new ideas. Located in the former Templar Community House on the slope of the main street of the German Colony, the new museum first opened its doors seven years earlier, but had thus far managed to attract neither visitors nor substantial public interest.[18] Sela clearly and succinctly explained her professional and political worldview in an interview with the Hebrew language newspaper *Haaretz* four days before the opening of an

---

[16] Haifa City Archives, HH 02581/14-58425.

[17] Tamir Goren, "The History of the Disappearance of the Old City from the Haifa Landscape", *Ofakim be-Geografia* 40-41 (1994), pp. 57-81 (in Hebrew).

[18] According to the visitors' report for the nine-month period between January and September 2007, the museum had only 2,572 visitors (an average of 286 per month, accounting for only 2.6% of the combined total number of visitors to all Haifa museums during the period).

exhibit cluster entitled *Crossed Histories*, the first museum project under her direction:

> Haifa epitomizes much of the pain and conflict in Israeli society, for example, the expulsion [of the Palestinian inhabitants] in 1948 and the forced exile that followed. I will deal with the charade that goes by the name of 'mixed city'....Until now all the exhibits that have been on display in the museum since its establishment in 2000 have told the Zionist narrative alone.

"I intend to tell all the stories," she clarified, noting that the museum's future exhibits would include some on the expulsion and the exile of the Palestinians.[19] The reaction was quick to come: none of the fourteen members of the Board of Directors of the Haifa City Museum attended the opening event of *Crossed Histories*. At the end of December 2007, with the conclusion of her first year of work at the museum, the Haifa Municipality did not renew her contract of employment and Sela was dishonorably relieved of her position. The mayor refused to meet with her, and as if to cover the tracks of the *Crossed Histories* exhibits, the Museum management quickly opened a new exhibit entitled *Masks and Magic* in March 2008, followed by the opening of *Haifa, 1948-1958: City of the Present*, an exhibit that would serve as the Zionist response to Sela's subversive work.

    It may be somewhat of an exaggeration to describe this episode as "stormy." After all, the museum quickly reverted back to its previous tranquil management, attracting virtually no visitors and little public interest and remaining alienated from its social surroundings within the German Colony. Nonetheless, the sudden appearance and disappearance of Rona Sela shed light on the ideological basis and the mode of operation of the mechanisms of defense, obfuscation, and denial at work alongside the construction of local identity. Regardless of its role as a minor artistic and community institution, the considerable efforts invested in shaping the program of the Haifa City Museum so that it serves the Zionist narrative alone and completely excludes the Palestinian narrative is worthy of consideration not only in the context of majority-minority relations in Israeli society but also in the local context. Haifa is a city whose leadership boasts of "co-existence" among the different segments of the local population but at the same time ignores the tragedy that befell the city's Palestinian inhabitants, and the city as a whole, in 1948. It also thwarts all expression of alternate narratives and the feelings of loss and frustration

---

[19] See the article by Danna Gillerman in the 18 September 2007's "Gallery Plus" Supplement of *Haaretz* (in Hebrew).

that continue to run deep among second and third generation *Nakba* Palestinians.

Fig. 2: Haifa City Museum

Some museums in Israel are located at historical sites that have been assigned Hebrew names (*'Ein Dor*, *Tel Hazor*, and *Tel Megido*, for example) in an attempt to achieve an ideological structuring of the landscape that creates seemingly natural continuity between the history of the geographical site and the history of the Zionist movement.[20] The case of the Haifa City Museum, however, is somewhat more complex. The museum is located in a historic German building in a part of the city that today is home to most of the Palestinian population of Haifa. In its endeavor to obscure the Palestinian past, the discourse surrounding the museum has employed the unique approach of highlighting the physical presence of the remains of the German Colony within the urban landscape, emphasizing the Templars' contribution to Zionist history while simultaneously downplaying the manifestations of German nationalist sentiment expressed before and during World War II. Moreover the Colony is portrayed as the city's oldest historical layer. As a result, the Palestinian

---

[20] Ariella Azoulay, "With Open Doors: History Museums in the Israeli Public Space", *Teoria u-Vikoret (Theory and Criticism)* 4 (1993), p. 82.

and Ottoman contribution to the physical, social, economic and cultural development of Haifa has gone relatively unexplored.

Although the undertaking has yet to be expressed publically, its ideological foundations can be recreated with the help of official documents such as the minutes of steering and advisory committees[21] and museum catalogues.

THE HAIFA CITY MUSEUM AND THE GERMAN COLONY

In the spring of 1870, the German Colony inaugurated its *Gemeindehaus*, or Community House, the first structure built by the Templars in Haifa and in Palestine as a whole, which served as a school and a house of worship. Today, after a period of renovation and reconstruction during the 1990s, the structure houses the Haifa City Museum.[22] During the 1980s, a long and difficult public campaign was waged to stop the grandiose construction projects planned for the gentle slope of Carmel Street/Ben-Gurion Boulevard. Had they been actualized, these projects would have threatened the natural landscape and architectural uniqueness of the German Colony. The following decade, the Municipality began a project to renovate and reconstruct the houses of the neighborhood, most of which had been neglected for years and some of which were falling apart. The home of the Würster family, with its residential and handicraft wings, is located near the top of the main street and was one of the first homes to be built in the Colony. Today, it houses Café *Fattush*.

The public campaign, the renovation of the main street, and the opening of the museum were undertakings that involved the development and dissemination of a historical narrative linking the history of the German colonial project with that of Zionist settlement in general and the history of Jewish Haifa in particular. In this context, Haifa-based historians of Templar settlement in Palestine played an active role. According to the narrative they advanced,

[T]he Templar settlements came to be synonymous with 'modernity,' 'progress,' and 'comfort' whereas the traditional landscape was characterized by unstructured villages, crowded meager homes, narrow streets, and the

---

[21] We consulted the minutes of the Community House Project Steering Committee and the 1997 Report of the Advisory Committee to Set a Program for Use of the Community House in the German Colony. The minutes we examined are stored in the Haifa Municipality's Engineering Department, not in the City Archives. They were neither filed nor numbered.

[22] Another building, which was constructed in 1902 behind the Community House to be used by the Templar school, is also designated to be incorporated into the museum complex.

absence of an organized system of spatial organization.... The Templars' spacious homes, large farm structures, straight tree-lined streets, public institutions, range of services, and economic success were a stark contrast to the Palestine landscape – 'a breathtaking cultural oasis on a semi-untamed beach'.... Their presence in the landscape and the many innovations they introduced were a source of inspiration for Jews, Arabs, and Turkish authorities alike.[23]

Contrary to this picture, research on the period suggests a more complex narrative that is represented neither in the museum exhibits nor in its publications. Indeed, the Templar community looked different to the country's Ottoman rulers and to the local inhabitants – Palestinians and Jews alike. This is clearly reflected in the Arabic and Hebrew press at the time and in documents of the Haifa *Shari'a* court. Repeated disregard for the law and for government authorities (local government, the municipality, and the courts), dishonest acts in land transactions, and the use of force against local Palestinians were all inseparable aspects of Templar settlement in Haifa. More than anything else, the Germans' profound contempt for and arrogance toward the Jewish and Arab communities, and the anti-Semitic tone of their writings and their debates with the Zionists, reveal the deep roots of radical nationalism that emerged among the younger Templar generation later in the Colony's history.[24]

---

[23] Ben-Artsi (1996), pp. 15 and 173-174. See also Carmel (2002), p. 116.

[24] Carmel (2002), p. 116; Mahmoud Yazbak, "Templars as Proto-Zionists? The 'German Colony' in Late Ottoman Haifa", *Journal of Palestine Studies* 4 (1999), pp. 40-54, especially p. 51. According to an October 1913 article in the Damascus newspaper *al-Qabas*: "They [the German settlers in Haifa and elsewhere] remained in their colonies as if on an isolated island. In their great self-centeredness, they never made an effort to share the benefits of their European way of life with the Ottomans in whose midst they lived. For this reason, they remained a marginal presence in the country." In his overall assessment of the Templars' contribution to the development of Haifa, Carmel acknowledges that it was the Ottoman-built Hijaz railway, with its link to the city (inaugurated in 1905), that gave Haifa the greatest push forward, Carmel (2002), p. 150.

The first narrative – with its emphasis on the Templars' pioneering contribution to the modernization of Haifa as a city and its visible and hidden connection with the Jewish settlement in Palestine is prevalent in other official publications as well. Also prominent is a tendency to portray the German Colony as the oldest neighborhood in Haifa [see the photo album *A Tour Through the Land* (1950) analyzed in the catalogue of *Haifa, 1948-1958: A City of the Present*, Exhibit Catalogue, Haifa City Museum (2008), pp. 6 and 8] and to ignore the complex relations between the Templars, the local authorities, and the inhabitants of the country. Particularly noticeable in these publications is the absence (or scant mention) of the final chapter of Templar history in Palestine, between World War II and the establishment of the State of Israel, during which many Templars embraced radical German nationalism. A succinct formulation of this narrative intended for Israeli youth can be found

Fig. 3: The Haifa City Museum

As we mentioned above, the Templar heritage was at the forefront of the working plan of the Haifa City Museum. The Advisory Committee's report of 6 May 1997 recommends that the site "be used as an active museum of the urban history of Haifa." According to the report, the museum was meant to focus on two display themes: commemoration of the activities of the Templars and their contribution to the development of

---

in *Our Haifa: An Information Book*, published by the Ministry of Education and the Haifa Municipality. In this book, the German Colony is the focus of the first chapter of the section on the city's old neighborhoods (neither the old city nor *Wadi al-Salib* appear in this section), and the Templars are portrayed as well-intentioned pioneers [Yehuda Zigman, et al., *Our Haifa: An Information Book* (2004), pp. 74-76 (in Hebrew)]. Like the historical survey that opens the booklet published jointly by the Council for the Preservation of Buildings and Settlement Sites and the Society for the Preservation of Nature during its campaign for the preservation of the Colony, this chapter contains no reference to the German settlers' final days in Haifa. See Council for the Preservation of Buildings and Settlement Sites and Society for the Protection of Nature, *Garden Towers on Red Roofs: The Campaign for the Preservation of the German Colony in Haifa* (1992), pp. 4-5 (in Hebrew).

Haifa, in the first place, and the development of Haifa's urban planning. The logical connection between these two themes is clear: if the German Colony was "the first settlement in the history of Palestine to be planned by a professional planner,"[25] while the "new city of Haifa" established by Dahir al-'Umar was "devoid of the most basic rules of building," had "narrow streets," and lacked "an organized system of spatial organization",[26] then the German settlement in Haifa assumes primary importance in the history of the architectural urban development of the city. In order to remove all doubts, the report emphasizes that "the museum *will make no pretense* [emphasis in original] of being a comprehensive museum of the history of Haifa addressing all aspects of the city's history"...."[27]

The museum did not always achieve the goals set by the Advisory Committee, as reflected in the list of exhibits that have been displayed there since its opening. However, in addition to an exhibit entitled *The Peace Crusade* (2002, Curator: Alex Carmel), which was dedicated in its entirety to "the German Contribution to Rebuilding Palestine in the 19th Century," the museum's connection to Templar heritage is highlighted in the introduction of the catalogue for the exhibit *Between the Mountain and the Sea* (Curator: Yehudit Matzkel), with which the museum opened in January 2000. "The restoration of the Community House and the school, and the preservation of the whole Colony, demonstrate our awareness of the debt of gratitude to the founding generation of the Templars and to the 'Churchmen' alike," writes Carmel in an article he authored for the catalogue, which makes special note of the "new impetus to the city's development" that stemmed from the rise of the German Colony. "Their pioneering contribution to rebuilding the Land of Israel, in the 19th century," he assures readers, "will not be forgotten."[28] Moreover, the

---

[25] Dan Goldman, *The Architecture of the Templers in Their Colonies in Eretz-Israel, 1868-1948, and Their Settlements in the United States, 1860-1925*, PhD Dissertation (2003), p. 200 (in Hebrew).

[26] Ben-Artsi (1996), p. 100.

[27] Nonetheless, in his 3 February 1999 written response to the proposed program submitted to the Municipality a few months earlier, the Chairman of the Advisory Committee noted the absence of two key issues in the history of the city: establishment and development of the New City, which was built by Dahir al-'Umar, and Haifa's linking to the Hijaz railway.

[28] *Between the Mountain and the Sea*, Exhibit Catalogue (2000), pp. 152-153 (in Hebrew). As an illustration of the theme of "progress," the article contains a photograph of the founders of the German Colony – the families of engineer Gottlieb Schumacher and teacher Friedrich Lange in clean, ironed, formal European attire – side by side with a photograph of rural Palestinian "olive suppliers to the oil and soap factory," dressed in traditional garb and sporting long beards, with one man sitting on a resting camel (p. 13).

catalogue contains more photographs of the German Colony than any other part of the pre-1948 city: nine, in comparison to two from "Ottoman Haifa," five from "Arab Haifa," and five from "Mandate Haifa."

The dissonance between the hard work invested in the preservation of the architectural heritage of the Templars on the one hand, and awareness of "the complex relations, to put it mildly, between the Temple Society and the renascent renewed Zionist community" on the other hand, is addressed only by architect Dagan Mochly at the beginning of his article "Conservation of the Templars' Community House" in the above-mentioned catalogue.[29] He resolves this internal contradiction by invoking "the 'first commandment'" of the ethics of conservation: "'To conserve the world's cultural heritage.' This means that the criteria of conservation are global, and are not necessarily linked to [a] geographical area or to the prevailing culture at a given time."[30]

In the spirit of its subversive approach which, as we have noted, marked a clear deviation from the museum guidelines, the *Crossed Histories* exhibit cluster undermined the role of Templar heritage on which the museum was founded. The curator's interpretation of Efrat Natan's piece entitled "Striding and Reaping," a sculpture constructed of scythes whose positioning evokes the general impression of the harvesting process, contains critique not only of Zionism but also of the Templar settlement that preceded it as a colonialist project in Palestine.[31]

The debate surrounding the connection of the museum, as an institution located in the heart of a mixed Palestinian-Jewish neighborhood, with its social and cultural surroundings also reflects the prevalent tendency among decision makers to focus the museum's work on the Templar and Zionist themes and to "shield" it from possible demands that it demonstrate greater openness to alternative narratives. After all, involvement in the community life of a mixed neighborhood is likely to raise expectations of a more prominent representation of the Haifa Palestinian narrative. In this spirit, a proposal that called for establishing a multicultural and multidisciplinary center for activity in the museum and for facilitating interaction between the museum, on the one hand, and the German Colony, with its ethno-nationally diverse population, on the other hand, was rejected.[32] Similarly, decision makers refused to accept a proposal to

---

[29] Ibid, p. 150.
[30] Ibid.
[31] *Crossed Histories*, Exhibit Catalogue (2007), "Introduction", p. 103.
[32] Proposal of Hanna Marwitz in the Program for Museum Activity, October 2003.

transfer management of the museum to *Beit ha-Gefen*, a Jewish-Arab community center that has been operating in the neighborhood for a number of decades.[33] Furthermore, upon their donation of funds for the renovation of the museum building, the Zeit Foundation and the City of Erfurt requested that the building be used to conduct meetings between Arabs and Jews. This stipulation, which has been repeatedly brought up at Steering Committee meetings,[34] has also yet to be met. It should be emphasized that during the period in question, neither of the relevant committees sought the membership of a Palestinian expert or public figure. Finally, *Crossed Histories* was the only exhibit in the history of the museum to make systematic use of the Arabic language, in addition to Hebrew and English, both in the exhibit captions and the published catalogue.

Fig. 4: The Old Templar School

---

[33] Steering Committee Meeting, 25 November 2003.
[34] For example, the minutes from the meetings of 28 October 2002, 25 November 2002, and 21 October 2003.

1948 HAIFA IN THE CITY MUSEUM

As we have seen, decision makers defined the museum as an "active museum of the urban history of Haifa," issued a directive that exhibits should be limited to achieving this goal alone, and stressed the fact that the museum was not meant to systematically address all aspects of the city's history.[35] This approach limited the mandate of the museum operators or, in other words, enabled them to avoid addressing the major rupture of 1948 which resulted in the departure of half the city's population within just a few months under circumstances that remain the subject of dispute. Rona Sela's 2007 reformulation of the aims of the museum, and the working program she prepared, completely contradicted the museum's approach during the previous decade.

Although Haifa itself is not the focus of the *Crossed Histories* exhibit cluster, its bold critical approach – when compared with the museum's activities during its first years of operation – clearly articulate the curator's attitude toward the city's history: multiple points of view and no obligation to predominant historical discourse. Each in its own way, the exhibits of the three female artists featured in *Crossed Histories* – Efrat Natan (*Striding and Reaping*, see above), Yael Bartana (*Summer Camp*), and Manar Zu'abi (*Without*) – address the official historical narrative and its colonialist elements and propose alternatives to them. Through her use of feminine materials, Zu'abi explores different aspects of the demarcation of borders, territorial marking, the geographic division of disputed territory, and the implications of these phenomena. Alluding to 1948 Haifa – the flight and expulsion of the Palestinians and the concentration of those who remained within the neighborhood of *Wadi al-Nisnas* – she erodes the standard masculine divisions that have been reflected in the formal schematic maps of Haifa since 1948 and constructs an abstract territory. In this way, and in the name she selected for the installation, Zu'abi expresses the personal and collective loss which the 1948 war brought upon the Palestinians of Haifa.[36]

Crossed Histories' divergence from the official approach delineated for the Haifa City Museum becomes even clearer when comparing the contents of the exhibit catalogue with the catalogue of *Between the Mountain and the Sea* (2000). According to the curator of the

---

[35] Advisory Committee Report, 6 May 1997; Steering Committee minutes, 16 May 2001.
[36] *Crossed Histories*, pp. 35-36.

latter exhibit, photography is a source of factual information, but can also convey "the feelings, the predictions, the ideas, the political and cultural urban concepts of the city."[37] "There has been a deliberate disregard for photographs which depict historical events in Haifa," she admits, "although there are quite a few which are nostalgic."[38] We ask: Nostalgic in whose eyes? Nostalgic for what? The Haifa in the exhibit is Hebrew Haifa, "which has *always* been the 'workers' city." [emphasis added] The refineries, the Nesher and Shemen factories, some of the initial industries of the pre-1948 Jewish community, represent the modernization which is replacing agriculture;[39] and indeed, the catalogue contains a large number of photographs of new buildings and industrial factories. The exhibit also includes the works of three Palestinian photography artists (7% of all the contributing artists), none of which carry an explicit political message except, perhaps, for Ashraf Fukhari's postcard series "I am a Donkey."[40] This may be read as an expression of longing for the naïve landscape that was obliterated by industrialization and modern transportation and a self-ironic perspective on the simplicity and humility of the Palestinian inhabitants of the country.

Although Eli Bruderman is the only artist in the exhibit to protest the dispossession implicated in the more recent "development" of Haifa, he too ignores the city's concrete history. His photographs[41] document the "conquest" of the lower city by government agencies – construction of the government office center, and the resulting reduced presence and exclusion of churches and mosques. The explanatory texts in the catalogue contain an element of protest, but, again, fail to directly address the relationship between the intentional destruction of the 1948's architectural legacy and the obliteration of memory by the aggressive construction of the 1990s.

If the exhibit *Between the Mountain and the Sea* delineated the ideological and educational approach of the Haifa City Museum and *Crossed Histories* represented a complete divergence from this approach, *Haifa, 1948-1958: City of the Present* (Curator: Batia Donner), which opened in September 2008, served to refocus the museum on its original aim. In the time-frame it adopted, the terminology it employed, and its incidental references to pre-1948 Haifa and the city during the war itself, the exhibit completely denied a voice not only to the Palestinian narrative

---

[37] *Between the Mountain and the Sea*, p. 145.
[38] Ibid., pp. 144-145.
[39] Ibid., pp. 143-144.
[40] Ibid., p. 38.
[41] Ibid., pp. 118-119.

but to the Zionist position that identifies with the pain of the refugees and that laments the physical and human destruction that Haifa experienced in 1948. The term "City of the Present" was coined by former Mayor Aba Hushi in the early 1950s in opposition to the utopian description of Haifa as a "city of the future," which appears in Theodor Herzl's *Altneuland*. The exhibit uses this concept not only as a justification for focusing its gaze on "events taking place here and now" within the confines of the Zionist narrative alone, but also as a pretext for refocusing the look from the recent past. The curator's explanation for her consciously self-imposed limitations with regard to the sources consulted and the points of view represented in the exhibit seem weak, and the apologetic tone is undoubtedly the product of her implicit dialogue with *Crossed Histories*. Noteworthy is her intentional failure to engage in critique of the sources, as she makes unqualified use of prevalent Zionist terminology when describing the events of April 1948 and the preceding months in Haifa and refrains from any expression of empathy toward the victims.[42] Also remarkable is the curator's disregard for the academic discourse of the past few decades on the 1948 war and its consequences.[43]

Haifa, 1948-1958 succeeded in getting the City Museum back on track after the shake-up caused by *Crossed Histories*. The subsequent exhibit on *Ottoman Haifa, 1516-1918* and two exhibits planned for the future – one on Haifa from the British perspective and another on the history of the Technion – ensure that the museum will continue implementing its policy of abstaining from addressing this painful chapter in the city's history and denying a platform for alternative, non-Zionist narratives. From this perspective, the Haifa City Museum is no different than other educational and propaganda mechanisms in Israel, which typically serve to erase remnants of Palestinian life in the country.

---

[42] This approach is even more pronounced in the section of the exhibit dedicated to the change of street names in Haifa after 1948. See *Haifa, 1948-1958: City of the Present*, pp. 136-137. Again, the facts are presented without historical contextualization and without an assessment of the psychological, moral, educational, and political significance of the campaign of erasing the remains of the Palestinian past, as if the changes were simply part of a natural process.

[43] See for example Baruch Kimmerling and Joel Migdal, *The Palestinian People: A History* (2003); Benny Morris, *The Birth of the Palestinian Refugee Problem Revisited* (2004); Ilan Pappé, *The Ethnic Cleansing of Palestine* (2006); Ilan Pappé, "Urbicide in Haifa", *Mediterraneans* 14 (2010), pp. 123-129.

PALESTINIAN CULTURAL REVIVAL ON BEN-GURION BOULEVARD: CAFÉ *FATTUSH*

Since the early 1950s, Haifa has been experiencing an Arabic cultural revival that has been largely rehabilitative in nature. Its focus has been on rebuilding the foundations of the city's lost intellectual and artistic life so that Haifa may once again assume its former position of cultural significance. However, Jewish rule in the country and the closed borders between Israel and the surrounding Arab region reduced the possibilities of this revival and confined it to a small area in the heart of the city known as *Wadi al-Nisnas*. It was there that the newspaper *al-Ittihad* continued to be published on a semi-weekly basis and that, in 1951, it was joined by the monthly cultural magazine *al-Jadid*. The communist party social centers emerged as a site of cultural and political activity, and the Zionist establishment also started sponsoring similar activities in the social centers of the Jewish Labor Organization (*Histadrut*) and the Federation of Working and Studying Youth (*ha-No'ar ha-'Oved ve-ha-Lomed*), in an effort to bolster "Jewish-Arab coexistence" in the city. This was also the aim of *Beit Belinsky*, which was established in the early 1960s and which is now known as *Beit ha-Gefen*.

A decade later, efforts began to break out of the borders of *Wadi al-Nisnas* by holding Arabic cultural activities at the *Histadrut*'s *Beiteinu* hall, which was periodically rented out to theater groups and to the communist party. Similar activities were also taking place at *Ahva* ("Brotherhood"), the communist party social center.

The diverse Arabic cultural activity in these centers were initiated primarily by the communist party and continued until the early 1990s, when they began to decline in the wake of the fall of the Communist Bloc, the first Gulf War, and the Oslo Accords, which overlooked the Palestinian citizens of Israel. This decline continued until the revival that began in the late 1990s.

In mid-July 1998, in a small basement at 38 Ben-Gurion Boulevard, Café *Fattush* opened its doors. The opening was attended by a small group of young men and women, including a number of artists and authors. It was the first café to open on the main thoroughfare since its renovation. From the outset, it was clear that Wadi' Shahbarat, the owner of the establishment, would do more than just serve food and beverages, and that he was also interested in transforming it into a center of cultural activity. He was about to fulfill his dream of opening a café that was different from other cafés in the city, from those that remained in *Wadi al-Nisnas* and from the European cafés in the Jewish neighborhoods of Hadar and Carmel Center. The new café was meant to offer a fusion of modern

European style and Arab authenticity. This aim is clearly reflected in the restaurant's design, with its arabesques, its Palestinian embroidery and *kufiyyah*s, and of course the name *Fattush*, referencing a popular Lebanese-Palestinian dish consisting of fresh vegetables, pieces of bread, and other traditional Arab ingredients, such as olive oil, spices, and even meat. The linking of East and West is also reflected in *Fattush*'s menu, which features a western platter of salamis, cheeses, and fresh vegetable garnishes alongside an "Arab platter" of sambousek with different fillings – spinach, hyssop, and cheese, and of course, breakfast from grandmother's kitchen.

Fig. 5: Café Fattush, July 2011

It is not every day that a writer is invited to speak at the opening of an Arabic restaurant. However, in the case of Café *Fattush*, just such an invitation was extended to Salman Natour, who used the occasion to speak about what he refers to as "the culture of chatter."

> Palestinian culture is rich and developed. However, it is for the most part a serious and forlorn culture that takes life too seriously. We write about Palestinian suffering and pain, resistance, and the dream of liberation, but we do not write about the leisure in our lives, the small minor details that people usually talk about. In other words we lack the culture of chatter. I hope this café helps us develop such a culture which, the world over, provides the foundation for novels, plays, films, soap operas, and even studies in sociology and anthropology.

Twelve years after the café's opening, Wadi' Shahbarat (born in 1972), explained:

> I got the idea to open a café of this kind when I was 20 years old. It was my dream. I dreamed of a cultural coffee house, and my friends encouraged me. I saw it as a great challenge, and I searched for a suitable location. I had initially thought about opening it in *Wadi al-Salib* or *Wadi al-Nisnas*, and by chance I learned that they were planning on renting out a building at 38 Ben-Gurion Boulevard in order to preserve it. The owner, a Jew of Egyptian descent, let me have it for six months free of charge, and I started thinking about the interior design. I didn't want to open an Arabic restaurant that

served hummous and ful like the rest of the Arabic restaurants in town, and I did not want to serve sandwiches, cheeses, and light meals. I was interested in opening a different type of restaurant – one that had special food and special music: Umm Kulthum, Fayruz, ethnic music, and African music. During the first three years I went to Ramallah a few times. There, I became familiar with the new restaurants and cafés that opened up before the second Intifada in which I saw many Jews enjoying themselves into the late hours of the night. I travelled to France, England, and Egypt, and I tried to bring everything that caught my eye in terms of design to *Fattush*. For me it is important that *Fattush* remain multicultural in character. At first, the young people who sat here were just trying to pass time and entertain themselves – making trouble and hassling the girls and the intellectuals. There were also some who tried to extort protection money. They would misbehave and break things, but we managed to establish an atmosphere of culture. My mother helped me a great deal from the very beginning. She cooked herself, but also took care of the place. We managed to get rid of the people who were causing problems, and they understood that this was not a place for them. I also announced that it was meant only for families. After some time passed, when everyone felt that the place was safe and respectable, I let individuals and young people back in. But they were not the only problem. The Municipality also made things difficult by not allowing us to use the yard. Inspectors would show up and write out tickets until the matter was finally dealt with. All people are equally welcome here. We get Arabs, Jews, and foreigners, and we hear different languages. Israeli soldiers also come in from time to time. We don't stop them from coming in, but carrying weapons is prohibited. Café *Fattush* is known throughout the country, in the Arab world, and in the world as a whole. When it first opened, it served as a place of meeting and leisure for young Arabs, especially for students from Haifa and from the villages of the Galilee and the Triangle. Here, they feel like they are in their natural environment, they speak Arabic without fear, and they dress in stylish clothes without worrying about the tradition which usually limits them. *Fattush* is even a meeting place for Arab lesbians. Many couples met here for the first time.

From the outset, Café *Fattush* attracted Arab intellectuals and artists who were in search of a place to hold cultural activities in the city. Hashim Diyab (born in 1960) of Tamra in the Galilee was one of *Fattush*'s first supporters and was involved in shaping its character. Diyab went to school in his village and then travelled to Europe, where he lived for 18 years. His first stop was Amsterdam. There, he made a living selling Shawarma, and then moved to the countries of Scandanavia, where he worked as a sculptor. When he could no longer stand the cold, he began migrating between Greece, France, Britain, Spain, and Germany. Diyab has been with *Fattush* since it opened, coming in every day and sitting with his fellow artists and writers. "This is my office," explains Diyab, who initiated cultural programs both inside and outside the café, along Ben-Gurion Boulevard. "We began with events, such as symposiums and poetry reading evenings that were open to the public. We invited mostly young poets who had not yet found a stage to read their work." One of the major happenings held at *Fattush* in 2003 was a festival entitled "Art is My Language," which was planned by "The First Night" group, led by Diyab.

Fig. 6: Café Fattush, July 2011

The idea evolved at *Fattush*, which is where I used to meet with a group of artists and intellectuals, and where we started to come up with ideas for cultural activity. 'The First Night' group consisted of 60 young artists from places throughout the country, from the al-Naqab/Negev to the occupied Golan Heights. They organized eight festivals, which were held first in Haifa and later in Nazareth and Acre. The festivals featured all types of artistic expression. For example, the third festival, which took place in May 2004, transformed Ben-Gurion Boulevard into an avenue that was teeming with culture.

The event received broad coverage in the Arab media. The following report appeared in the Arabic language newspaper *al-Ittihad*:

> The festival was attended by thousands of people from the Carmel and the Galilee, including many Jews who came to encourage and enjoy the Arab artistic expression. A large number of Arab artists, musicians, and singers took part in the festival, including classical singers and rap artists. Traditional and modern dance was performed on stages in the yards of four cafés: *Fattush, Havana, Dahan,* and the *Back Door*. The *Back Door*'s stage featured theatrical and musical performances for children from morning through 4 p.m., and from early evening through midnight it featured performances for adults, like the other stages. In addition to the musical performances, the festival also featured book and painting exhibitions.

The organizers' initiatives did not stop with the "Art is My Language" festival, which was one of the most important cultural projects to take place in Haifa in recent years. Rather, they continued holding regular cultural evenings and exhibits at *Fattush*, and also began initiating theatrical productions at the *al-Maydan* theater in town. In 2007, they organized the "Summer Nights", which the festival program described as follows:

> Summer Nights at *Fattush* 2007 brings us the beauty and splendour of Haifa and will be different from any other summer. High quality art... Music for desire... Pleasure for the soul... Joy of sight and deep heart beat. 2007 will become the core of creating culture and introducing world artists to us ... opening all the doors of the universe....

"Summer Nights," which lasted for more than a month, included a wide variety of activities, including the screening of concerts of well known singers from the Arab world and other parts of the world. The same year, the Ben-Gurion Gallery displayed works of Jewish and Arab artists along the Boulevard. In addition, the entire month of Ramadan featured evening entertainment and artistic activity, complete with theater actors and stand-up comedians. This constituted a revival of a longstanding pre-1948 Haifa tradition of Ramadan evening entertainment in all neighborhoods of the city, and particularly in its cafés.

Reviving these performances after more than sixty years was another attempt to restore Haifa's Arab cultural character, and this effort faced significant obstacles and difficulties from the outset. According to Diyab,

> The Municipality did not expect Arabs to open businesses along Ben-Gurion Boulevard, and when they did, it not only failed to support them but actually presented them with problems.... At first, the Municipality threatened to call the police in order to stop our activities. We held them in the courtyards of the cafés. We put up stages. For us, the challenge was ensuring that there would be no acts of theft or violence, and we were successful....

During the period of Israeli Independence Day, the Arab cafés on Ben-Gurion Boulevard remain closed, as their owners and most of their customers feel disconnected from the celebration. At first, crowds of Jews out to celebrate the holiday would come to Ben-Gurion Boulevard. However, when they realized that everything was closed, they moved to Herzl Street in *Hadar ha-Carmel*. "Our programs were aimed at restoring Haifa's pre-1948 cultural atmosphere," explains Diyab.

> We worked based on our consciousness of the city's history. The establishment of the State of Israel resulted in the scattering of the Arab population and left no threads linking them together. We were seeking just such a connection when we transformed Ben-Gurion Boulevard into a meeting place. It ... is a place where close relationships between bands and artists and Arabs from cities and villages around the country develop. We were not looking for financial gain. The activities here have had a positive effect on other cities, like Acre and Nazareth. It is the cultural alternative to the blue [Israeli] ID card. We tried to create a Haifa of our own. In Haifa, we are ready to absorb many different identities and to derive strength from the diversity. All the religious groups, nationalities, and colors are equal, and everyone has the right to live on the basis of mutual respect.

Over the past decade, the cultural work at Café *Fattush* and around blossomed between two tragic events that were traumatic for Jews and Arabs alike: one that accelerated the activity and another that halted the festivals and forced organizers to limit themselves to more reserved endeavors. In October 2000, with the outbreak of the second *Intifada*, 13 young Palestinian citizens of Israel were killed by the police force during demonstrations that erupted in the Galilee and Triangle regions in expression of solidarity with their Palestinian brothers and sisters in the occupied territories. The October events caused a rupture in Arab-Jewish relations within Israel. Jews stopped coming to centers of commerce and leisure in Arab villages and mixed towns, and Arabs, for their part, refrained from visiting Jewish commercial and leisure centers. Arabs in general, and students from the Galilee and the Triangle in particular, saw *Fattush* and the other cafés in the neighborhood as free and open leisure sites in which they could feel comfortable to talk and joke with one another in their native language without receiving suspicious looks.

Fig. 7: Café Fattush, July 2011

Another event was the second Lebanon war of July 2006. During the war, a large number of missiles fired by Hizballah struck Haifa, and particularly the Arab neighborhoods and the German Colony. "The Lebanon war brought an end to the festivals," explains Diyab.

> We organized a festival during the war in order to make it clear that missiles would not stop everyday life in the city. This was the first festival that received the support of the Municipality. However, the war left its mark on the feelings of Jews and Arabs. During the war, what is known as Jewish-Arab 'coexistence' in the city was badly and perhaps fatally injured. Later, in early 2009, when life was starting to return to normal, the war in Gaza broke out. During the war, the Jews abandoned the neighborhood out of the fear caused by the tensions.

Some young Arabs refer to Ben-Gurion Boulevard as "the street of love and wine," others call it "Abu Nuwwas Street" in reference to the Abbasid period Baghdadi poet of wine and love. In any case, the street is not an island isolated from the broader Israeli-Palestinian reality. Rather, it is part of these realities and impacted by the events, moods, and alternating periods of tension and calm that characterize relations in the region. Still, "It is a fact that the German Colony is unique within the Israeli-Palestinian landscape, and perhaps the only place in the country in which Jews and Arabs spend time together by choice, knowing that members of both groups are simultaneously present in the same space."[44]

An effort to expand the Arab cultural activity to another part of the city was unsuccessful. In 2004, a café called *Elika* opened in *Hadar ha-Carmel* on Masada Street, which is populated primarily by Arab families and new Jewish immigrants from the former Soviet Union. The project was undertaken by 'Ali Nicola, son of Jabra Nicola, one of the most important Palestinian intellectuals who ever lived in Haifa (1906-1974). Although the café attracts artists and conducts cultural activities, such as the screening of Palestinian films and evening poetry readings and musical performances, it has not succeeded in creating a cultural setting like that of the German Colony.[45]

Fig. 8: Café Fattush, July 2011

---

[44] Yusuf Rafik Jabarin, "The Meaning of Place among Jews and Arabs: The German Colony in Haifa as a Space of Trust", *Ofakim be-Geografia* 73-74 (2009), p. 211 (in Hebrew).
[45] Interview with Salim Abu Jabel.

CONCLUSION

Historical museums – which serve to preserve the past and shape collective memory – play an important role in the struggle over cultural hegemony. This is particularly true in societies like Israel, which tend to deal with the past a great deal. By positioning the Jewish people and the Zionist movement at the center of their representations of the past, museums of the history of the organized pre-1948 Jewish community in Palestine and, subsequently, Israel have excluded the "other" – first and foremost the Palestinian other – from their exhibits and displays, robbing them of their status as a "speaker" out of fear that they will propose their own representation of the past.[46] The Haifa City Museum, situated in the old Community House of the German Colony, offers a good example of this dynamic with a unique local twist: the attention it pays to Templar history, and the efforts to integrate it into the Zionist narrative in general and that of Jewish Haifa in particular. All of this takes place in a city where the remnants of a past Palestinian existence have been either completely obliterated or neglected to the point of collapse. The reaction to the short episode of the *Crossed Histories* exhibit cluster, and its attempt to open up to the Palestinian narrative and to place it, without fear, on the same plane as the Zionist narrative, provides us with a better understanding of the typical approach of the museum decision makers.

In an article based on interviews with Jews who grew up in Haifa during the 1950s, Dan Rabinowitz sheds light on the mechanism of forgetting that his interviewees (as well as Jews in other mixed towns) applied as individuals to cope with the departure of the Palestinians and the impact of this development. According to Rabinowitz, the Palestinians "have been swept off the physical and social landscape, and then from Jewish Israeli memory and consciousness almost instantly."[47] By adopting Hallbwachs' thesis that memory, by its very nature, is collective, and that seemingly personal memories are also shaped in communal frameworks, he concludes that his interviewees

> ... were socialized into a collective which, while built on the ruins of Palestinians, was heavily invested in blanket denial of their previous

---

[46] Azoulay (1993), pp. 80-82, 88 and 90; Tamar Katriel, *Performing the Past: A Study of Israeli Settlement Museums* (1997), pp. 2, 8 and 11.

[47] Dan Rabinowitz, "'The Arabs Just Left': Othering and the Construction of Self amongst Jews in Haifa Before and After 1948", in Daniel Monterescu and Dan Rabinowitz (eds.), *Mixed Towns, Trapped Communities: Historical Narratives, Spatial Dynamics, Gender Relations and Cultural Encounters in Palestinian-Israeli Towns* (2007), p. 52.

existence in the territory... Palestinians, now absent physically, were not allowed a space in memory, and were successfully erased from recollection even in those who clearly saw and recognized their presence prior to the war. Negating return is thus not merely a political project. It is a trajectory which involves identity and can be reflected in socialized individual memory as well.[48]

Despite its marginal role in the city's cultural life of the German Colony and the city as a whole, the Haifa City Museum illustrates how this mechanism of forgetting operates on the level of public education as an indivisible component of the construction of Jewish collective memory.

In contrast, we are also witness to a clear and deeply rooted endeavor on the part of Palestinians in the country to construct Palestinian collective memory and a Palestinian narrative in opposition to the Zionist one. The Palestinian cultural activity in Haifa, based largely on sporadic non-official initiatives, provides a foundation and fertile ground for this effort. The events that took place in the German Colony over the past decade supply clear expression of the desperate attempts to restore the Arabic cultural past of Haifa, as it existed before the *Nakba*.

In early 2010, the Palestinian Authority's Ministry of Education declared 13 March, Mahmud Darwish's birthday, Palestinian Culture Day. In Haifa, the event was marked with a week of activity centered around the cafés on Ben-Gurion Boulevard. Poems by Darwish and other Palestinian poets were read aloud inside the cafés, in addition to the screening of movies and video clips.

The new Palestinian generation in search of "spaces of trust"[49] has found them here. Their aim is not merely to live freely, but to re-establish a national and cultural identity, and in this way to strengthen their connection to the generation of 1948 whose identity was obliterated by the *Nakba*. As far as the Palestinians are concerned, the *Nakba* is not simply a historical occurrence that started and ended in 1948; it is an ongoing experience that has continued for more than 60 years, and that will continue until a Palestinian state is established and a solution to the refugee problem is found. Through diverse cultural events, the Palestinians are attempting not only to commemorate the tragedy that marks the beginning of their new national history, but also to construct a memory of life, renewal, and connection with Arab and world culture, on the one hand, and with Hebrew-Jewish culture on the other. They are not attempting to establish a

---

[48] Ibid., pp. 60 and 62.
[49] Jabarin (2009), pp. 194-213.

fictional, forced "coexistence" along the lines of what the Israeli establishment has been trying to create for the past 60 years, but rather an equal multicultural encounter.

The "war of names" being waged over the main street of the German Colony between the official name, which commemorates the founding father of the State of Israel, and the "underground" name invoked by its Palestinian residents and visitors, commemorating the ancient Arab "cultural hero" Abu Nuwwas, is indicative of the "dialogue between the deaf" currently underway between the Haifa City Museum, officially charged with shaping local memory, and the Palestinian inhabitants of the neighborhood, whose story the museum completely disregards. With no explicit intention of doing so, Café *Fattush*, with its cultural initiatives and the space it provides for spontaneous encounters between members of the young Palestinian generation, has emerged as an alternative locus of activity that serves to counterbalance the City Museum and its approach to Jewish-Arab relations in Haifa.

HAIFA UMM AL-GHARIB:[1]

HISTORICAL NOTES AND MEMORY OF INTER-COMMUNAL RELATIONS

REGEV NATHANSOHN AND ABBAS SHIBLAK

PREFACE

We, Abbas and Regev, first met in Salzburg, Austria, in the winter of 2009. Abbas arrived there directly from Oxford (UK), and Regev from Ann Arbor, Michigan (USA), to participate in the IHJR's Haifa Project. We sat next to each other in the introduction session, and the personal chemistry was immediately felt, overriding the decades of life experiences that set us apart. It was this personal interaction, or our shared interest in personal interactions – the focus of this paper – that brought us into this joint journey to Haifa of 1948.

Geared with an imperative optimism, this journey blended our personal and intellectual motivations. For Regev, this journey was part of his PhD research in Anthropology, focusing on the history and practice of "coexistence" in Haifa. But it was also a personal journey for him as an Israeli citizen who was born more than two decades after the 1948 war, and is concerned about the future of the region which cannot evade its past. For Abbas, a Palestinian academic who lives and works in England, this journey allowed revisiting Haifa, the place of his birth, to which he returned for the first time since 1948 in the autumn of 1994 (see the article by Yazbak and Weiss in this book). During our conversations Abbas recalled that visit:

> It was my first visit to the family house in Haifa's Hadar ha-Carmel. My mother, who didn't join me, asked me to bring her a photo of Sara, our red haired Jewish neighbor. My friend companion the novelist Emil Habibi knocked at the door, and a lady with red hair opened it, looked curiously, and exchanged a few words in Hebrew with Emil. She then stepped ahead,

---

[1] *Umm al-Gharib* in Arabic means the mother of the stranger.

hugged me and switched into Arabic: "of course I remember Abbas! He is the curly haired shoes collector!" Sara invited us in and started to recall the days with my parents. She was flooded with memories and couldn't stop talking about the good time they had together. How, during the time of escalating violence, my father (her landlord) allowed her to bring her frail father to live with her, and didn't charge any extra rent. My father also told her to ignore the municipality's objection to convert her balcony into a living space for her father.[2]

We agreed to meet the next day and bring my wife, too. I asked Sara whether it would be possible to video-record our conversation, as my mother had wished, and she agreed and asked to see a recording of my mother as well: 'I would like to know how Zahiyyah looks like now,' she said, and I promised her to do so. On our way out Sara pointed at two photos of a young man and a young woman in military uniform. 'These are my son and daughter,' she said, 'they are no longer in the army... they are successful professionals now. They live with their families close to Haifa, and would love to meet you, too.'

That evening Sara called: 'Abbas,' she said, 'there is no need to come with your friend Emil or to bring your video camera tomorrow. My children are not going to make it ... do not worry, we are going to have a long chat with you and your wife in a nice Arabic café'.

Abbas's recollection of his encounter with Sara reveals both the strength of interpersonal neighborly relations that survive in memory through the decades of divulsion, as well as the strength of the attempts to redefine communities according to mutually exclusive national categories through the same decades. The warmth of Sara's welcoming and her reconsideration of the nature of interaction with Abbas show how these opposing forces are played out. Ignoring this simultaneity might lead to overestimating the strength of one of these forces.

This paper is aimed at showing Haifa's two-fold experience of solid inter-communal relations and strategies of segregation. Since we come from different academic disciplines, for our joint journey Shiblak mainly traced the history of interactions between communities making use of his family memoirs, while Nathansohn mainly conducted oral history interviews with veteran residents of Haifa.

---

[2] See the article by Yazbak and Weiss in this collection.

Fig. 1: Fadil and Zahiyyah Shiblak with their Son Khalil in Haifa, late 1930s

Fig. 2: Abbas Shiblak (front) with his brother Khalil and sisters Ra'ifa (right) & Ra'isa (left) in Haifa, 1946

Fig. 3: Zahiyyah Shiblak's tombstone in Oxford, 2007. Photo by A. Shiblak[3]

INTRODUCTION

With the establishment of "New Haifa" in the mid-18th century, it became a home for a Muslim majority as well as for Christian and Jewish minorities. The reality of Arabs (both Muslims and Christians) and Jews living together in Haifa transformed throughout the years, as an outcome of the British colonization, the rise of nationalism, and other socio-economic and political forces which resulted in the expulsion of most of Haifa's Palestinian population and the creation of a Jewish state in 1948.

Traditional accounts of 1948 events stress a notion of rupture, and focus the narration on the transformation from communities sharing the same space and living together in coexistence, to an atmosphere of growing hostility, violent clashes, and expulsion. What we are asking here is how this transformation was experienced on the interpersonal level? What happened to the long history of shared life and personal relations? Did the rupture indeed erase all relationships established before the 1947/1948

---

[3] The words on the lower section of the tomb stone were requested by Zahiyyah Shiblak prior to her death; "Oxford – Haifa, 3200 Km", together with a quote from the late Palestinian poet Mahmoud Darwish: "I am from there and I have memories."

violence and block relationships between individuals within and between communities during the war? Through an analysis of moments of intersubjectivity, when one sees the other and engages with the other, as they are described in personal accounts of daily life of both Jews and Palestinians who experienced the war, we will show that the rupture was not firm.[4] Despite the dramatic changes in relationships between communities, some relationships between Jews and Palestinians continued to exist, even to the extent of rescue attempts during the peak of violent events in the city. Putting the focus on these attempts, and on ways of seeing the "other", could allow a richer narrative of Haifa in 1947/1948, which contrary to traditional and official Israeli and Palestinian historiography, does not focus solely on the national rupture narrative.

Our paper describes the history of coexistence and tolerance in Haifa, and the transformations it went through, based on primary and secondary sources focusing on personal accounts. We then move on to describe and analyze moments of intersubjectivity occurring in 1947/1948, when individuals of both sectors were engaged with each other, and negotiated and renegotiated their notions of "self" and "other". We offer here an analysis of oral history interviews and personal memoirs and show how they present intersubjective moments between Palestinians and Jews – and in particular between Palestinians and Mizrahi[5]/Arab-Jews – while at the same time other descriptions of 1948 tend to ignore such intersubjective experiences. As we will argue, by ignoring the Palestinian-Jewish intersubjective spaces, the social relationships between Jews and Palestinians are re-constituted as separate and distinct, thus serving a narrative of national divide.

It is our assumption that the rupture narrative described in mainstream historiographies is too simplistic, as it is mostly based on methodological nationalism[6] and state-centered epistemology. The rise of nationalism, accompanied by the widening of ethno-religious conflict and hostility, leading to violence and expulsion cannot assume totality, especially not in a place with a long history of coexistence and tolerance. We argue that moments of intersubjectivity, of relationships and

---

[4] For intersubjectivity in Anthropology, see Michael Jackson, *Minima Ethnographica: Intersubjectivity and the Anthropological Project* (1998).
[5] The term *Mizrahi Jews* refers to Jews of Middle Eastern, North African, Central Asian and Caucasian origins but first and foremost to Jews from Arab countries.
[6] See Ulrich Beck, "New Critical Theory with Cosmopolitan Intent", *Constellations* 10 (2003), pp. 453-468.

interactions between individuals, are most important to dwell on especially when dealing with a condition of sectarian violence. Both Israeli and Palestinian traditional narratives not only stress the rupture narrative, but are also organized – methodologically and theoretically – in a way that denies the shared Jewish-Palestinian relationships throughout the war.

It is both our theoretical and political conviction that the dominance of nationalism in the construction of reality should not reduce the practice of historiography to methodological nationalism whereby moments of intersubjectivity are suppressed.

HAIFA'S COMMUNITIES' RELATIONS IN THE LATE OTTOMAN PERIOD

The expansion of the economic infrastructure in Haifa, as described in this book's introduction, with the increasing numbers of immigrants from Muslim, Christian and Jewish communities, allowed Haifa to become an open and tolerant city which facilitated a slow but steady flourishing.[7] It is following these transformations in Haifa that Palestinians gave it the name *Umm al-Gharib* (Mother of the Stranger).[8]

A glimpse of interactions between communities at the time is described by 'Abdullah 'Udih based on the memoirs of his family.[9] According to 'Udih, some of the Jewish families who lived in the old Muslim neighborhood *al-Hara al-Sharqiyya* were Mizrahi/Arab-Jews who went into trade with Palestinian Arabs, and there were also cases of mixed marriages between these religious communities.

In Haifa, much like in other places in the Islamic Arab societies under the Ottoman rule, the communities of Mizrahi/Arab-Jews shared common culture with the Palestinian Arabs, both speaking Arabic, enjoying the same music style, same cuisine, and in many cases celebrating religious festivals together. The early Jewish immigrants from Europe, who arrived in the area in 1880 following the growing anti-Semitic persecutions, seemed to have also integrated well in the Palestinian society at the time. The renowned cartoonist Naji al-'Ali recalls in his biography the presence of the Jewish community in his village *al-Shajarah* in the Galilee which in the early stage of their arrival from Europe under the Ottoman rule enjoyed

---

[7] Mahmoud Yazbak, *Haifa in the Late Ottoman Period, 1861-1914: A Muslim Town in Transition* (1998).
[8] See Mahmoud Yazbak, "Haifa before the Nakba", *Mediterraneans* 14 (2010), pp. 22-26.
[9] 'Abdullah 'Udih, *The History of Kababir Village until the End of the British Mandate* (1980) (in Arabic).

good relations with villagers before they moved out to live in a newly constructed Jewish settlement in the late 1940s under the shadows of conflict.[10]

It is incorrect, therefore, to describe the Jewish communities in Palestine at that time as homogeneous. There is evidence that the cultural gap between the indigenous Jewish communities in the Arab and Muslim societies and that of the European Jewry mirrored the cultural gap between the local societies and that of Europe. "[I]ntraconfessional boundaries could occasionally be as strong as, or at time even stronger than, interconfessional ones", argued Michelle U. Campos lately in her book *Ottoman Brothers*, describing the relations between Muslims, Christians, and Jews in early 20th century Palestine.[11] From a different angle Sociologist Yehouda Shenhav mentions that the Zionists emissaries reported that Jews in Iraq had totally assimilated to the Arab Culture.[12] Similarly, Sami Zubida highlights the fact that Jews of Iraq shared common popular culture with the local Muslims.[13] The same could be said about indigenous Jewish communities in Palestine. For instance, the main shrine in Haifa was visited and the three religions were practiced there. For the Jews it is called *Elyahu ha-navi Cave*, for the Christians *Mar Elyas*, and for the Muslims *al-Khadir*.[14] Zahiyyah Shiblak, Abbas's mother, who was born early in the 20th century, used to tell her children stories on how religious festivals brought all three religious communities together in a festival of joy and fun for days, and how she and her Jewish and Christian neighbors and friends used to exchange homemade sweets and gifts in their religious festivals.

Zahiyyah, like many of the Palestinians of her generation, used to call the indigenous Jews in their midst *Yahud Awlad 'Arab* (Jews of Arab

---

[10] Khalid al-Faqih, "Naji Al-'Ali's Biography", *Kan'an e-Newsletter* 9/1961 (July 2009).
[11] Michelle U. Campos, *Ottoman Brothers. Muslims, Christians, and Jews in Early Twentieth-Century Palestine* (2011), p. 18.
[12] Yehouda Shenhav, *The Arab Jews: A Postcolonial Reading of Nationalism, Religion, and Ethnicity* (2006), pp. 170-181.
[13] Sami Zubaida, *Islam, the People and the State: Political Ideas and Movements in the Middle East*, 2nd ed. (1993). See also Mahmoud Yazbak, "Holy Shrines/Maqamat in Modern Palestine-Israel and the Politics of Memory", in Marshall J. Breger, Yitzhak Reiter and Leonard Hammer (eds.), *Holy Places in the Israeli-Palestinian Conflict: Confrontation and Co-Existence* (2010), pp. 231-249; Josef W. Meri, "Re-appropriating Sacred Space: Medieval Jews and Muslims Seeking Elijah and al-Khadir", in Larry J. Simon (ed.), *Medieval Encounters: Jewish, Christian and Muslim Culture* in Confluence and Dialogue 5 (1999), pp. 1-28.
[14] See Yazbak (2010).

descent). This is also echoed in the works of Palestinian literary authors at the time such as Khalil al-Sakakini and Wasif Jauhariyyah.[15] In his study on Iraqi Jews, Shiblak used the term "Arab-Jews", arguing that the indigenous Jewish communities in Palestine and the Arab region did not necessarily identify themselves at the time in national or ethnic terms.[16] They used religious categories instead. Shenhav argues that after the rise of nationalism in the region, and Zionist nationalism in particular, in order to be included in the national collective, the Arab-Jews had to be "de-Arabized", and their notion as Arab-Jews has been "forgotten or suppressed from collective Israeli memory".[17] According to Shenhav, religion came to be a mechanism for distinguishing Arabs from Arab-Jews, thus cultivating national identity among the Arab-Jews. Today, according to Tamari, the term "Arab-Jews" is widely considered to be full of contradictions, and even "an oxymoron".[18]

The writings of Ishaq Shami, an Arab-Jew, who lived in the early 20th century under Ottoman rule, mostly in Haifa, highlight the significant differences between the indigenous Arab-Jews in Palestine and Jews who emigrated from Europe. According to Shami, both groups had a distinctive social and cultural history, thus Zionism tried to transform the first group.[19]

BRITISH MANDATE AND THE DUAL TRACKS OF TRANSFORMATION

Much like in descriptions of life under the Ottoman rule, there is not much literature on the daily life or social and cultural interactions between the different communities in Haifa under the British Mandate. Most of the available historiographies of the period have been written from a national paradigm which resulted in abandonment of the history of Jewish communities in Arab and Muslim societies. Conversely, Zachary Lockman

---

[15] See Salim Tamari, *Mountain against the Sea: Essays on Palestinian Society and Culture* (2009), pp. 228-230.
[16] Abbas Shiblak, *The Lure of Zion; The Case of the Iraqi Jews* (1986), 2nd ed. published under the title *Iraqi Jews: History of Mass Exodus* (2005). Other scholars followed in using the term "Arab Jews" like Salim Tamari, Yehouda Shenhav, Ella Habiba Shohat, and Sasson Somekh.
[17] Shenhav (2006), p. 136.
[18] Tamari (2009), p. 226.
[19] Quoted by Tamari, "Ishaq al-Shami and the Predicament of the Arab Jew in Palestine", in ibid.

suggests the dual society paradigm as a lens by which Mandatory Palestine should be interpreted.[20]

In fact, one could argue that there were two main dynamics of transformation that had profound effects on community relations in Mandatory Palestine and best illustrated in the city of Haifa as the most mixed and prosperous city at the time. These two dynamics could be seen as contradicting in their motivations and directions: The first was the rapid development of the city as a successful colonial enterprise that allowed for a communal coexistence; the second was a parallel track of development that laid the ground for establishing "a Jewish national home" that motivated segregation and conflict.

The first dynamic seems to be essentially inclusive. From the outset, all communities were supposed to share the prosperity by creating more investments, more job opportunities and more daily human interactions among the various communities. It was a process that brought these communities together rather than segregated them. In this sense, Haifa was likely to be the most culturally diverse, open and tolerant city in Mandatory Palestine. It was a dynamic that was supposed to bring a sense of normality and peace based on economic developments.

The opening of the Kirkuk-Haifa oil pipeline, the railway warehouses and the oil refinery offered new job opportunities and attracted further investments in oil and chemical companies such as Imperial Chemical Industries (ICI), Shell, Vacuum Oil and IPC. The major expansion of the port, the airport, the improvement of roads network and railway links helped the city to be the main industrial city in Palestine within a short period of time. The trade and industrial directory of 1928 shows that Haifa's share constituted 90% of the total industry in the country with more than 35% of the total investment capital in the country.[21]

As a result of the developments Haifa experienced during those years, it became the fastest growing city in Palestine, expanding south and

---

[20] Zachary Lockman, *Comrades and Enemies: Arab and Jewish Workers in Palestine, 1906-1948* (1996). Scholars, such as Shmuel Noah Eisenstadt, Dan Horowitz and Moshe Lissak embraced this model. However, as Talal Asad points out, Palestinian Arabs play virtually no role whatsoever in Eisenstadt's analysis: the *Yishuv* appears to have developed in a vacuum, entirely disconnected from and uninfluenced by the Arab society in its midst. See Sari Hanafi, "Haifa and Its Refugees: The Remembered, the Forgotten and the Repressed", *Kyoto Bulletin of Islamic Area Studies* 3-1 (July 2009), pp. 176-191.

[21] Mahmoud Yazbak, *Arab Immigration into Haifa*, M.A. Thesis, University of Haifa (1987) (in Hebrew), p. 23.

west and becoming the administrative and economic center of Northern Palestine. The city became a magnet, attracting Arab entrepreneurs and labor force from neighboring countries and beyond, and it increasingly offered diversity with respect to the "other", and openness and tolerance towards the newcomers. The social, economic and cultural transformations of the city's communal life affected Arabs and Jews alike.[22]

However, there was little social interaction. This signifies the second dynamic which was essentially exclusive, divisive, and based, on the Jewish side, on segregation towards building a "Jewish National Home" in Palestine. The Zionist movement aspired to create parallel economies and administrative infrastructure in order to achieve its political goal, statehood. Indeed, the emergence of National Socialism in Germany and the persecution of Jews in Europe had encouraged large scale influx of Jewish immigrants to Palestinian in the 1930s. Ultimately, it constituted the seeds for forthcoming conflict that consequently led to bloodshed and the exodus of the majority of the Palestinian Arab inhabitants of the city, estimated to have been between 70,000 and 75,000.[23]

It was already under the influence of the Zionist ideology that Jews gradually preferred living in exclusively-Jewish neighborhoods and towns and not in mixed areas.[24] In Haifa, a significant number of Jews, namely those of European descent, moved to live in the newly established Jewish neighborhood, Herzliah, during the first decade of the 20th century. A number of Jews also moved out of Haifa's mixed neighborhoods either temporarily or permanently following the violence that erupted in 1929 and during the Palestinian Arab uprising of 1936-1939 against the immigration of Jews to Palestine. Nevertheless, large number of Jews remained living in Arab neighborhoods, and according to official British figures, until the late 1940s when violence broke out following the United Nations Partition Resolution 181 in November 1947, more than a third of the Jewish

---

[22] Sahar Huneidi, *Broken Trust: Herbert Samuel, Zionism and Palestinians* (2001). See also Yosi Ben-Artsi and Mordechai Naor, *Haifa and Its Development, 1918-1948* (1989) (in Hebrew); Daphna Sharfman (ed.), *The Secrets of Coexistence: Jews and Arabs in Haifa during the British Mandate in Palestine, 1920-1948* (2007).
[23] Benny Morris, *1948: A History of the First Arab-Israeli War* (2008); Ilan Pappé, *The Ethnic Cleansing of Palestine* (2006).
[24] On the creation of Mount Carmel as a segregated Jewish residential space, separated from Haifa's mixed city during the British Mandate, see Yosi Ben-Artsi, *The Creation of the Carmel as a Segregated Jewish Residential Space in Haifa 1918-1948* (2004) (in Hebrew).

community remained in Haifa's Arab neighborhoods such as *Wadi al-Nisnas, Wadi al-Salib* and *Hallisa*.[25]

Leftist and union activists worked closely together in the trade unions and the Communist Party, yet both seemed to be paralyzed or split when the conflict intensified and the nationalistic divide took over the class unity.[26] The same happened in the municipality when the Arab members resigned during the rebellion of 1936, which effectively paved the way for the Jewish council members to play a more dominant role in running the city.[27]

Moreover, not the entire Arab population of the city benefited from Haifa's boom. Indeed big landlord families such as Khayyat, Murad, Shukri, Qaraman, and Khuri owned large lands, while traders, construction contractors and industrialists had less. However, they had to compete with local Jewish traders and industrialists who had more resources and stronger links with the British authorities. More importantly, Arab entrepreneurs had to compete with foreign imported goods with little or no tax mainly by British but also by European-Jewish owned companies.[28] The conditions in rural areas were also declining, and *Fallahin* (farmers) suffered from the Mandatory policy as well. High taxes on agricultural land pushed the *Fallahin* to an unfair system of borrowing that led them to lose the land and work for the new owners or abandon working in agriculture and look for work in the city instead.[29]

With regards to living conditions, it was estimated at the end of 1945 that 40 % of the Arab residents of Haifa were living in slums. Figures at the time show that 27,000 Arabs and 3,700 Jews lived in the poor areas of

---

[25] Yazbak (1987), p. 139.
[26] Musa Budeiri, *The Palestine Communist Party 1919-1948; Arabs & Jews in the Struggle for Internationalism* (1979). See also Bulus Farah, *From the Ottoman to the Hebrew State* (1985) (in Arabic), and The League of National Liberation, "The Palestinian Problem and the Way to Resolve It", *Three Historical Documents* (January 2001).
[27] For background on relations between Jewish and Arab members in Haifa's municipal council, see Tamir Goren, *Cooperation in the Shadow of Confrontation: Arabs and Jews in Local Government in Haifa during the British Mandate* (2008) (in Hebrew).
[28] See the article by Mustafa Abbasi and David De Vries in this collection.
[29] Yazbak (1987), pp. 139-143. On Kababir's transformation from Fallahin to workers in Haifa see 'Udih (1980), pp. 31, 46-49, 80.

the city: the old city and the poor quarters of the suburbs such as *Hawwasa* and *Ard al-Ramil* between Haifa and Acre.[30]

As the violence broke out in November 1947, cracks started to appear between and among the local Arab leadership of Haifa, as well as in other cities, and with the national Palestinian leadership represented by the Mufti Hajj Amin al-Husayni, the head of the High Arab Committee, who was in exile in Lebanon at the time. Rashid al-Hajj Ibrahim, the leader of the National Committee of Haifa at the time, referred to disagreements with Amin al-Hussayni on the plan to defend the city and on his proposal for truce with the Zionist paramilitary groups to save the city. Hajj Ibrahim reported being rejected by al-Husayni and being received with deaf ears by the Haganah commanders.[31]

Although less apparent, there were disagreements also between the Haganah commanders and the civil Jewish leadership of the city. While the Haganah commanders, who, following the redeployment of the British forces, quickly took control of the city, called upon its Arab population to leave, the moderate Jewish Mayor Shabtai Levi, who until then seemed to believe that coexistence between the two communities was possible, was reported to have implored the city's Arabs to stay "with tears streaming down his face."[32] His calls, however, were brushed aside.

It is very doubtful that Haifa's local leadership could have changed the course of events. According to historian Benny Morris, a plan was designed to evacuate the Arabs "by attacks or fear of attacks".[33] Ilan Pappé introduces the terminology "ethnic cleansing" to describe the expulsion of the Palestinian Arabs.[34] The Haganah and other paramilitary groups began to carry out the plan in December 1947, a few days after the United Nations adopted the Partition Resolution.

According to Pappé, the fate of Haifa was sealed on 10 March 1948 when Zionist leaders and generals decided after a long period of

---

[30] A survey of Palestine is quoted by Yazbak (1987), pp. 139-143. Sheikh Nimr al-Khatib, a prominent Haifawi leader, estimated their number in 1947 to be 80,000 with no reference to source. Sheikh Nimr al-Khatib, *The Legacy of Nakba* (1951) (in Arabic).
[31] Rashid al-Hajj Ibrahim, *Defending Haifa and the Problem of Palestine: The Memoirs of Rashid al-Hajj Ibrahim, 1891-1953* (2005) (in Arabic).
[32] Quoted by Childers B. Eraskine, "The Other Exodus", *The Spectators*, 12 May 1961. On the collaboration between the British Army and the Haganah commanders during the redeployment of the British forces in Haifa see Motti Golani, *The British Mandate for Palestine, 1948: War and Evacuation* (2009), pp. 71-73 (in Hebrew).
[33] Benny Morris, *The Birth of the Palestinian Refugee Problem, 1947-1949* (1987), p. 59.
[34] Pappé (2006), p. 58.

deliberation, to finalize their master plan, Plan Dalet, to extend the cleansing to Palestine as a whole. Indeed, as Pappé mentions, there were times of coexistence, but "the early eruption of violence put a sad end to a relatively long history of workers' cooperation and solidarity in the mixed city of Haifa".[35] "The Jews," Pappé adds, "wanted the port city but without the 75,000 Palestinians who lived there, and in April 1948, they achieved their objective".[36] In July 1948, the Israeli military commander of Haifa forced the 3-5,000 Palestinians that still stayed in the city to move within 4 days from the various parts of the city where they were living into one single neighborhood, the crammed and small quarter of *Wadi al-Nisnas*, one of the city's poorest areas.[37] The rest became refugees and were listed in Israel as "absentees".

Indeed, the violence gave a major blow to the little trust remaining among the communities of Haifa. Their fate was taken over by the hands of the armed groups and the human stories were buried with the nationalist collective discourse.

HAIFA'S OTHER NARRATIVE: INTER-COMMUNAL INTERACTIONS IN 1947/1948

The extent to which growing hostility between communities affects each of their individuals is difficult to measure. The fact that 'Adnan Shiblak, a Muslim-Palestinian, still recalls that as a teenager in the 1940s he was fond of a young Jewish girl who emigrated from Poland and lived nearby in the same neighborhood of *Wadi al-Nisnas*, is only one evidence that shows how the tense atmosphere and the rising hostility during these years did not redefine what is affectionable for the non-adults.[38] For 'Adnan, the Jewish girl was not an enemy who should be hated. The fact that he recounted these feelings decades later highlights how what seemed normal to him as a teenager is understood in retrospect as an exceptional experience worth mentioning.

But there were other exceptions to the growing hostility, such as the case of Abu Muti' Qazaq, a Palestinian who is said to have saved the life of a Jew who lived in the neighborhood of *Wadi al-Salib*. This was at the

---

[35] Ibid.
[36] Ibid., p. 93.
[37] Ibid.
[38] Interviewed by A. Shiblak, London, 22 August 2009.

beginning of violence when some fighters from outside the neighborhood arrested a Jewish resident there and were on the verge of killing him.[39]

Fig. 4: Shiblak's house in Wadi al-Nisnas, with a Palestinian flag on the occasion of the prophet Muhammad birthday, 1935

Salma Qazaq, who was then a married woman in her 20s, also recalls the phone calls from her family's Jewish neighbors in *Wadi Al-Salib* and *Hadar ha-Carmel*, which continued even after her family moved to live in the German Colony which was a safer area.[40] The Jewish neighbors were updating the family on developments in the neighborhood, and alerting them when young men, members of the family, were wanted by the Haganah and thus should avoid returning to the neighborhood. Salma Qazaq recalls that their Jewish neighbors also helped her mother pay frequent visits to the family homes, which were under their protection, in order to bring stuff.

Can historiography ignore such accounts which are being recounted as personal experiences and which do not follow the hegemonic national narratives? As Olick and Robbins point out, the distinction between history and memory "is a matter of disciplinary power rather than of

---

[39] Zahiyyah Qazak (Shiblak), Interviewed by A. Shiblak, Oxford, 9 June 2004.
[40] This was confirmed by Mansour Al-Sharif, the son of the house owner in the German Colony, interviewed by A. Shiblak, 8 June 2009, Cairo.

epistemological privilege".[41] Thus, when compared to traditional historiography, oral histories can offer a perspective on events which is different from historiographies which are based on military, state, and diplomacy archives: the experience of women, of children, and of ordinary men. In fact, by expressing the awareness of the historicity of personal experience and of the individual's role in the history of society, oral histories can undermine the notion of "event" that is widely accepted in the established discipline of history.[42]

The following pages present and examine oral history interviews which reveal moments, opportunities, denials and deferrals of social interactions between Jews and Palestinians in Haifa in the midst of rising violence. The interviewees, both Jews and Palestinians, are the first generation to the 1947/1948 events in Haifa, and were, in fact, too young to participate in the events as described in institutional historiography. Therefore, it is mostly the perspective of children (boys and girls), from which we examine here inter-communal engagements.[43]

Miryam (Christian-Palestinian, born in Haifa, 1931)[44]

Miryam started her narrative with descriptions of 1948's events, delivering a sense of terror and confusion, partly because it was not always easy to tell who was who in the mixed-neighborhood of *Wadi al-Nisnas* where she lived:

> We left the house three days before the fall of Haifa. We were right in the middle of fighting between the Jews and the Arabs. Every night we heard the explosions. The last week was really difficult for us. We were alone, our neighbors had already left the house, and we were hit by some 100 bullets. When I climbed up to the second floor the Arabs shot at me because they

---

[41] Jeffrey K. Olick and Joyce Robbins, "Social Memory Studies: From 'Collective Memory' to the Historical Sociology of Mnemonic Practices", *Annual Review of Sociology* 24 (1998), pp. 105-140. For Olick and Robbins's discussion on oral history, see ibid., pp. 126-128.
[42] Alessandro Portelli, *The Battle of Valle Giulia: The Art of Dialogue in Oral History* (1997), p. 6. On the essentiality of personal narratives to the understanding of the Israeli-Palestinian conflict, see Efrat Ben-Ze'ev, *Remembering Palestine in 1948* (2011).
[43] All interviews conducted by Nathansohn were held in Hebrew, and the names of the interviewees were changed to obtain confidentiality. The excerpts are presented here with only minor editing, which keeps the content untouched, while translating the narrative from Hebrew to English and from an oral to a written form. See Rebecca Jones, "Blended Voices: Crafting a Narrative from Oral History Interviews", *Oral History Review* 31/1 (2004), pp. 23-42.
[44] Interviewed by Nathansohn, 26 August 2008.

thought I'm Jewish. It's only a miracle that I survived. *Why did they think you were Jewish?* Because it was a mixed neighborhood. Not only Arabs lived here. And those who shot didn't know who's who.

So one of our friends told us 'you're suffering enough, just leave'. When we left the house all the windows were already broken and the beds were covered with glass. We moved to my cousin's place, a block away. A couple of days later Haifa fell.

Later in the interview, Miryam brought some photographs, and in one of them, which was taken before the war, she is photographed with her classmates in the Christian Orthodox School (Figure 5).

Fig. 5: Miryam and her classmates in the Christian Orthodox School

Of all the girls you see here, some are Jewish. Almost all classes were in English, but when we went to Arabic classes, they went to Hebrew classes. After the war I was in touch only with one of them. Every class had some two-three Jewish girls. We even had Jewish neighbors. We rented the lower floor to a Jewish family who escaped from Germany before the Second World War. They had two boys and three girls, and we were playing together every day. One of the girls was coming to my place to play and to eat with us. There was no difference, and such good relationships between neighbors. […] There was no sense of me being an Arab and her being Jewish. It wasn't like that at all.

Miryam's narrative shows both the brutality of the attempts to rearrange the space and its population according to national categorizations, as well as the imperfect success in fulfilling this mission.

Leah and Nehama (Jewish sisters, born in Haifa in 1933 and 1935)[45]

As little girls, Leah and Nehama had an Arab nanny, named Mayy, who arrived in Haifa from Lebanon to take care of them and their little sister, Dalia, who was born in 1943. In order to communicate with Mayy, the sisters had to learn Arabic quickly. At that time both of their parents were already fluent in Arabic. Their mother was born in Jerusalem at the beginning of the 20th century, learned the language and used it, like many others. Their grandfather immigrated to Palestine in 1844, settled in Hebron, and learned Arabic there. Their story shows how everyday intimacy in the domestic sphere was stronger than the mobilization to national categories and led to a rescue attempt.

> *Nehama*: When our little sister Dalia was born, in 1943, our parents hired an Arab nanny from Lebanon, named Mayy, to take care of us three.
>
> *Regev*: Why from Lebanon?
>
> *Nehama*: Domestic workers came from Lebanon, from Syria...
>
> *Leah*: Look, our parents were very connected with the Arabs. There wasn't anything strange about it.
>
> *Nehama*: Jews and Arabs lived together, really together. So, when Mayy arrived, our father said: from now on we speak only Arabic at home. So I told him: Okay, just tell me how do you say in Arabic: 'Ma Ze?' [What's that?], and he replied: 'Shu Hada?' At night, when Mayy came to say goodnight, I was pointing at the window, and asking: *shu hada?* and she replied: *shubbak*. I was pointing at the door, asking: *shu hada?* – *Bab*. And you know what? Quickly we spoke fluent Arabic.
>
> *Leah:* We were very close to Mayy, and in 1947 mom told her that she's afraid that she's going to get hurt, so she advised her to move to her sister's place in Acre, because the atmosphere in Haifa was getting heated. Mayy left, and then, one day in 1948 she came back to the store where mom worked. Mom asked her: *'How did you get here? It's dangerous! How did you get here?'* Those days it wasn't easy to travel like that. So she replied that she took the risk in order to save us. But since she can't save us all, she only asks mom to give her Dalia. At least Dalia she could save. She wanted to save Dalia!

---

[45] Interviewed by Nathansohn, 8 August 2009.

Nehama: She said: '*They are going to slaughter*'. It was clear that they are going to slaughter all of us.

Leah: Mayy said: '*they are going to slaughter all of you so give her to me, I cannot save all of you so let me save Dalia*'. But mom refused and told her '*if they will slaughter her, they will slaughter all of u*'. Then Mayy went back. And today, when they come and tell me that Arabs were expelled from Haifa, I tell them: They ran away! They left the food on the table and they ran away! Because they were sure we're going to do to them what they were planning to do to us. They took whatever they had on them, got into boats and ran away in the direction of Acre. But no one expelled. They did not expel Arabs from Haifa. I tell you that from personal knowledge. And the proof is what Mayy did to save Dalia because they were planning to slaughter all of us.

When talking with Leah and Nehama about the larger context and experiences of Haifa in 1948, in particular, and about living in a mixed city in general, it was important for them to contextualize Mayy's story politically, and to relate it to their knowledge of the "new historians" with their claim of expulsion. "In memory," Dominick LaCapra argues, "one is both back there and here at the same time, and one is able to distinguish between (not dichotomize) the two. In other words, one remembers [...] what happened then without losing a sense of existing and acting now."[46] For Leah and Nehama, when relating their intersubjective experience to the here-and-now, their experience surpasses.

Joseph (Christian-Palestinian, born in Haifa, 1934)[47]

Like both of his parents, Joseph was born in Haifa. When the 1947/1948 war broke out he was 14 years old and was taken by his school teacher to Lebanon for a period which was planned to be of two weeks but ended up being three years. For Joseph, the 1947/1948 events should be understood as a "thunder" which disrupted all familiar relationships with the Jews. His narrative of the war is not restricted to violent clashes, but rather emphasizes the difference from the pre-war relationships. It started by describing what he remembered about the relationships with the Jews:

> Our family had many Jewish friends. We went together each year to Lebanon to spend some time there – ten, fifteen days. They all wore fez (*Tarbush*). We didn't know what is a Jew or what an Arab is. We called the Jews *Yahud Awlad-'Arab* [Jews of Arab descent]. [...] We didn't know what hatred is.

---

[46] Dominick LaCapra, *Writing History, Writing Trauma* (2001), p. 90.
[47] Interviewed by Nathansohn, 11 July 2007.

We were friends with many Jewish families, and there was no such thing that someone will harm the other. We didn't know what a Jew or what an Arab is.

As mentioned above, like in other mixed cities of that time, there was a great cultural proximity between Palestinian Arabs and Jews who had either lived in the area for several generations, or had emigrated from Muslim countries during the British Mandate. All spoke Arabic and shared a similar lifestyle. According to the description shared by Joseph, the formation of identity and difference through inter-group interactions was practiced simultaneously. Jews and Arabs had the same lifestyle, and supposedly did not know who was who. Emphasizing the cultural proximity, while at the same time mentioning that they used to call the Jews *Yahud Awlad-'Arab* indicates that distinctions were noticeable, but these were probably understood as based on religion, rather than on nationality.

According to Shenhav, the Arab-Jews (or *Yahud Awlad-'Arab*, in Joseph's narrative,) "have been forgotten or suppressed from collective Israeli memory".[48] Joseph's description shows how the relations between Arabs and Jews contained paradox and ambiguity, affirming both identity and difference.

When clashes in the city intensified, Joseph was taken to continue his studies in Lebanon, but two weeks before he left Haifa, there was a knock on the door:

> We were at home, on one of the evenings, when three guys knocked on our door. They entered with weapons, one of them spoke a little Arabic, asking – 'what are you doing here at home?' – We live here, we answered – 'There is no such a thing,' the man replied. He wanted to shoot at our father. My father started crying, kissing their feet, and said: 'We already have a son who disappeared, take whatever you want and leave the house'. My father begged, and they left the house.

When asked whether he knew who these three guys were, Joseph's reply showed familiarity with the various Zionist paramilitary groups of that time:

> You know, history repeats itself. During that war it was the same as what we have today among the Palestinians. There is the *Fatah*, there is *Hammas*, and there is the *Jihad Islami*. Same as it was back then with the Jewish forces: the *Palmach* and the *Haganah* – their handling of things was softer, but there

---
[48] Shenhav (2006), p. 136.

was the *Etzel* and the *Lechi* of Menahem Begin and Yitzhak Shamir and all this gang. They only knew how to kill. Whoever they caught they killed on the spot.

This intimacy with Zionist politics, so it appears, may have saved Joseph's father's life:

> So, my father begged and they left us and said: 'we'll come back tomorrow, and if you stay here we'll kill you'. We had many Jewish friends, so my father called them, and they said they will send someone from the *Haganah* to guard us. My father told the girls and my mother to leave, so they left to the village of *Pqi'a*, where my father's cousin lived. That was around February. Two weeks later I left for Lebanon.

In Joseph's experience, this simultaneity of various "others", those who come to evict, and those who offer to protect, was brought to an end with his departure to Lebanon as a refugee. Joseph was allowed to return to Haifa in 1951, and joined his family who was by then relocated to a house in *Wadi al-Nisnas*. Upon entering the house, Joseph found the place to be familiar. It was the house where a classmate of his had lived with his family before the war, a classmate who became a refugee and stayed in Lebanon, not being allowed to return.

Moshe (Jewish, born in Haifa, 1939)[49]

Moshe spent his childhood in the Hadar ha-Carmel neighborhood, which at that time was a Jewish neighborhood where people could live without having any contact with the Arab community. His story, therefore, reveals how events were experienced when no direct interactions between communities were practiced. Moshe's knowledge about events was channeled to him by other people. His narrative here shows how he got to learn about the other side by means ranging from rumors at the time when events were unfolding, to historiographies written decades later.

> My dad had this special diet, so my mom used to make him sandwiches, which I used to bring him every day to the bank where he worked. The bank was on Ha'halutz Street, and there, from both sides of the bank there was a protecting wall, which was built by the Jews as soon as the relations with the Arabs started to deteriorate, so it didn't bother my mom to send me with the sandwiches. There was a section I had to walk along the wall. It was a wall that was shot at from the other side. They didn't shoot at me. But it was

---

[49] Interviewed by Nathansohn, 6 July 2009.

known that they were shooting. I remember taking these sandwiches, and walking while bending down, although I really didn't need to because the wall was taller than I was. But you know, they tell you that they shoot. *Did you hear shootings yourself?* I don't remember shootings, but I remember the atmosphere. There were snipers, and in *Geulah* Street, for example, there was a segment of some 100 meters that it was forbidden to walk there. Although it was a Jewish neighborhood, it was right in the line of fire. *And your dad used to go to work every day?* Every day. *Even in April when there were real battles in the city?* Yes, yes. Life didn't stop for a single moment. Look, all this period of Haifa's pre-Occupation was very short. And look, I read today all kinds of new historians. It's all stories. I remember it as if it was today, I remember the loudspeakers, and I remember dad saying that it's Shabtai Levi calling the Arabs not to leave the city. I remember that. They cannot tell me all these stories on expulsion and stuff. *Did you know about Arabs leaving Haifa at that time?* We were kids, we didn't know exactly who left and who didn't leave.

As a young boy, the only means available for Moshe to learn about Haifa's Arabs was by various representations and mediators: the protecting wall, rumors about shootings, living room conversations with his father, and historiography, which he rejected when it contradicted his own memory, much like in Leah and Nehama's narrative.

Emil (Christian-Palestinian, born in Haifa, 1937)[50]

In 1948 I was a kid, aged ten, maybe nine, and everyone in Haifa heard that the priest in the church here was murdered. I remember it as if it just happened. Then this disorder in Haifa started. Some came to school to pick up their kids. And there was this high school kid that the teachers asked him to take me home. So we were climbing up on Stanton Street, today's *Shavei Tzion* Street, and then I saw some of the cars turned upside down, and a lot of guys, aged 15 or 16, each carried two pistols, standing in the corner. I still didn't understand it then, but my father realized that the situation was starting to deteriorate.

This story that I want to tell you, it moved me then and it is moving for me now. Down the street, there was a Jewish man, and he had a small workshop where he used to make wooden toys for kids. My brother used to work there (he was two years older than me). So there were these riots, after they killed the priest, and one day, two weeks later, that person came back to see what had happened with his business. He came at around seven in the

---

[50] Interviewed by Nathansohn, 12 June 2007.

evening, and people saw him, and started chasing after him. A lot of people chased after him. He climbed up the stairs close to our house and entered our neighbor's place. That neighbor was a well known figure in Haifa. And he protected him. I was standing at the door, looking outside to see what was happening. Those who chased after him were saying: hand him over to us, hand him over! So he replied: he came to my house, he is a human being. And then, after they had left, he released him.

Experiences like this, of rescuing the other during violent events, are rarely shared in descriptions of Haifa's 1947/1948 events. One may argue that these events carry no historical significance on the larger scale since historical significance could be determined only according to the effects of the event. Indeed, this act of rescue (much like the experiences shared by other interviewees) probably did not change the course of the war or the course of the Zionist-Palestinian conflict, although it might have saved one life. However, this event can be regarded as evidence for possibilities of alternative historical developments, as well as of alternative narrations of events. Seen in this light, experiences such as the one shared by Emil enrich our knowledge of how participants in the actual event, as well as participants in the act of narrating the event, negotiate and engage with their notions of self and other. The person who rescued, the person who was saved, the crowd that asked to hand him over, the observers, and the listeners/readers of the narrative – this event calls for inter-communal engagement from all of them, across time, space and identities.

CONCLUSION: FROM AN ALTERNATIVE PAST TO AN ALTERNATIVE PRESENT

What do these personal accounts teach us? As we have shown, a long history of inter-communal interaction, sometimes coupled with cultural and spatial proximity, cannot be assumed to be annulled and sweepingly surrendered to national divides. Clearly, the national conflict had – and still has – a forceful recruiting affect on individuals and communities. As Salma Qazaq recalls, when her family moved out from *Wadi al-Salib* to the German Colony due to the ongoing attacks, those who were members of the paramilitary Zionist forces were happy to see their backs. But at the same time, some of their Jewish neighbors were warning the family, and keeping them updated on the situation.

In his study on Haifa's Palestinian refugees, Hanafi argues that oral histories better reflect the social heterogeneity of the Palestinian society around the world, but they are often overlooked in favor of a unified national character.[51] What we have shown here is that personal accounts of interactions between people of different communities can also work against the narrative of a comprehensive national divide, as is so often reflected in traditional historiography.

Our effort here was not to ignore the dramatic events which had shaped the lives of generations of Palestinians and Jews but to work against the suppression of the residues of a long history of inter-communal relationships, which in some cases surpassed attempts to rearrange the social sphere according to a national logic. The non-binary and the indefinite possibilities are not a terrain comfortable for whoever is adopting the national logic of social life as a way to live, think, interact, and write histories. Institutional historians' narrations, and even more so – their silences and denials of human interaction, makes it difficult for a non-binary and ambiguous option to be developed in the visions of the past. The results of these silencing practices might be the sharpening of notions of difference: a difference between communities, and a difference between historical periods, where 1948 marks the break. As Nathansohn has written elsewhere,[52] the analysis of moments of intersubjectivity during the 1947/1948 violent events in Haifa can both create alternative forms of knowledge production and circulation, as well as contribute in forming new political possibilities in the context of the Israeli-Palestinian conflict. What we have tried to show here is that another past existed, thus also another present.

---

[51] Hanafi (2009).
[52] Regev Nathansohn, "Imagining Interventions: Coexistence from Below and the Ethnographic Project", *Collaborative Anthropologies* 3 (2010), pp. 93-101.

BIBLIOGRAPHY

ARCHIVAL COLLECTIONS

Central Zionist Archive (Jerusalem)
Haganah Archive (Tel Aviv)
Haifa City Archives (Haifa)
Haifa History Society Archives (Haifa)
Haifa Municipality Archives, Department of Conservation and Reservation (Haifa)
Haifa Municipality, Engineering Administration Archives (Haifa)
Israel State Archives (Jerusalem)
Labor Movement Archives, Lavon Institute (Tel Aviv)
Yad Yaari, Hashomer Hatsair Archives (Givat Haviva)

NEWSPAPERS

Al-Difa' (Jaffa)
'Al-Hamishmar (Tel Aviv)
Al-Ittihad (Jaffa)
Al-Karmil (Haifa)
Al-Madina (Haifa)
Al-Mihmaz (Haifa)
Davar (Tel Aviv)
Filastin (Jaffa)
Haaretz (Tel Aviv)
Hamashkif (Tel Aviv)
Hatzafon (Haifa)
Ma'ariv (Tel Aviv)
Palestine and Near East Economic Magazine, 1926-1932
Palestine Post (Jerusalem)
Ha-Tzvi (Jerusalem)

PUBLISHED PRIMARY SOURCES

Abbott, Andrew. "Temporality and Process in Social Llife", in Andrew Abbott, *Time Matters* (Chicago: The University of Chicago University Press, 2001), pp. 209-239.

Aharonowitz, Haimm. *Hadar ha-Carmel: Masekhet Amal ve-Yetzira shel Dor ha-Meyasdim ve-Habonim* [*Hadar ha-Carmel: A Story of the Labor and Creativity of the Generation of Founders and Builders*] (Haifa: Va'ad Hadar ha-Carmel, 1958) (in Hebrew).

Aleph, Yael (Editor and Documenter). *Beit ha-Qeshatot Wadi Salib Haifa*, Haifa Municipality, Long-term Planning Department, Physical Survey by Edward Kollick, Conservation Sphere (Jerusalem: Antiquities Authority, 1995) (in Hebrew).

BIBLIOGRAPHY

Al-Faqih, Khalid. "Naji al-'Ali's Biography" (*Kana'an e-Newsletter*, 9/1961, 23/7/2009).

Al-Hajj Ibrahim, Rashid. *Al-Difa' 'An Hayfa Wa-Qadiyyat Filastin, Mudhakarrat Rashid al-Hajj Ibrahim*, introduced by Walid al-Khalidi (Beirut: Mu'assasat al-Dirasat al-Filastinyya, 2005) (in Arabic).

Al-Hut, Bayan. *Al-Qiyadat w-al-Mu'sassat fi Filastin 1917-1948* (Acre: Al-Aswar, 1984) (in Arabic).

Al-Khatib, Sheikh Nimr. *The Legacy of Nakba* (Damascus: al-Mataba'a al-'Umumiyya, 1951) (in Arabic).

Al-Quds, Ibn. *The Qassami Commander 'Adnan Mahmud al Ghul* (2007).

Anderson, Benedict. *Imagined Communities: Reflections on the Origin and Spread of Nationalism* (London: Verso, 1991).

Anglo-American Committee of Inquiry on Jewish Problems in Palestine and Europe, Report (London: Her Majesty's Stationery Office, 1946).

Appadurai, Arjun. "The Production of Locality", in Arjun Appadurai, *Modernity at Large: Cultural Dimensions of Globalization* (Minneapolis: University of Minnesota Press, 1996), pp. 178-200.

'Asqalani, Gharib. *The Rain* (2009), www.daralkashkol.com (in Arabic).

Avitsur, Shmuel. *Apparatuses in Landscapes: Chapters in Palestine's Industrial Archeology* (Tel Aviv: Histadrut, 1994) (in Hebrew).

Avitsur, Shmuel. *Manufacturing: On the History of Industry in Palestine* (Tel Aviv: Milo, 1974) (in Hebrew).

Avitsur, Shmuel. "Nahum Wilbusch: From Traditional to New Industries", in *Inventors and Adaptors: The Makers of the Revolution in Palestine's Manufacturing* (Jerusalem: Yad Izhak Ben-Zvi, 1985), pp. 122-128 (in Hebrew).

Avitsur, Shmuel. "The Production of Olive Oil in the Galilee and Its Dimensions at the Beginning of the Century", *Ofakim be-Geografia* 20 (1987) (in Hebrew).

Azaryahu, Maoz and Rebecca Kook. "Mapping the Nation: Street Names and Arab-Palestinian Identity: Three Case Studies", *Nations and Nationalism* 8 (2002), pp. 195-213.

Azoulay, Ariella. *Consistent Violence, 1947-1950: A Genealogy of a Regime and 'the Catastrophe from Their Point of View'* (Tel Aviv: Resling, 2009) (in Hebrew).

Azoulay, Ariella. "With Open Doors: History Museums in the Israeli Public Space", *Teoria u-Vikoret (Theory and Criticism)* 4 (1993), pp. 79-95 (in Hebrew).

Bar On, Nili and Idit Shelomi. *Beit Tuma Simtat ha-Nevi'im 3 Haifa* [*Tuma House, 3 ha-Nevi'im Lane Haifa*], Documentation File, Sites Conservation Unit, Haifa Municipality (2010) (in Hebrew).

Barron, John B. (ed.). *Palestine Report and General Abstracts of the Census of 1922* (Jerusalem: Government of Palestine, Census Office, 1922).

Beck, Ulrich. "New Critical Theory with Cosmopolitan Intent", *Constellations* 10 (2003), pp. 453-468.

Ben Arieh, Yehoshua. "The Population of Large Towns in Palestine during the Eighty Years of the Nineteenth Century According to Western Sources", in Moshe Ma'oz (ed.), *Studies on Palestine during the Ottoman Period* (Jerusalem: Magness Press, 1975), pp. 49-69.

Ben-Artsi, Yosi, *From Germany to the Holy Land: Templar Settlement in Palestine* (Jerusalem: Yad Izhak Ben-Zvi, 1996) (in Hebrew).

Ben-Artsi, Yosi. "Ha-'Ir ha-'Atiqa (Haifa Betokh ha-Homot)" ["The Old City (Haifa within the Walls)"], *Haifa ve-Atareha* [Haifa and Its Sites], *Ariel Ketav Et le-Yedi'at Eretz Yisrael* 37-39 (1985), pp. 201-204 (in Hebrew).

Ben-Artsi, Yosi. *The Creation of the Carmel as a Segregated Jewish Residential Space in Haifa 1918-1948* (Jerusalem: Magnes, 2004) (in Hebrew).

Ben-Artsi, Yosi and Mordechai Naor. *Haifa and Its Development, 1918-1948* (Jerusalem: Yad Izhak Ben-Zvi, 1989) (in Hebrew).

Ben-Bassat, Yuval. "On Telegraph and Justice: The Petitions of Residents of Jaffa and Gaza to the Great Wazir of Istanbul in the Late Nineteenth Century", *The New East* 49 (2010), pp. 30-52 (in Hebrew).

Ben-Ze'ev, Efrat. *Remembering Palestine in 1948* (Cambridge, N.Y.: Cambridge University Press, 2011).

Bernstein, Deborah S. *Constructing Boundaries: Jewish and Arab Workers in Mandatory Palestine* (Albany, N.Y.: State University of New York Press, 2000).

Bigger, Gideon. "Shekhunot ha-Ganim – Tikhnunan ve-Hitpathutan be-Reishit ha-Shilton ha-Briti, 1917-1925" ["The Garden Neighborhoods – Their Planning and Development in the Early Years of British Rule, 1917-1925"], *Katedra* 6 (1977) (in Hebrew).

Bitan, A. and P. Ben-Rubi. "The Distribution of Snow in Israel", *Geojournal*, Vol. 2/6 (1978), pp. 557-567.

Bontemps, Véronique. "Mémoire et Identité locale. L'industrie du Savon à Naplouse", in David Meulemans (ed.), *La Mémoire, Outil et Objet de Connaissance* (Paris: Aux Forges de Vulcain, 2008), pp. 213-235.

Budeiri, Musa. *The Palestine Communist Party 1919-1948; Arabs & Jews in the Struggle for Internationalism* (London: Ithaca Press, 1979).

Burke, Peter. "The Invention of Leisure in Early Modern Europe", *Past and Present* 149 (February 1995), pp. 136-150.

Buroway, Michael. "What Is to Be Done? Theses on the Degradation of Social Existence in a Globalizing World", *Current Sociology*, Vol. 56/3 (2008), pp. 351-359.

Campos, Michelle U. *Ottoman Brothers. Muslims, Christians, and Jews in Early Twentieth-Century Palestine* (Stanford, California: Stanford University Press, 2011).

Candea, Matei. "Arbitrary Locations: In Defense of the Bounded Field-Site", *Journal of the Royal Anthropological Institute* 13 (2007), pp. 167-184.

Carmel, Alex. *Haifa under the Ottomans* (Haifa: Haifa University's Jewish-Arab Centre, 1977) (in Arabic).

Carmel, Alex. *The German Settlement in the Holy Land by the End of the Ottoman Era* (Haifa: Haifa University and the Society for the Protection of Nature in Israel, 1990) (in Hebrew).
Carmel, Alex. *The History of Haifa under Turkish Rule* (Haifa: Haifa University, 1977 and 2002, 4th ed.) (in Hebrew).
Carmel, Alex. "The Templars' Community House and School in Haifa: The German Settlers in Palestine", in *Between the Mountain and the Sea*, Exhibit Catalogue (Haifa: Haifa City Museum, 2000), pp. 152-156.
Carmeli, Amos, Shlomo Shhori and Ariela Hareuveni (eds.). *Haifa 1948-1968 – Events of 20 Years* (Tel Aviv: Davar Publishing House, 1968) (in Hebrew).
Cassirer, Ernst. *An Essay on Man: An Introduction to a Philosophy of Human Culture* (New Haven: Yale University Press, 1962).
Casto, Ray E. "Economic Geography of Palestine", *Economic Geography* 13/3 (July 1937), pp. 235-259.
Chakrabarti, Dipesh. "The Climate of History: Four Theses", *Critical Inquiry* (Winter 2009).
Childers, Eraskine, B. "The Other Exodus", *The Spectators*, 12 May 1961, London.
Cohen, Shaul Ephraim. *The Politics of Planting: Israeli-Palestinian Competition for Control of Land in the Jerusalem Periphery* (Chicago: University of Chicago Press, 1993).
Darwazza, Muhammad 'Izzat. *One Hundred Palestinian Years*, Vol. I (Damascus: Matba'at Samed, 1984) (in Arabic).
David, Tova and Tzilla Reiser. *Seqer Eikhuyot le-Shimur be-Shekhunat Abbas be-Haifa* [*Qualities Survey for Conservation in the 'Abbas Neighborhood of Haifa*] (Haifa: Haifa Municipality, Engineering Administration, Long-term Planning Department, Building Conservation Unit, 2004) (in Hebrew).
Davidon, Yaakov. *Hayyo hayta haifa* (Haifa: May, 1952) (in Hebrew).
De Vries, David. *Idealism and Bureaucracy in 1920s Palestine: The Origins of 'Red Haifa'* (Tel Aviv: Hakibbutz Hameuchad, 1999) (in Hebrew).
Diamond, Jared. *Collapse: How Societies Chose to Fail or Succeed* (N.Y.: Penguin, 2005).
Doumani, Beshara. *Rediscovering Palestine: Merchants and Peasants in Jabal Nablus, 1700-1900* (Berkeley: University of California Press, 1995).
El-Eini, Roza I.M. "Trade Agreements and the Continuation of Tariff Protection Policy in Mandate Palestine in the 1930s", *Middle Eastern Studies* 34/1 (January 1998), pp. 164-191.
El-Eini, Roza I.M. *Mandated Landscape: British Imperial Rule in Palestine, 1929-1948* (London & New York: Routledge, 2006).
Fabian, Johannes. *Time and the Other* (N.Y.: Columbia University Press, 1983).
Farah, Bulus. *From the Ottoman to the Hebrew State* (1985) (in Arabic)
Farah, Bulus. *Meha-shilton ha-'othmani la-medina ha-'ivrit*, translated by Udi Adiv and Yusuf Mansour (Haifa, 2009) (in Hebrew).
Farah, Bulus. *Min al-'Uthmaniyya ila l-Dawla l-'Ibriyya* (Haifa: al-Sawt, 1985) (in Arabic).

Friedland, Uriel. "Palestine's Oil Industry", *The Palestine Economist Annual* (1948), pp. 102-106 (in Hebrew).
Garden Towers on Red Roofs: The Campaign for the Preservation of the German Colony in Haifa (Haifa: Council for the Preservation of Buildings and Settlement Sites and Society for the Protection of Nature, 1992) (in Hebrew).
Gerber, Haim. "The Population of Syria and Palestine in the Nineteenth Century", *Asian and African Studies* 13 (1979), pp. 58-80.
Gilbar, Gad. "Megamot ba-hitpathut ha-demografit shel 'arviyei eretz Israel", *Katedra* 45 (1987), pp. 43-56 (in Hebrew).
Gilbar, Gad. "Trends in the Demographic Development of the Palestinians, 1870-1914", *Sekirot* 108 (1989), pp. 3-59 (in Hebrew).
Golan, Arnon. "The War of Independence in the Mixed Towns of Palestine", in Yair Safran (ed.), *Haifa in 1948: A Collection of Articles, 60 Years of the State of Israel* (Haifa: Haifa History Society, 2008) (in Hebrew).
Golani, Motti. *The British Mandate for Palestine, 1948: War and Evacuation* (Jerusalem: The Zalman Shazar Center for Jewish History, 2009) (in Hebrew).
Goldman, Dan. *The Architecture of the Templars in Their Colonies in Eretz-Israel, 1868-1948, and Their Settlements in the United States, 1860-1925*, PhD Dissertation (Cincinnati, Ohio: The Union Institute and University, 2003).
Gonen, Amiram. *Between City and Suburb: Urban Residential Patterns and Processes in Israel* (Avebury: Aldershot, 1995).
Goodsell, Charles T. "The Concept of Public Space and Its Democratic Manifestations", *American Review of Public Administration* 33/4 (December 2003), pp. 361-383.
Goren, Tamir. *Cooperation in the Shadow of Confrontation: Arabs and Jews in Local Government in Haifa during the British Mandate* (Ramat Gan: Bar Ilan University Press 2008) (in Hebrew).
Goren, Tamir. "Ganim tziburiyyim ve-tipuah ha-'ir bi-tquftat ha-mandat", in Yair Safran (ed.), History of Haifa Association, *Haifa be-tashah, 1948* (Haifa: History of Haifa Association, 2008), issue No. 5, pp. 5-12 (in Hebrew).
Goren, Tamir. *Haifa ha-Aravit be-Tashah: Otzmat ha-Ma'avak u-Meimadei ha-Hitmotetut* [*Arab Haifa in 1948: The Intensity of the Struggle and the Dimensions of the Collapse*] (Beersheba: Ben-Gurion Institute, Ben-Gurion University/Ministry of Defense, Haganah History Archive, 2006) (in Hebrew).
Goren, Tamir. *Iriah Meshutefet be-Ir Me'urevet: Hitgabshuto u-Fo'alo shel ha-Shilton ha-Munitzipali be-Haifa be-Tequfat ha-Mandat* [*A Joint Municipality in a Mixed City: The Crystallization and Operation of the Municipal Authority in Haifa during the Mandate Period*], PhD Dissertation (Haifa: Haifa University, 2000) (in Hebrew).
Goren, Tamir. *Mitlut le-Hishtalvut: Ha-Shilton ha-Yisra'eli ve-Arviei Haifa, 1948-1950: Behina Historit ve-Geografit* [*From Dependence to Integration: The Israeli Regime and Haifa's Arabs, 1948-1950: A Historical and*

Geographical Examination], Part 2 (Haifa: Haifa University, The Jewish-Arab Center, 1996) (in Hebrew).

Goren, Tamir. "Naming the Streets of the City during the British Mandate", *Haifa: Journal of the Haifa History Society* 4 (2004), pp. 2-13 (in Hebrew).

Goren, Tamir. "The History of the Disappearance of the Old City from the Haifa Landscape", *Ofakim be-Geografia* 40-41 (1994), pp. 57-81 (in Hebrew).

Government of Palestine. *A Survey of Palestine: Prepared in December 1945 and January 1946 for the Information of the Anglo-American Committee of Inquiry* (Jerusalem: Government Printer, 1946).

Government of Palestine. *Palestine Royal Commission Report* (London: Her Majesty's Stationery Office, 1937).

Government of Palestine. *Report by His Majesty's Government in the United Kingdom of Great Britain and Northern Ireland to the Council of the League of Nations on the Administration of Palestine and Trans-Jordan for the Year 1929* (London: Colonial Office, 1930).

Gozansky, Tamar. *The Development of Capitalism in Palestine* (Tel Aviv: Mifalim Universitaiim, 1988) (in Hebrew).

Gross, Nachum. "Haifa at the Beginning of Jewish Industrialization in Palestine", *Riv'on Le-Kalkala* (September 1980), pp. 308-319 (in Hebrew).

Grossman, David. *The Yellow Wind* (New York: Farrar, Straus, and Giroux, 1988) (Original title in Hebrew: *Ha-zeman ha-tsahov* (*The Yellow Time*) (Jerusalem: Keter, 1987)).

Hacohen, David. *Et Lesaper* [*Time to Relate*] (Tel Aviv: Am Oved, 1974) (in Hebrew).

Haifa City Museum. *Between the Mountain and the Sea*, Exhibit Catalogue (Haifa: Haifa City Museum, 2000) (in Hebrew).

Haifa City Museum. *Crossed Histories*, Exhibit Catalogue (Haifa: Haifa City Museum, 2007) (in Hebrew).

Haifa City Museum. *Haifa, 1948-1958: City of the Present*, Exhibit Catalogue (Haifa: Haifa City Museum, 2008) (in Hebrew).

Haifa Labor Council. *The Histadrut in Haifa, 1933-1939* (Haifa: Histadrut, 1939) (in Hebrew).

Halbwachs, Maurice. *On Collective Memory* (NY: Harper & Row Colophon Books, 1980).

Hanafi, Sari. "Haifa and Its Refugees: The Remembered, the Forgotten and the Repressed", *Kyoto Bulletin of Islamic Area Studies* 3-1 (July 2009), pp. 176-191.

Handelman, Don. "Micro-historical Anthropology: Towards a Prospective Perspective", in Don Kalb and Herman Tak (eds.), *Critical Junctions: Pathways beyond the Cultural Turn* (Oxford and New York: Berghahn Books, 2004).

Hasan, Manar. *Ha-Nishkahot: ha-'Ir ve-hanashim ha-falestiniyot, ve-hamilhama 'al ha-zikaron*, unpublished PhD Dissertation (Tel Aviv: Tel Aviv University, 2009) (in Hebrew).

Huneidi, Sahar. *Broken Trust: Herbert Samuel, Zionism and Palestinians* (London and New York: I.B. Tauris, 2001).
Ibrahim, Hanna (ed.). *Hanna Naqqara: Muhami al-Ard wa l-Sha'b* (Acre: Dar al-Aswar, 1985) (in Arabic).
Ighbariyya, Husayn. *Haifa – al-Ta'rikh wa l-Dhakira* (Haifa: The Social Development Committee, 2001) (in Arabic).
Jabarin, Yusuf R. "The Meaning of Place among Jews and Arabs: The German Colony in Haifa as a Space of Trust", *Ofakim be-Geografia* 73-74 (2009), pp. 194-213 (in Hebrew).
Jackson, Michael. *Minima Ethnographica: Intersubjectivity and the Anthropological Project* (Chicago: University of Chicago Press, 1998).
Joha, Michelle. *Mary 'Ajami* (Beirut: Riyad al-Rayyis l'il Kitab w'al-nashr, 2001) (in Arabic).
Jones, Rebecca. "Blended Voices: Crafting a Narrative from Oral History Interviews", *Oral History Review* 31/1 (2004), pp. 23-42.
Kabha, Mustafa. "Hayei ha-tarbut be-haifa ha-'aravit be-shalhey ha-mandat", in Yair Safran (ed.), History of Haifa Association, *Haifa be-tashah, 1948* (Haifa: History of Haifa Association, 2008), issue No. 5 (in Hebrew).
Kamen, Charles. "After the Disaster: The Arabs in Israel, 1948-1950", *Mahbarot le-Mehkar u-le-Vikoret* 10 (1984), pp. 5-91 (in Hebrew).
Kanafani, 'Abd al-Latif. *15 Shari' al-burj – Haifa, dhikrayat wa-'ibar* (Beirut: Baysān, 1996) (in Arabic).
Karlinsky, Nachum and Avi Bareli (eds.). *Economy and Society in Mandatory Palestine, 1918-1948* (Beer Sheva: Ben-Gurion University, 2003) (in Hebrew).
Katriel, Tamar. *Performing the Past: A Study of Israeli Settlement Museums* (Mahwah, New Jersey and London: Lawrence Erlbaum Associates, 1997).
Khalaf, Issa. "The Effect of Socioeconomic Change on Arab Social Collapse in Mandate Palestine", *International Journal of Middle Eastern Studies* 29 (1997), pp. 93-112.
Khasawneh, Diala. *Memories Engraved in Stone: Palestinian Urban Mansions* (Ramallah: Riwaq Center for Architectural Conservation and the Institute of Jerusalem Studies, 2001).
Khuri, Yusuf (ed.). *Al-Sahafa l-'Arabiyya fi Filastin, 1876-1948* (Baqa al-Gharbiyya: Dar al-Shams, 1992) (in Arabic).
Kimmerling, Baruch and Joel Migdal. *The Palestinian People: A History* (Cambridge Mass.: Harvard University Press, 2003).
Klein, Itzhak. "The Arabs in Haifa under the British Mandate: A Political, Economic and Social Survey", *Occasional Papers on the Middle East* (Haifa: Haifa University), No. 5 (1987) (in Hebrew).
Koestler, Arthur. *Arrow in the Blue* (New York: McMillan, 1952).
Korsholm Nielsen, Hans Chr. and Jakob Skovgaard-Petersen. "Introduction: Public Places and Public Spheres in Transformation – The City Conceived, Perceived and Experienced", in Hans Chr. Korsholm Nielsen and Jakob

Skovgaard-Petersen (eds.), *Middle Eastern Cities 1900-1950* (Aarhus: Aarhus University Press, 2001), pp. 9-19.

Kroll, Zvi (ed.). *The Oil Jug: Shemen's Twenty Year Anniversary* (Haifa: Shemen, 1945) (in Hebrew).

Kushner, David. *Palestine in the Late Ottoman Period* (Jerusalem: Yad Izhak Ben-Zvi, 1986).

LaCapra, Dominick. *Writing History, Writing Trauma* (Baltimore: Johns Hopkins University Press, 2001).

Levine, Michael. *'Ir Levana, Adrikhalut ha-Signon ha-Beinle'umi be-Yisra'el, Diuqana shel Tequfa* [*White City: The Architecture of the International Style in Israel, Portrait of a Period*] (Tel Aviv: Tel Aviv Museum and the Jewish Museum of New York, 1984) (in Hebrew).

Levy, Dalia. *Seqer Shimur Beit Majdalani, Rehov Yavneh 3, Haifa* [*Conservation Survey of Majdalani House, 3 Yavneh Street, Haifa*] (Haifa: Sites Conservation Unit, Haifa Municipality, 2001) (in Hebrew).

Lloyd, Edward Mayow Hastings. *Food and Inflation in the Middle East, 1940-45* (Stanford: Stanford University Press, 1956).

Lockman, Zachary. *Comrades and Enemies: Arab and Jewish Workers in Palestine, 1906-1948* (Berkeley: University of California Press, 1996).

Malak, Hana. *Al-Judhur al-yafiyya* (Jerusalem: Matba'at al-Sharq al-'Arabiyya, 1996) (in Arabic).

Manderstam, L.H. "Continuous Hydrogenation in the Oil Hardening Industry", *Journal of the American Oil Chemists' Society* 16/9 (September 1939), pp. 166-172.

Mansour, Johnny. "Ha-'aravim be-haifa bi-tqufat ha-mandat ha-briti, hitpathuyot u-tmurot hevratiot, kalkaliot ve-tarbutiot", in Dafna Sharfman and Eli Nahmias (eds.), *Tei al Mirpeset ha-Qazino, Du-Qium be-Haifa be-Tequfat ha-Mandat ha-Briti 1920-1948* [*Tea on the Casino Verandah: Coexistence in Haifa during the British Mandate Period 1920-1948*] (Haifa: Mishpaton, 2006), pp. 239-301 (in Hebrew).

Mansour, Johnny. *Haifa Arab Streets* (Haifa: The Social Development Committee, 1999) (in Arabic).

Mansour, Johnny. *Hajazi Railway Line: History and Development of Dir'a-Haifa Rail* (Jerusalem: Institute of Jerusalemite Studies, 2008) (in Arabic).

Mansour, Johnny. "The Hijaz-Palestine Railway and the Development of Haifa", *Jerusalem Quarterly* 28 (2006), pp. 5-21.

Marcinkowski, Nelly. *Rain on a Clear Day* (Haifa: Society for the Protection of Nature and Council for the Preservation of Buildings and Settlement Sites, 1994) (in Hebrew).

Mazzotti, Massimo. "Enlightened Mills: Mechanizing Olive Oil Production in Mediterranean Europe", *Technology and Culture* 45/2 (2004), pp. 277-304.

Meri, Josef W. "Re-appropriating Sacred Space: Medieval Jews and Muslims Seeking Elijah and al-Khadir", in Larry J. Simon (ed.), *Medieval Encounters: Jewish, Christian and Muslim Culture in Confluence and Dialogue* 5 (1999), pp. 1-28.

Metzer, Jacob. "Economic Growth and External Trade in Mandatory Palestine: A Special Mediterranean Case", in Sevket Pamuk and Jeffrey G. Williamson (eds.), *The Mediterranean Response to Globalization before 1950* (London & New York: Routledge, 2000), pp. 363-383.

Metzer, Jacob. *The Divided Economy of Mandatory Palestine* (Cambridge: Cambridge University Press 2002).

Morris, Benny. *1948: A History of the First Arab-Israeli War* (New Haven: Yale University Press, 2008).

Morris, Benny. *1948: The Annals of the First Arab-Israeli War* (Tel Aviv: Am Oved, 2010) (in Hebrew).

Morris, Benny. *The Birth of the Palestinian Refugee Problem, 1947-1949* (Cambridge: Cambridge University Press, 1987).

Morris, Benny. *The Birth of the Palestinian Refugee Problem Revisited* (Cambridge: Cambridge University Press, 2004).

Morris, Benny. *The Origins of the Palestinian Refugee Problem* (Oxford: Clarendon Press, 1994).

Nadan, Amos. *The Palestinian Peasant Economy under the Mandate: A Story of Colonial Bungling* (Cambridge, Mass.: Harvard University Press, 2006).

Nahmias, Eli. "Aravim ve-Yehudim be-shuq Avoda Dinami ve-Energeti be-Haifa ha-Mandatorit" ["Arabs and Jews in a Dynamic and Energetic Labor Market in Mandatory Haifa"], in Dafna Sharfman and Eli Nahmias (eds.), *Tei al Mirpeset ha-Qazino, Du-Qium be-Haifa be-Tequfat ha-Mandat ha-Briti 1920-1948* [*Tea on the Casino Verandah: Coexistence in Haifa during the British Mandate Period 1920-1948*] (Haifa: Mishpaton, 2006) (in Hebrew).

Nathansohn, Regev. "Imagining Interventions: Coexistence from Below and the Ethnographic Project", *Collaborative Anthropologies* 3 (2010), pp. 93-101.

Nimr, Ihsan. *The History of Nablus Mountain and Balqa*, Vol. II (Nablus: Matba'at al-Nasir, 1961) (in Arabic).

Olick, Jeffrey K. and Joyce Robbins. "Social Memory Studies: From 'Collective Memory' to the Historical Sociology of Mnemonic Practices", *Annual Review of Sociology* 24 (1998), pp. 105-140.

Orell, Aluf and Dror Orell. *Binyamin Orell: Adrikhal Lelo Diploma* [*Binyamin Orell: Architect without a Diploma*] (Haifa: Private Publication, 2008) (in Hebrew).

Owen, Roger (ed.). *Studies in the Economic and Social History of Palestine in the Nineteenth and Twentieth Century* (London: Macmillan, 1982).

Pappé, Ilan. *The Ethnic Cleansing of Palestine* (Oxford: Oneworld, 2006).

Pappé, Ilan. "Urbicide in Haifa", *Mediterraneans* 14 (2010), pp. 123-129.

Peled, Amatzia (ed.). *A Street Guide to Haifa* (Haifa: University of Haifa and the Municipality of Haifa, 2007) (in Hebrew).

Philipp, Thomas. *Acre: The Rise and Fall of a Palestinian City, 1730-1831* (New York: Columbia University Press, 2001).

Portelli, Alessandro. *The Battle of Valle Giulia: The Art of Dialogue in Oral History* (Madison, Wis.: University of Wisconsin Press, 1997).

Qaraman, Su'ad. *Hoveret Ma'amarim: Haifa Maqom le-Ta'asiya, Atidam shel Mivnim Historiyim* [*Collection of Articles: Haifa as a Site for Industry, the Future of Historic Buildings*] (Haifa: The Center for the Study of Architectural Heritage, the Technion, 2009) (in Hebrew).

Rabinowitz, Dan. "'The Arabs Just Left': Othering and the Construction of Self amongst Jews in Haifa Before and After 1948", in Daniel Monterescu and Dan Rabinowitz (eds.), *Mixed Towns, Trapped Communities: Historical Narratives, Spatial Dynamics, Gender Relations and Cultural Encounters in Palestinian-Israeli Towns* (Aldershot: Ashgate, 2007), pp. 51-64.

Rabinowitz, Dan and Khawla Abu-Baker. *Coffins on Our Shoulders: The Experience of the Palestinian Citizens of Israel* (Berkeley: University of California Press, 2005).

Ramón-Muñoz, Ramón. "Specialization in the International Market for Olive Oil before World War II", in Sevket Pamuk and Jeffrey G. Williamson (eds.), *The Mediterranean Response to Globalization before 1950* (London & New York: Routledge, 2000), pp. 159-198.

Rashid, Harun Hashim. *Haifa wa l-Buhayri: Madina wa-Sha'ir* (Damascus: Dar al-Hayat, 1975) (in Arabic).

Raz, Danny and Semadar Raz. *Heikhal Iriat Haifa – Seqer Miqdami* [*The Haifa Municipality Building – Preliminary Survey*] (Haifa: Haifa Municipality, 2008) (in Hebrew).

Roll, Itzhak and Yaakov Yasuur. "Shemen and the Development of Jewish Haifa", in *Haifa – 1954: Municipality Book* (Haifa: Haifa Municipality, 1955), pp. 270-273 (in Hebrew).

Ron, Mordechai. *Haifa shel yemei yalduti (The Haifa of My Youth)* (Jerusalem: Ariel, 1993) (in Hebrew).

Rosenzweig, Rafael N. *The Economic Consequences of Zionism* (Leiden & New York: E.J. Brill, 1989).

Rotbard, Sharon. *'Ir Levana, 'Ir Shehora* [*White City, Black City*] (Tel Aviv: Bavel, 2005) (in Hebrew).

Said, Himadeh B. *Economic Organization of Palestine* (Beirut: American University Press, 1939).

Scholch, Alexander. *Palestine in Transformation 1856-1882* (Washington, D.C.: Institute for Palestine Studies, 1993).

Seikaly, May. *Haifa: Transformation of a Palestinian Arab Society, 1918-1939* (London: I.B. Tauris, 1995).

Seikaly, Sherene. *Meatless Days: Consumption and Capitalism in Wartime Palestine 1939-1948*, unpublished PhD Dissertation (New York University, 2007).

Sharfman, Daphna. "Ha-anashim, ha-eru'im veha-meqomot she-'assu historya", in Daphna Sharfman and Eli Nahmias (eds.), *Tei al Mirpeset ha-Qazino, Du-Qium be-Haifa be-Tequfat ha-Mandat ha-Briti 1920-1948* [*Tea on the Casino Verandah: Coexistence in Haifa during the British Mandate Period 1920-1948*] (Haifa: Mishpaton, 2006), pp. 173-238 (in Hebrew).

Sharfman, Daphna (ed.). *The Secrets of Coexistence: Jews and Arabs in Haifa during the British Mandate in Palestine, 1920-1948* (Booksurge, 2007).

Shenhav, Yehouda. *The Arab Jews: A Postcolonial Reading of Nationalism, Religion, and Ethnicity* (Stanford, California: Stanford University Press, 2006).

Shiblak, Abbas. *Iraqi Jews: History of Mass Exodus* (London: Saqi Books, 2005).

Simmel, George. "The Metropolis and Mental Life", in Gary Bridge and Sophie Watson (eds.), *The Blackwell City Reader* (Malden, M.A.: Blackwell, 2002).

Smith, Barbara. *The Roots of Separatism in Palestine: British Economic Policy, 1920-1929* (Syracuse: Syracuse University Press, 1993).

Sofer, Arnon. *Industrial Location in Haifa Bay Area*, PhD Dissertation (Jerusalem: Hebrew University, 1971) (in Hebrew).

Sorek, Tamir. "Leumiyut Falastinit ba-medina ha-mandatorit: medor ha-sport ke-sokhen zehut", *Zmanim* (Tel Aviv), 70 (Spring 2000), pp. 15-22 (in Hebrew).

Sorek, Tamir. *Zehuyot be-mishaq* (Jerusalem: Magnes, 1996) (in Hebrew).

Stein, Kenneth W. *The Land Question in Palestine, 1917-1939* (Chapel Hill: University of North Carolina Press, 1984).

Stern, Shimon. *The Development of Haifa's Urban Network, 1918-1947*, PhD Dissertation (Jerusalem: Hebrew University, 1974) (in Hebrew).

Tamari, Salim. *Mountain against the Sea: Essays on Palestinian Society and Culture* (Berkeley: University of California Press, 2009).

Tamari, Salim. "The Vagabond Café and Jerusalem's Prince of Idleness", in Salim Tamari, *Mountain against the Sea: Essays on Palestinian Society and Culture* (Berkeley: University of California Press, 2009), pp. 176-189.

'Udih, 'Abdullah. *The History of Kababir Village until the End of the British Mandate* (Shafa 'Amr: Dar Al-Mashriq, 1980) (in Arabic).

Vashitz, Yosef. *Ha-'Aravim be-eretz Israel: kalkala ve-hevra, tarbut u-mediniyut* (Merhavya: Sifriyat Po'alim, 1947) (in Hebrew).

Vashitz, Yosef. "Social Changes in Arab Society during the British Mandate: Merchants, Entrepreneurs and Others", in Nachum Karlinsky and Avi Bareli (eds.), *Economy and Society in Mandatory Palestine, 1918-1948* (Beer Sheva: Ben-Gurion University, 2003), pp. 393-439 (in Hebrew).

Vashitz, Yosef. *Social Changes in Haifa's Arab Society under the British Mandate*, unpublished PhD Dissertation (Jerusalem: Hebrew University, 1993) (in Hebrew).

Vatikiotis, P.J. *Among Arabs and Jews* (London: Weidenfeld and Nicolson, 1991).

Weiss, Yfaat. *A Confiscated Memory: Wadi Salib and Haifa's Lost Heritage* (New York: Columbia University Press 2011).

Weiss, Yfaat. *Wadi Salib: ha-Nokheiah veha-Nifqad* (Jerusalem: Van Leer Institute and Ha-kibbutz ha-Me'uhad, 2007) (in Hebrew).

Wirth, Louis. "Urbanism as a Way of Life", *American Journal of Sociology* 44(1) (July 1938), pp. 1-24.

Yakhluf, Yahya. *Water from the Sky/A Novel* (Amman: Dar al-Shuruq, 2008).

Yazbak, Mahmoud. *Administrative Systems and Social Structures in Haifa at the Late Ottoman Period (1870-1914)* (Nazareth: al Nahda, 1994) (in Arabic).

Yazbak, Mahmoud. *Al-Hijra al-'Arabiyya Ila Hayfa fi Zaman al-Intidab* (Nazareth, 1988) (in Arabic).

Yazbak, Mahmoud. *Arab Immigration during the Mandate Period* (Nazareth: al-Qabas, 1996) (in Arabic)

Yazbak, Mahmoud. *Arab Immigration into Haifa*, M.A. Thesis (Haifa: Haifa University, 1987) (in Hebrew).

Yazbak, Mahmoud. "Ha-hagira ha-'aravit le-haifa, 1933-1948: nituah kamuti 'al pi mekorot 'arviyim", *Katedra* 45 (1987), pp. 131-146 (in Hebrew).

Yazbak, Mahmoud. "Haifa before the Nakba", *Mediterraneans* 14 (2010), pp. 22-26.

Yazbak, Mahmoud. *Haifa in the Late Ottoman Period, 1864-1914: A Muslim Town in Transition* (Leiden: Brill, 1998).

Yazbak, Mahmoud. "Holy Shrines/Maqamat in Modern Palestine-Israel and the Politics of Memory", in Marshall J. Breger, Yitzhak Reiter and Leonard Hammer (eds.), *Holy Places in the Israeli-Palestinian Conflict: Confrontation and Co-Existence* (London and New York: Routledge, 2010), pp. 231-249.

Yazbak, Mahmoud. "Templars as Proto-Zionists? The 'German Colony' in Late Ottoman Haifa", *Journal of Palestine Studies* 4 (1999), pp. 40-54.

Yehoshu'a, Ya'acov. *Ta'rikh al-Sahafa l-'Arabiyya fi Filastin, 1919-1929* (Haifa: The University of Haifa, 1981) (in Arabic).

Yuval-Davis, Nira and Floy Anthias (eds.). *Women-Nation-State* (London: Macmillan, 1989).

Zemach, Shlomo. *Seed Flax Growing* (Tel Aviv: Hapoel Hatsair, 1928) (in Hebrew).

Zigman, Yehuda et al. *Our Haifa: An Information Book* (Haifa: Ministry of Education, Culture, and Sport and the Municipality of Haifa, 2004) (in Hebrew).

Zu'bi, Nahla. "The Development of Capitalism in Palestine: The Expropriation of the Palestinian Direct Producers", *Journal of Palestine Studies* 13/4 (1984), pp. 88-109.

Zubeida, Sami. *Islam, the People and the State: Political Ideas and Movements in the Middle East*, 2nd ed. (London: I.B. Taurus, 1993).

Zweig, Ronald W. "Restitution of Property and Refugee Rehabilitation: Two Case Studies", *Journal of Refugee Studies* 6/1 (1993), pp. 56-64.

The League of National Liberation. "The Palestinian Problem and the Way to Resolve It", *Three Historical Documents* (January 2001)

"The Olive Oil Industry", in Report of the Olive Oil Sub-Committee, 10 November 1941, ISA/672/AG/38/1/2.

INDEX

1948 War   12, 22, 33, 63, 117, 121, 154, 165, 167, 181, 198

A

Aba Hushi   167
'Abbas Street   52, 130
'Abd al-Ghani, 'Usman   58
Abi Nadir-Swidan, Simon   95
Abi Nadir family   49
Abu al-'Asal, Bishara   152
Abu Muti', Qazaq   193
Abu Nassur beach   85-6
Abu-Qatnah, Ahmad   132, 145
Abu-Qatnah, Fatima   132, 145
Acre   vii, 101-3, 117, 124, 126, 151, 172, 174, 192, 197-8
Advisory Committee   159, 161-2, 165
Afula   127, 143, 148
Al-Ahmar Mosque (Safad)   83
Ahuza (neighborhood)   133
'Ajami, Mary   90-1
Amin Cinema   73
Aleppo   63
Alex Carmel   104, 153-4, 162
Alexandria   105
Allenby Street   72, 151
Amman   24, 82
Amphi Cinema   73
Anielevich (Mordechai) Street   155
Appinger Hotel   154
'Aqid   13
Aram Tsova Synagogue   64
Ard al-Billan (quarter)   15
Ard al-Ramil neighborhood   192
Armon Cinema   73, 77, 143
'Asfur family   49, 51
'Asqalani, Gharib   119, 128-9
Association of Arab Women in Haifa (*jam'iyyat al-ihsan al-'amm lil-sayyidat al-'arabiyyat fi* Haifa)   88
Atid   101, 104-5
'Atlit   86
Ha-'Atzma'ut Street   131, 151
Auschwitz   32
Austria   49-50, 181
Aviv Cinema   73
'Azar, Na'im   93

B

Bab al-Manatir (quarter)   39
Baha'i gardens, Temple   27, 41
Balad al-Sheikh (village)   37, 73, 152
Balfour Street   87
Al-Bard, Sha'ban   54
Bartana, Yael   165
Bat Galim   74, 93
Bauhaus School   48
Baydun, Rafiq   95
Beer-Sheva (Bi'r al-Sabi')   124
Begin, Menahem (Menachem)   199
Beirut   ix, 8, 15, 18, 25, 102-3
Beit ha-Gefen Community Center   164, 168
Beit ha-Ta'asiya (Industry House)   44
Ben-Gurion, David   36-7, 156
Ben-Gurion Boulevard   87, 151, 156, 159, 168, 170, 172, 174-5, 178
Ben Yehouda Street   142
Billan   15
Binyamin, Gan (park)   73, 84
Birqin (village)   132
Black September   25
Bondi, Beter   32
Bonshtein, Pesach   93
Borra, Giovanni   52
British Mandate   8, 12, 14, 44, 53, 57-8, 62, 72, 75, 82, 99, 102, 104, 154-5, 190-2
Brock, Haya   58
Bruderman, Eli   166
Bucharest   49
Burj   18, 44, 73
Al-Burj Street   18, 44, 73
Burke, Peter   70-1
Bustan al-Inshirah Café   73, 75
Bustan al-Balad (Gan ha-'Ir) Cinema   48, 73, 75, 152, 155
Al-Bustan Street   152, 155
Bustani, Emil   48, 152
Al-Bustani, Wadi'   152
Butaji (Tall Emile/Dado) beach   86, 95
Butaji family   86

C

Caesarea   104-5
Cairo   ix, 25, 112, 194
Canada   25, 48

INDEX

Carmel, Alex 104, 153-4, 162
Ha-Carmel Hospital 62-3
Carmel Mountain 57, 133
Carmel Street 151, 154, 156, 159
Carmelites 153
Casino 53, 57, 72, 74-5, 84, 86, 93
Catafago, Salim Bey 102
Catafago family 102-3
Central Carmel 47, 133, 140-1
Chaikin, Benjamin 48-9
Christian Arabs/clubs 103, 88-93
Christian Orthodox School 196
Ha-Cohen, David 57
Cold War 138
Coliseum Cinema 72
Communist Party 128, 130, 146, 191
Crusaders Road 28, 31, 39, 41
Custodian of Absentees' Property 63, 65
Czechoslovak Immigration Association 32

D

Daliyat al-Karmil (village) 133, 149
Damascus 7-8, 22, 91, 133, 144, 160
Darwish, Mahmud 53-4, 178, 184
Dead Sea 124
Derekh Hayam (road) 140, 143, 148
Development Authority 26, 65
Diaspora 3, 5, 147
Dik, Hasan 56
Diyab, Hashim 171-5
Donner, Batia 166
Duzan Restaurant 151

E

Eastern Rice Marketing Company, The 56
Eden Cinema 72-3, 152
Edmon Café 152
Educational Athletic Club (al-Nadi al-Riyadi al-Tahdhibi) 92
Egged buses 126
Egypt 25, 38, 54, 63, 82, 101, 106, 110, 112, 114, 122, 152, 154, 171
Egyptians 8, 90
'Ein Dor Cinema 73, 75, 77-8, 152, 158
Ein Shemer transition camp 125
Elika Café 176
Elisha Hospital 136

England 25, 107, 141, 171, 181
Eqron Street 58
Erman, Menashe 109
Etzel 199
Europe 9, 11, 21, 46-8, 50, 60, 69, 71, 111, 116, 122, 143, 147-8, 155, 186-8
Even va-Sid company 57

F

Al-Fakhura (neighborhood) 14
Fallaheen 116, 191
Farid Café 152
Faris, Ahmad 12, 15, 48, 90
Faris, Asma' 90
Fassuta (village) 38
Fattush Café 151, 171-4
Filastin (newspaper) 36, 77-8, 80, 82-5, 87-93
French Carmel 51
Fukhari, Ashraf 166

G

Galilee vii, 101, 113, 116, 122-4, 127, 171, 173-4, 186
Ha-Ganim Street 156
Gaza 17, 37, 119, 131, 175
Gaza Strip 119, 131
Geddes, Patrick 47
Ha-Gefen Street 52, 151, 156, 164, 168
Gemeindehaus (The Templar Community House) 159
General Philanthropy Association of Arab Women in Haifa 88
George Café 151-2
German Colony in Haifa 153, 161, 176
Germany 9, 13, 47, 154, 171, 190, 196
Gershon, Mazal 119, 144
Gerstel, Leopold v, 5, 43-6, 48-54, 57-62, 67
Gerstel, Moshe 5, 43-54, 57-62, 67
Ghattas, Yusif 103, 117
Goldstien, Giza 18, 19
Goodsell, Charles 70
Greek Catholic Church 130
Greidinger, Kalman 119, 141
Grossman, David 121
Gubernik, Miriam 119, 141, 143

218

H

Habash, Sonya 82
Habibi, Emil 181
Hadar ha-Carmel 12, 15, 17, 43-5, 47, 54, 57, 73, 75-7, 125, 137, 140, 155, 174, 176
Hadar ha-Carmel Committee 45
Haddad, Hilana 83
Haddad, Nasrallah 87
Haganah 18, 23, 44, 74, 96, 152, 192, 194, 199-200
Haggar, I. Engineer 39, 41
Haifa v, vii-ix, 1-12, 14-41, 43-54, 56-8, 61-4, 69-97, 99-119, 123-47, 151-63, 165-8, 171-9, 181-93, 195-203
Haifa Association for Assistance and Education 56
Haifa Chamber of Commerce 56
Haifa Christian scouts 72
Haifa City Museum v, 6, 149, 154, 156-61, 165-7, 177-9
Haifa Drama Club 92
Haifa Municipality 15-16, 18-19, 21, 27, 30-1, 35, 48-9, 52, 58, 64, 155, 157, 159, 161
Haifa University 133
Haifo'im v, 6, 121-2, 140, 144, 147
Hajj Ibrahim, Rashid 14, 192
Hakawati 72
Halissa (neighborhood) 44
Hamburg ix-x, 2, 4
Hamburger Institute for Social Research (HIS) 2-3, 6
Hapo'el 72, 80-1
Ha-Shahar (bus company) 136
Havana Café 173
Hawwasa (neighborhood) 192
Hayfawis 6, 121-2, 129-30, 133, 144, 146
Al-Hammuz Café 24
Al-Hara al-Gharbiyya (neighborhood) 103
Al-Hara al-Sharqiyya (neighborhood) 7, 65, 186
Hebron 197
Hertzliyya (Herzliah), Jewish neighborhood 73
Herzl, Theodor 8, 167, 174, 190
High Arab Committee 192

Hijaz Railway 7, 22, 102-3, 160, 162
Hillel Cinema 95
Histadrut, the Jewish Labor Organization 128
Hoffman Street 155
Holy Land 122, 153-4
Horef Hamishim 147
Hotel Zion 141
Hunayni 54
Huri, Agnes 52
Al-Husayni, Hajj Amin 192
Hushi, Aba 167

I

Ibin-Sina Street 49
Ibrahim, Mu'ayyad 14, 131, 192
Ibtin (village) 53, 57, 61
'Ifara, Emil 133-5
'Ifara family 119, 134-5, 145
Ijzim (village) 115
Institute for Historical Justice and Reconciliation (IHJR) ix, 1
International Red Cross, The 132, 136, 145
International Style of Architecture 5, 27, 48-50
Intifada 171, 174
Iraq Street (Kibbutz Galuyot) 8, 12, 75, 127, 187
Irbid 24-5, 129, 145
'Isifya (village) 133
Islamic Association 56
Islamic Sports Club 91-2
Israel vii-viii, 2-3, 10-11, 24-7, 35-7, 62, 88, 115-16, 119, 121-6, 128, 147, 154-6, 167-8, 174
Israeli Communist Party (MAKI), The 130
Italian hospital 131
Italy 102
Al-Ittihad (newspaper) 74, 77, 128, 130

J

Jabal Iskandar 14, 18, 24
Jabal Jarmaq 83
Jabbur, Ilyas 129
Al-Jadid Literary Magazine 168
Jaffa 2, 36-7, 72-3, 77, 81-2, 91-2, 96, 101, 130-1, 151

INDEX

Jaffa Road, Street 131
Jahshan, Jamila 84
Jamal Pasha, Ottoman Governor 91
Jam'iyyat Ta'awun al-Qura 115
Jauhariyya, Wasif 188
Jenin 132
Jericho 124
Jerusalem vii, 2, 72, 79, 92, 103, 106, 116, 122-4, 136-8, 142-3, 146, 151, 197
Jezrael Valley 126
Jordan 24-5, 57, 82, 114, 118, 122, 129, 131, 147
Jordanians 8
Al-Jreini (Al-Jurayna) Café 152
Jurayna 74
Al-Jurayna Mosque 74

K

Al-Kababir (village) 14, 133, 186, 191
Kanafani, 'Abd al-Latif 74-5, 85
Karkabi, Maggie 86, 93, 95
Karkabi, Zahi 130
Karma 52, 156
Al-Karmil (newspaper) 103, 110-13, 115, 151
Al-Karmil Street 52, 156
Kaufmann, Richard 46
Ka'war, Najwa 89-90
Al-Kawkab Café 82, 152
Al-Khadra, Subhi 17
Khammash, Rawi 54
Al-Khatib Alley (road) 143
Khayyat (al-'Aziziyya) beach 75, 84-5
Al-Khayyat, 'Aziz 84
Al-Khayyat family 75, 84-5, 191
Al-Khuri family 191
Al-Khuri, Jiryis , 90
Al-Khuri, Najib 36
Al-Khuri, Rashid 90
King George Street 143, 151
Kings Street 74-5, 151-2
Klibanov, Avraham 58
Knesset 29, 146
Kracauer, Leopold 48
Kufur 'Inan (village) 102, 116

L

Lamam, Subhi 53, 95
Lugashi, Rahamim 18

Le Grand Moulin 8
Lebanese 8, 169
Lebanon 25, 63, 82, 118, 120, 122, 128, 131, 147, 175, 192, 197-200
Lechi 199
Levi, Gershon 119, 144
Levi, Shabtai 57 192, 201
Levy, Yosef 31-2
Lod International Airport 145
Lod Road 13, 24, 26
London 3, 99, 104, 193
Lower Carmel 48
Lubban al-Sharqiyya (village) 24, 131

M

Maccabi 72, 81
Magen David Adom (health emergency service) 139
Ha-Maginim Street 151
Majdal 'Asqalan (village) 119
Majdalani, Iskandar Café 152
Majdalani family 49
Makhluf, Eugene 124
Malas, Khalil 58
Mandate period v, vii, 2, 4, 9, 53, 56-7, 64, 72, 75, 97, 99-100, 117
Mannasi, Taufiq 12, 15
Al-Mansi (village) 132
Mansur, 'Awad Ahmad 58, 103, 116
Mansura (village) 38
Mar Ilyas Monastery 133
Al-Marfa' Street 87
Marj 'Uyun (village) 131
Matabbi 52
Mat'am al-marfa (wharf restaurant) 87
Matzkel, Yehudit 162
Al-Mawaris (Qiryat Eliezer) 74
Al-Maydan Cinema 173 Mendelssohn, Erich 46, 48
Menkes, Theodor 48
Mixed neighborhoods 154, 163
Mizrahi/Arab-Jews, Yahud Awlad 'Arab 185-6
Mochly, Dagan 163
Modern Press of Palestine (*matba'at filastin al-haditha*) 93
Moriya Cinema 73, 88, 95
Moriya Street 133
Morris, Benny 36, 121, 167, 190, 192
Moshav Merhavia 143

220

INDEX

Mount Carmel 8, 14, 41, 44, 46, 50, 95, 125-6, 130, 133, 136, 138-9, 142-3, 148-9, 153
Mount Kan'an 83
Mughar (village) 102
Municipality of Haifa 27, 33, 40
Murad family 191
Musamsam 52
Muslim Association 36
Muslim quarter 121
Al-Mustashfa Street 155

N
Nablus 15, 18-21, 24, 53-4, 56, 100-1, 103, 107, 110-14, 131
Al-Nabulsi family 111-13, 116-17
Al-Nabulsi, Hajj 'Abdul-Rahim Afandi 112, 116Al-Nabulsi, Hajj Hasan 111
Al-Nabulsi, Hajj Nimr 111, 113
Al-Nabulsi, Sabih 24
Nachshon, Galia 119, 125, 128, 141-3
Al-Nadi al-Riydi al-Islami 74, 92
Al-Najah National School for Girls 24, 92
Nakba 1, 4, 11-12, 17, 24-5, 37, 43, 63-4, 158, 178, 186, 192
Naqqara, Hanna 152
Nassar, Najib 8, , 112
Nassar, Sadhij 90
Natan, Efrat 163, 165
National Committee of Haifa 192
National Orthodox School 91
National Socialism 9, 190
Nationalism 147, 187
Nazareth vii, 56, 83, 89, 124, 126, 130-1, 145, 172, 174
Nazi 154-5
Negev 122, 124, 172
Nesher 8, 110, 166
Neufeld, Yosef 46
Neveh Sha'anan (neighborhood) 61
Ha-Nevi'im Steps 48
Nordau Street 84
North Africa 122
Nur al-Fayha' 91

O
Ohanna, Nissim, the Chief Rabbi of Haifa 66

Old Carmel Hospital 62
Old City 156
Olive Oil Sub-Committee 113
Ora Cinema 73
Orell, Binyamin 49
Ottoman 7-8, 14, 22, 71, 73, 91, 94, 101-3, 153-4, 159-60, 163, 167, 186-8, 191
Ottoman Empire 101
Oxford viii, 19, 25, 181, 184, 194

P
Paenson, Ilia Eliyahu 104-5
Palestine vii-viii, 7-10, 24-5, 34-6, 46-50, 52, 55-6, 69-70, 79-81, 91-3, 99-118, 151-4, 159-60, 162-3, 187-93
Palestine Arab party 56
Palestine Electric Company 36
Palestine Football Association 73, 79
Palestinian Arab uprising (1936-1939) 190
Palestinian Authority 3, 178
Palestinian General Sports Association 79
Palestinian refugees 4, 12, 26, 129, 131, 147, 202
Palmach 199
Pappé, Ilan 167, 190, 192-3
Pidy, Carmen 93-4
Plan Dalet 193
Poland 49, 143, 193
Population (Haifa) 73, 165
Portugal 84
Pross Café 87
Public gardens/parks 71, 73, 75, 79, 83-4, 94
Public sphere/space 5, 33, 69-70, 81, 83, 89, 94, 96-8

Q
Qada 7
Qaraman, 'Abd al-Ra'uf 53-4
  Qaraman, al-Hajj Tahir 5, 8, 46, 53-4, 56, 58-63
Qaraman, Darwish 53-4
Qaraman, Hajj 'Arif 53
Qaraman, Su'ad 53-4, 57
Qaraman family 49, 54, 57, 62-3, 66

221

INDEX

Qaraqoz/ karagöz (operators of street puppet-shows) 72
Al-Qassam, 'Izz al-Din 9, 14
Qazaq, Hasan 12, 14-15, 17-19, Qazaq, Salma 194, 202
Qazaq, Abu Muti' 193
Qazaq family 14-9
Qiryat Eliezer 74
Qisariya 94
Qutran, Sulayman 60

R

Rafah 129
Ramat Gan 114
Ramih (village) 77, 102-3
Ramil 192
Ramla 82, 89
Rayyis, Raja 49
Ha-Re'ali School 141
Rechter 61
Red Cross 132, 136, 145
Resolution 181 10, 190
Reznik, Ya'akov 64
Rizq, Widad 83-7, 94, 97
Romania 49-50, 54
Rosenthal, A. Engineer 64
Rotbard, Sharon 66
Rothschild Boulevard 142
Rothschild Hospital 136
Rumaysh (village) 39
Rupin Road 136
Russia viii, 104, 141
Ruthenberg 36

S

Al-Sabah Café 152
Sa'd, Fu'ad 102-3, 112
Sa'd, Jubran 102-3
Sa'd, Musallam 48
Sa'd family 102-3, 117
Safad vii, 83, 124
Sahat al-Khamra (Khamra Square) 52
Sahyun family 52, 95
Sajur (village) 102, 117
Sakakini, Khalil 188
Salam family 49
Salamih, Hanna 89
Salzburg ix, 1-4, 181
Salzburg Global Seminar 1
Samir Café 87

Sanat al-Thaljih (The Year of the Snow) 119, 129
Sanduq al-'aja'ib 72
Sankari Café 152
Saraqibi, Shafiq 58
Saraqibi family 54, 58-9
Saudi Arabia 25
Sela, Rona 156-7
Sha'arawi, Huda 54
Shabab al-'Arab 74, 80-1
Shabib, Salih 95
Shabib family 49, 95
Shabtay Levi Street 131
Shafa 'Amr 129
Shahbarat, Wadi' 168, 170
Shalom, Haya 58
Shami, Ishaq 188
Shamir, Yitzhak 199
Sharbiv family 58
Sharon, Arieh 46, 61, 66
Sharqawi, Munir 119, 132-3, 144-5
Al-Shawwa, Usama 54
Shenhav, Yehouda 187-8, 199
Shiblak, 'Adnan 193
Shiblak, Abbas ('Abbas) 6, 19, 23-5, 181-184, 187
Shiblak, Fadil 12-26, 33, 58, 183 Shiblak, Hamza 24-5
Shiblak, Hasan (Abu Nayif) 14
Shiblak, Khalil 14-5, 18, 24-5, 183
Shiblak, Ra'ifa 24-5, 145, 183
Shiblak, Ra'isa 19, 24-5, 183
Shiblak, Zahiyyah 12, 15, 17-8, 22-5, 183-4, 187
Shiblak family 4, 12, 14-15, 24-6, 131, 145, 183-4
Shihadih, Hayfa 83
Shukri, Hasan 49
Shukri family 49, 191
Simhon, David 58, 66
Simmel, Georg 95-6
Sirkin Street 63
Slitzan, Shmuel 109
Slovakia 143
Solel Boneh 126
Southern Carmel 47
Soviet embassy 142
Spain 101, 171
Sports 79, 91-2

INDEX

Stanton, Alexander (British Governor of Haifa District) 47
Stanton Street 66, 201
Steel Brothers & Co. 33-4
Stella Maris 14, 51, 133
Sudanese 8
Swidan, 'Afifa 31
Swidan, Farid 38
Swidan, Hanna 27, 29,
Swidan, Jad 130
Swidan, Jean 31
Swidan, Malik 28, 31
Swidan, Mubadda 36
Swidan family 4, 29, 31, 37
Swidan House 12, 27-35, 39-42
Switzerland 104
Syria 25, 54, 101, 103, 107, 110, 113, 118, 132, 147, 197
Syrians 8

T

Talpiot Market 45, 47, 57, 59, 62, 66
Taltish 58-9
Tamari, Salim 188
Tanzim Road 39
Technion 8, 50, 125, 167
Tel-'Amal (neighborhood) 44
Tel Aviv vii, ix, 37, 110, 123-4, 126, 137, 142, 149
Teltsch Hotel 49
Templars 7, 101-2, 153-4, 158-63
Thabet, Anton 49
Theater 92-3, 152
Tiberias vii, 96, 124
Al-Tamimi, Najah 86 Al-Tirsana 74
Tobzi 52
Trans-Jordan 114, 118
Tsurel, Yona 18
Tunisia 14-15, 25
Turkey 122, 147
Tyre 39
Tzefat (Safad) 124

U

'Udih, 'Abdullah 186, 191
Al-'Umar, Dahir 156, 162
Umayya Café 72
Umm al-Gharib (Mother of the Stranger) 7, 186
Union of Arab Clubs 151

Union of Arab Orthodox Clubs 89
United Nations 10, 24, 28, 190, 192
United Nations Partition Resolution 181 (November 1947) 190, 192
UNRWA 24, 120, 132
Urbanization 81
'Uwayda, Subhi 95

V

Vaad Hatsirim (Delegates' Committee) 104
Vashitz, Yosef 115
Vatikiotis, P.J. 74-6
Vienna Café 87
Vienna University 49

W

Wadi al-Jimal (Ein ha-Yam) (neighborhood) 12-15, 23, 49, 168, 170, 191, 193-5
Wadi al-Nisnas (neighborhood) 11-12, 14, 32, 35, 38, 76, 153, 165, 168, 170, 191, 193-5, 200
Wadi al-Salib (neighborhood) 12-13, 15, 23, 54, 65, 144, 161, 170, 193, 202
Wadi al-Siyyah 14
Wadi Rushmiya 44
Wadud, Shakib 131
Weizman, Chaim 37, 104
West Bank 131-2
Western Carmel 47
Wilbushewitz, Gedalia 104, 109
Wilbushewitz, Nachum 104, 109
Williamson, Jeffrey G. 100-1
Wirth, Louis 81
Women's Literary Club in Damascus 91
World War I 8, 10, 47, 49, 72, 91, 100-1, 104, 109, 111, 153-4
World War II 18, 20-1, 23-4, 60, 99, 101, 115, 155, 158, 160
Würster family 159

Y

Yahya Yakhluf 129
Yavneh Street 49
Al-Yawm (newspaper) 128
Yehi'el Street 66
Yemen 125

INDEX

Yishuv 189
Yitah 37, 39
Yitzhar 114
Young Christian Society in Jaffa 91
Young Women's Christian Association 90

Z
Zahir Café 152
Zakka, Juliet 94
Zarubi, Hanna 94
Zichron Yaakov 103
Zion Theater in Jerusalem 92
Zionism 61, 109, 147, 156, 163, 188, 190
Zionist 6, 8, 36, 50, 104-5, 107-10, 147-9, 157-9, 163, 167-8, 177-8, 190, 192, 199-200, 202
Zohar, Eric(k)a 119, 143
Zohar, Yehezkel 49
Zu'abi, Manar 165
Zubeida, Sami 187
Zucker, Natan 58